GENDER AND THE OPEN METHOD OF COORDINATION

Gender and the Open Method of Coordination

Perspectives on Law, Governance and Equality in the EU

Edited by

FIONA BEVERIDGE and SAMANTHA VELLUTI
University of Liverpool, UK

ASHGATE

Published by

Ashgate Publishing Limited
Gower House
Croft Road
Aldershot
Hampshire GU11 3HR
England

Ashgate Publishing Company
Suite 420
101 Cherry Street
Burlington, VT 05401-4405
USA

www.ashgate.com

British Library Cataloguing in Publication Data

Gender and the open method of coordination : perspectives
on law, governance and equality in the EU
1. Sex discrimination in employment - European Union
countries - Congresses 2. Manpower policy - European Union
countries - Congresses
I. Beveridge, Fiona II. Velluti, Samantha
331.4'133

Library of Congress Cataloging-in-Publication Data

Beveridge, Fiona.
Gender and the open method of coordination : perspectives on law, governance and equality in the EU / by Fiona Beveridge and Samantha Velluti.
p. cm.
Includes index.
ISBN 978-0-7546-7343-9 (alk. paper)
1. Sex discrimination--Law and legislation--European Union countries. 2. Equality before the law--European Union countries. I. Velluti, Samantha. II. Title.

KJE5142.B48 2008
344.2401'4133--dc22

2008017886

ISBN 978-0-7546-7343-9

FSC Mixed Sources
Product group from well-managed forests and other controlled sources
www.fsc.org Cert no. SA-COC-1565
© 1996 Forest Stewardship Council

Printed and bound in Great Britain by
MPG Books Ltd, Bodmin, Cornwall.

Contents

List of Tables

List of Contributors

Dr. Ayse Idil Aybars is a Postdoctoral Research Fellow at the Centre for European Studies, Middle East Technical University (METU). She holds an MSc from the London School of Economics and a Ph.D. from the University of Ulster. She has been involved in several international projects on Turkish social policy, social dialogue, and the development of civil society in Turkey. Her research interests include comparative analysis of welfare regimes, gender equality in employment, patterns and mechanisms of Europeanization, social policy and welfare regime in Turkey and EU-Turkey Relations. She is the co-editor of *Bridging the Real Divide: Social and Regional Policy in Turkey's EU Accession Process*, METU Press, 2007.

Professor Fiona Beveridge is Professor of Law at the University of Liverpool. She has written extensively on gender law and policy in the European Union and the Member States. Her current research focuses on gender mainstreaming in the European Union, the Member States and in International Economic Institutions. Her publications include *Making Women Count: Integrating Gender into Law and Policy Making* 2000, Dartmouth, Ashgate (with Nott S. and Stephen K.) (eds.); 'Feminist Perspectives in International Economic Law' in Buss D. and Manji A. (eds.) *Feminist Perspectives on International Law* 2004, Oxford, Hart; and 'Building Against the Past: The Impact of Mainstreaming on EU Gender Law and Policy' 2007, *European Law Review.* In 2002 she co-edited a *Special Issue* of *Feminist Legal Studies* on *Mainstreaming Gender in European Public Policy* (with Shaw J.).

Professor Małgorzata Fuszara is Professor at Warsaw University where she is Head of the Centre for Socio-Legal Studies on the Situation of Women and Director of the Gender Studies Program. Her areas of teaching and research focus on sociology of law, sociology of culture, gender discrimination and women's rights. In 1995 and in 2002 she gave lectures on Women's Rights at Ann Arbor, University of Michigan, in the US and at the Oniati Institute of Sociology of Law, in Spain, respectively. Professor Fuszara is also member of the advisory board of *Signs. Journal of Women in Culture and Society* and member of the international editorial board of the *European Journal of Women's Studies*. Between 1996 and 1998 she was also a member of the *ad hoc* group of experts on Gender Mainstreaming at the Council of Europe. She has published extensively on women's rights in Polish, English, German, Slovak and Romanian.

Dr Roberta Guerrina is a Senior Lecturer in the Department of Political, International & Policy Studies, University of Surrey. Her research interests lie in the area of European Social policy and gender equality, particularly the politics of gender, equality rights and maternity; women's human rights; and, the gendered nature of citizenship. Recent publications include *Mothering the Union: The*

Politics of Gender, Equality and Maternity Rights in the EU 2005, Manchester, Manchester University Press; *Europe: History, Ideas and Ideologies* 2002, Arnold; and "Constitutional Politics in Europe: Continuing Trends in the Politics of Gender" (2006) 8 *Identities: Journal for Politics, Gender and Culture*. She has also edited with Marysia Zalewski a special issue of *Review of International Studies* (2007) on "Women's Human Rights".

Dr Kristina Koldinská is a researcher at Charles University, Faculty of Law, Department of Labour Law and Social Security Law in Prague, Czech Republic. Her current research interests focus on European Social Law and Policy and on legal aspects of gender equality. She has published extensively on issues such as social protection, gender equality and social assistance and in this context the level of implementation of EC law in the Czech Republic. She has also participated in various projects and studies for the Ministry of Labour and Social Affairs of the Czech Republic and delivered papers at international conferences. She is a member of the Commission's network of legal experts on the application of Community law on equal treatment for women and men.

Professor Julia S. O'Connor is Professor of Social Policy at the University of Ulster. Her main areas of research are welfare states in comparative perspective and social inequality, poverty and social exclusion. Current research includes studies of convergence in social policy in the EU in the context of changes in the governance of social policy and EU enlargement; precarious employment and income security; and multicultural policy in Canada in terms of its relevance for the UK and Ireland. Her work has been published in several journals including the *British Journal of Sociology*, the *Canadian Review of Sociology and Anthropology*, the *Canadian Review of Higher Education*, *Current Sociology* (a trend report *From Women in the Welfare State to Gendering Welfare State Regimes*), *Policy and Politics, Research in Political Sociology, European Societies, Journal of European Social Policy* and in several edited collections. She is co-author with Orloff A. S. and Shaver S. (1999) of *States, Markets, Families Gender, Liberalism and Social Policy in Australia, Canada, Great Britain and the United States* (Cambridge: Cambridge University Press, 1999).

Dr Amparo Serrano Pascual is researcher and Lecturer at the Complutense University in Madrid (Faculty of Political Sciences and Sociology). Her main research interests are comparative employment, social and activation policies; gender policies; the deconstruction of EU discourses; and monitoring the European employment strategy. Some of her most recent publications are *Reshaping welfare states and activations regimes* 2007, Brussels: Peter Lang (with Magnusson L.); *Unwrapping the European Social Model* 2006, Bristol: Policy Press (with Jepsen M.); *From Welfare to Knowfare* 2006, Brussels: ETUI (with Mósesdóttir L. and Remery C.) (eds); *Activation policies in international perspective* 2004, Brussels: ETUI; *Equal pay and gender mainstreaming in the European employment strategy.* Brussels: ETUI; *L'approche intégrée du genre dans la stratégie européenne pour l'emploi*, 2002, Paris: L'Harmattan (with Behning U.) (eds.).

Dr Samantha Velluti is Lecturer in Law at the University of Liverpool. She has researched extensively in the area of EU governance and open method of co-ordination in the context of EU social law and policy. She is particularly interested in the effectiveness of soft law instruments in ensuring the implementation of EC law and the relationship between the OMC and the *acquis communautaire* in relation to the strengthening of EU social governance. Velluti's publications include: 'Towards the Constitutionalisation of New Forms of Governance: A Revised Institutional Framework for the European Employment Strategy' (2002) 22 *Yearbook of European Law* 353, 'What European Union Strategy for Integrating Migrants? The role of OMC soft mechanisms in the development of an EU immigration policy' (2007) 9 *European Journal of Migration and Law* 53; 'Promotion of Gender Equality at the Workplace: Gender Mainstreaming and Collective Bargaining in Italy' (2008) 16(2) *Feminist Legal Studies*, forthcoming.

Acknowledgements

This collection of chapters arose from a one-day colloquium on Gender and the OMC held in Liverpool in 2006, organized by the Feminist Legal Research Unit, Liverpool Law School. Financial support for that event was received from the Dean of the Faculty of Social and Environmental Sciences, University of Liverpool. We are grateful to both the Feminist Legal Research Unit and the Dean for their support. We would also like to thank the participants in that event for their helpful thoughts and comments.

We are extremely grateful to all the contributors to this collection for their time and effort in producing their chapters, to Dianne Scullion for her efficient work and help in the final stages of the book, and to the production team at Ashgate Publishing Ltd.

We hope that this collection will be a useful addition to the growing literature on the OMC and that it will contribute to understandings of EU social governance. We hope also that it offers fresh insight into the practice of gender mainstreaming and to the conduct of gender politics in the EU.

Professor Fiona Beveridge
Dr. Samantha Velluti
Liverpool, March 08

Chapter 1

Introduction – Gender and the OMC

Fiona Beveridge and Samantha Velluti

This collection of chapters focuses on the intersection between a long-standing area of EU policy, gender equality, and a relatively new mode of policy-making, the Open Method of Co-ordination (OMC). Invoking a range of disciplinary perspectives, each contributor examines gender in the OMC in a different context, sometimes at a general EU level, sometimes at a Member State level, all asking in different ways how effectively OMC has served as a conduit or medium for the advancement of gender equality.

Central to these enquiries is the concept of gender mainstreaming which suggests that a gender equality perspective should be incorporated "in all policies at all levels and at all stages, by the actors normally involved in policy-making" (Council of Europe 1998: 10). Different chapters assess how effectively gender mainstreaming has worked in the context of the OMC and what aspects or elements of OMC processes have been particularly helpful or detrimental to the development of effective gender mainstreaming policies and practices.

Setting the Scene

Gender Equality: From 'Cinderella status' to Queen without a Crown?

Gender equality made its appearance in the founding Treaties of what is now the European Union (EU) through the inclusion of an equal pay principle in Article 119 of the Treaty of Rome. In the 50 intervening years this somewhat isolated provision has served as the bedrock for the development of what has proved to be a robust and dynamic area of EU policy. The focus on equal pay (now Article 141 EC) has given way to a broader equality agenda, extending from equality between women and men to the elimination of inequality based on sex, racial or ethnic origin, religion or belief, disability, age or sexual orientation (Article 13 EC). Legal obligations now extend beyond the workplace into the provision of services, the exercise of free movement and citizenship rights and the many other areas of activity where Member States must exercise their national powers in accordance with the principle of gender equality established in the Treaty and now regarded as a constitutional obligation. A gender mainstreaming duty in Article 3(2) EC requires the Community to seek to eliminate inequality and promote equality between women and men in all its activities. Meanwhile, in the 'soft' law realm, Community equality policy now extends to issues such as domestic violence and healthcare, previously the exclusive domain of Member States (European Commission 2006).

The progressive deepening and widening of EU gender policy has come about in a piecemeal, somewhat organic fashion, reflecting broader concerns about the commitment of the EU to social policy more generally, the turn in EU politics towards a concept of citizenship, developing discourses about the constitutional features of the EU legal order and the progress of market integration, among other elements. Enlargement has also played its part bringing both new leaders and new laggards on gender equality into the EU, and focussing attention on what has (and has not) been achieved. Throughout this process both soft and hard tools have been used: the Commission has played an important role using soft tools such as Programmes of Action and Recommendations to orientate its own activities and the attention of the states in new directions; meanwhile, both the legislature and the European Court of Justice (ECJ) have played significant roles, enacting and bringing to life respectively the hard law provisions which have significantly extended legal protection beyond the issue of pay discrimination between women and men. Despite these developments women and men remain far from equal in the EU. High levels of employment segregation, persistent pay gaps, the widespread acceptance of gender stereotypes and tolerance of sexism, together with unacceptable levels of domestic violence and persistent homophobia and sexual orientation based discrimination tell a different story. Of EU gender equality policy, then, a common if trite conclusion might be that it has made a start, but that it has a long way to go.

The turn towards gender mainstreaming can be understood as a response to perceptions of failure (Beveridge 2007). Mainstreaming offers new understandings of 'the problem' and of 'the solution' (Beveridge and Nott 2002), and is often taken to require the development of a new toolkit to tackle gender discrimination. Moreover, mainstreaming has been taken by some parties to call into question not only the tools used to tackle discrimination but also the whole process of decision-making about what constitutes a 'problem' and what should be done about it. It can be said, therefore, that gender mainstreaming entails a paradigm shift from previous equality measures such as equal treatment, equal opportunities and positive action. Gender mainstreaming addresses the problem of gender inequality at a more structural level in comparison with previous generations of equal treatment and equal opportunities measures which are largely based on a representative form of democracy and a complaints-led model. These types of measures emphasize an individualization of rights whereby the individual is considered to be autonomous and self-sufficient and capable of protecting his or her freedom of choice and action ignoring "both the value of social interaction and the ways in which breaches of rights operate in a collective and institutional way" (Fredman 2005: 351). Thus they mainly provide for a set of equality rights and create the conditions for exercising them but still hold individuals primarily responsible for exercising them. Much of the literature regarding these rights has focussed on issues of discrimination, redistributive justice and prejudice.

In addition, gender mainstreaming is based on a more systematic approach. It identifies gender biases in current policies assessing the impact of gender biases in the reproduction of gender inequality (Verloo 2005) and it is based on a proactive model whereby the measures to counter discrimination are enacted by policy-makers, service providers and civil society groups as well as employers rather than being merely a reactive response to individual claims brought in litigation cases (Fredman 2005: 373). Thus mainstreaming has helped to refocus attention on issues of political participation and, more generally, to raise issues about governance and participatory modes of democracy (Rai 2003; Shaw 2005; Squires 2005).

The OMC as a New Constitutional Architecture for EU Social Governance

OMC refers to the mode of governance developed by the EU working in conjunction with Member States whereby areas of policy competence are addressed through a range of non-binding measures which have been the subject of common agreement and which are designed to pursue an agreed set of policy goals. Typically, OMC has been introduced in areas where policy competence remains largely with the Member States with the EU institutions playing a coordinating role, and where the assent of Member States is thus essential. Like other areas previously dealt with through inter-governmental arrangements, this requirement for consent is an essential requirement and safeguard for the Member States.

Key elements of OMC include:

- the reliance of this strategy on political, rather than legal suasion and on partnership and participatory democracy;
- the strong element of multilateral surveillance (by the Commission), leading to regular benchmarking, peer review and a 'naming and shaming' ritual as a 'soft' means of enforcement;
- the iterative elements of the process – giving capacity to shape debate (Mosher and Trubeck 2003);
- the drawing up of pan-European guidelines and use of joint language (Eurodiscourse), including the construction of a common or shared view of the 'problem';
- the development of a common knowledge base, including indicators;
- the systematic dissemination of knowledge – benchmarking, mutual learning, peer review (Jacobsson 2004).

OMC first developed as the *modus operandi* of the Community and the Member States in the area of employment policy. Employment policy, previously a Member State preserve, acquired a Community dimension as a result of the incorporation of a new 'Employment' chapter in the EC Treaty by the Treaty of Amsterdam in 1997 and the consequent development of what became known as the European Employment Strategy (EES). While the Treaty recognized that primary responsibility for employment issues remained with the Member States, attaining a 'high level of employment' became one of the 'objectives' of the Community (Article 2 EC) which was subsequently changed to 'full employment' (Presidency Conclusions, European Council 2000). The Community institutions were charged with "the promotion of coordination between employment policies of the Member States with a view to enhancing their effectiveness by developing a coordinated strategy" (Article 3(1)(i)

EC). Thus the process is a multi-level one, involving a broad range of actors including the social partners (Velluti 2003).

In 1997 the Council adopted Guidelines for Member States' Employment Policies which utilized a range of 'soft' tools to encourage states to bring their employment policies into line. This was significant since annual review by the Commission and Council was anticipated in these Guidelines: as Jacobsson notes, compared to other 'soft law' processes in the EU the OMC used in the context of the EES included a "more systematic system of monitoring with clear procedural mechanisms" (Jacobsson 2004: 358). In subsequent years the EES has gathered momentum and it has been developed into a *quasi*-fully-fledged mode of governance introducing new institutional arrangements at both European and national levels with the establishment of further objectives and indicators and thus maintaining employment high on the agenda of the EU.

From its inception, the EES addressed gender equality issues, as it had already been recognized that the forces of economic integration and the development of the Single Market might result in a potential worsening of the situation of women but equally, and in a more strategic manner, that the objective of high employment in the EU could only be achieved in numerical terms by taking into account women's employment and working conditions. Further, the setting up and launch of the EES must be understood in the context of the development of a platform for action on gender equality at the 1995 UN summit on women in Beijing which explains in part the increase in importance of gender equality at European level (Rubery 2005:392).

Relying on the findings of a report into the impact of the Single Market on women's employment the Commission concluded in 1998 that "active policies to promote the equal sharing between men and women of work and family responsibilities are needed to avoid that women are harder hit than men by the cuts in public spending caused by convergence policies in Member States, increased competition, added pressure on wages and social standards and the de-regularization of employment." (CEC 1998: 12). Equal opportunities formed one of the four 'pillars' of the first set of guidelines and was also integrated into the implementation of the other pillars and to evaluation of the results. Thus the promotion of gender equality became one of the key objectives of EES and one of the key measures of its success with equal opportunities between women and men being established as one of the four pillars of the EES and the commitment to gender mainstreaming being included as one of the guidelines of the strategy. Moreover, gender equality targets have been developed with a specific female employment rate objective for 2005 and 2010 and targets for the provision of childcare. These developments have been included in the new phase of the EES despite the disappearance of the fourth pillar and the objective of equal opportunities between women and men being reduced to one guideline following the review and simplification of the EES and its synchronization with the economic coordination process resulting in integrated guidelines.

The OMC has now assumed centre stage as the key method of governance in relation to both the EES and the Social Policy Agenda, two areas of policy-making where gender is acknowledged to have a central role. These two policy areas are now key arenas for the development of EU gender equality policy. The launch in 2000 of the Lisbon Strategy, a strategy for economic management based on the objectives of long term sustainable economic growth, full employment, social cohesion, and transition to a knowledge based society, gave added political impetus to these processes, and the OMC has now also been extended to other areas of policy-making. Though the precise form of OMC varies from area to area, the key characteristics identified above are common features.

The use and spread of OMC has led to its interrogation as a form of governance within the EU and this has given rise to different and conflicting views as to its nature, value and effectiveness. Those in favour of the OMC have defined it as the 'Lazarus of European integration', as promoting experimental learning and deliberative problem-solving, as a 'third way' for EU social policy, as a middle course between regulatory competition and harmonization and inter-governmentalism and supranationalism and as a tool for achieving convergence of results whilst respecting national diversity. On the other hand, critics of the OMC have argued that it allows the EU to pursue its creeping agenda of Europeanization in fields that are the domain of national decision-making or that, conversely, it represents a potential threat to the Community Method, that it lacks transparency, accountability and enforcement mechanisms and that it is thus ineffective as an instrument of policy learning and transfer. These contrasting interpretations of the OMC confirm the challenge it poses to scholars in attempting to situate it in clearly definable theoretical contexts.

Like the turn to gender mainstreaming, OMC has given rise to the development of new tools and new approaches to policy-making, as well as new and different forms of engagement between key stakeholders in employment policy. This raises important questions about capacities and the effectiveness of different methods, as well as issues about governance. One particular concern is the impact of enlargement and the experiences of new Member States in dealing with OMC processes which present distinct challenges by comparison with hard law measures (Koldinská; Fuszara, in this collection; Velluti 2005).

Key Themes and Structure of the Book

This collection of chapters represents the result of a one-day workshop held in Liverpool in 2006 which brought together scholars and researchers involved in studies of the OMC's processes and outputs to explore the contribution of OMC to EU gender policy. The collection draws on the discussions and preliminary conclusions of this seminar and its aim is to provide new insights and fresh perspectives into the interaction between these two policy concerns: gender policy and the OMC. In particular it considers how well OMC can serve as a policy instrument for the advancement of gender policy, what opportunities and risks are attached to the use of OMC as a tool for gender policy, and what its limitations are in the context of the recent enlargement and transition from an EU of 15 Member States to one of 27. Further, it offers a valuable insight into the practice of gender mainstreaming and the conduct of gender politics in these new policy arenas.

Collectively and separately, the chapters explore four key themes:

- *Gender and the Nation State*. Diversity between Member States; the usefulness/appropriateness of models (for example, models of the welfare state); the directions and forces of policy transfer; the question of Europeanization.
- *Visions of Gender Equality*. The meanings of gender equality promoted under OMC; ideals of gender equality; the relationship between ideals and models of nation states.
- *Strengths and limitations of 'soft' approaches*. How does the choice of 'hard' versus 'soft' or vice versa relate to EU political commitment on the one hand and Member State acceptance/compliance on the other? What is the contribution of the OMC and gender mainstreaming modes of governance to our understanding of policy-making at European and national levels? Does the dichotomy 'soft'/'hard' stand?
- *Actors*. Who are the actors participating in the OMC, who doesn't and why? In what way does the involvement or absence of certain actors determine OMC processes?

The contributions examine the applicability of the OMC to differing aspects of gender policy at national level, some exploring the themes theoretically, others more concretely by having a geographic spread and relying on the use of *ad hoc* case studies (Aybars, Koldinská, Fuszara, Velluti). In particular, the chapters provide new insights into the study of European integration for domestic political institutions and policy processes which are summarized by the concept of 'Europeanization.' The contributions analyze the relationship between EU-level governance arrangements and domestic transformations, which are examined in terms of changes in domestic policies, discourses and institutions including the role of law in adapting to change from a gender perspective.

This collection opens with an introductory chapter by Fiona Beveridge in which she introduces and traces the development of the two central issues of EU gender equality policy and the OMC. The emergence of gender mainstreaming as a strategy and its resonance and disconnects with OMC are noted and discussed. Finally this chapter discusses the key themes of the book which recur throughout the collection and offers some thoughts on how these should be approached.

In chapter 3, Roberta Guerrina, focuses on demography and fertility rates, an important underlying issue often given less attention than is due in discussions of gender equality. In particular, the chapter looks at the link between women's activation policies and demographic trends in the EU and asks whether the EES provides an adequate framework for the development of a multidimensional approach to gender equality encouraging higher female participation in the official labour market whilst, at the same time, challenging traditional power structures in the family. Her analysis of employment policies is centred on three interrelated issues: (1) gender power hierarchies in the family; (2) women's choices about mothering/motherhood; (3) fertility rates.

Julia O'Connor, in chapter 4, considers the potential and limitations of the OMC for enhancing social policy objectives in the EU, in particular the potential for broadening the possibilities for gender equality beyond the labour market participation objectives of the EES. This is discussed with reference to the development of EU gender equality measures since the mid-1990s including the adoption of gender mainstreaming initiatives. O'Connor highlights a mismatch between the theoretical promises of the OMC and what has been achieved so far: its failure to ensure deliberative modes of democracy, the gap between commitment and implementation at national level in terms of policy learning and underlying tensions between different policy discourses at the basis of the EES. She concludes with a discussion of the potential of the OMC process for gender equality objectives in the context of the 2008 synchronization of the economic and employment OMC processes with the social exclusion OMC.

Ayse Idil Aybars then turns the spotlight fully onto the EES in an examination of the impact and implications of EES in different Member States. The four states chosen – Spain, Denmark, France and the UK – each represents a different type of welfare state and the four case studies together demonstrate the differing relevance and impact of EES in states with diverse welfare approaches and differing legacies in relation to gender equality. Aybars employs a 'Europeanization' analysis to consider whether the EES has produced significant convergence between these diverse states. She demonstrates that while the EES has fuelled parallel developments driven by common targets, each state has sought to preserve key elements of its national approach, so that diversity has also survived.

In chapter 6, Malgorzata Fuszara challenges some of the assumptions underlying accepted definitions of the OMC, at least as they apply in some of the newer Member States. Focussing on Polish experience, particularly with twinning projects, she argues that some of the perceived benefits of the OMC – its flexibility, its discursive nature, its respect for subsidiarity and its promotion of mutual learning; overall its soft character – cannot be relied on to deliver improvements in gender equality in the particular circumstances of Poland. This chapter points to the importance of domestic political commitment on the one hand, and indigenous capability in relation to gender equality on the other, as twin pre-requisites for successful implementation of equality policy through OMC processes.

Kristina Koldinská's chapter focuses on the 2004 enlargement more generally and the pre-and post-accession engagement of five states – the Czech Republic, Slovakia, Slovenia, Estonia and Poland – with the EES and the Social Exclusion Strategy, questioning the effectiveness of the OMC in advancing gender equality in these states. While it is early days for these states, there are signs that the process is having only very limited effect in orientating domestic policies towards the issue of gender equality. Indeed, based on the first round of national reports, it seems that there are broad divergences between different states' interpretations of the objectives of these processes from a gender perspective and wide gaps in levels and modes of engagement with the OMC-based agendas.

In chapter 8, Samantha Velluti turns the spotlight back onto two 'old' Member States in her case study on gender mainstreaming in the labour markets of Italy and Denmark. Velluti's concern is with a particular element of the EES, that is, its ability to bring about changes in the way in which gender equality issues and goals are articulated in the context of labour market policies. This is important since, in the countries under scrutiny, the social partners (employer and employee organizations) play a central role in the organization of the labour market and hence it is their behaviour that must change if labour-related gender equality issues are to be tackled effectively. Thus this chapter offers a rare insight into the penetration of gender mainstreaming elements of EES into the world of workplace organization. In so doing it focuses attention on issues which are crucial to the effectiveness of OMC processes generally, as well as of gender equality elements.

Chapter 9, by Amparo Serrano Pascual, asks a key question: whether the EES has created additional political resources for the promotion and pursuit of gender equality. Her concern is particularly with the gender mainstreaming paradigm and the potential advantages which OMC offers to pursue mainstreaming, by comparison with other forms of governance. It focuses attention on the methodological implications of mainstreaming and the resonance between these and elements of the OMC, and considers how OMC accordingly presents a new and potentially fruitful set of opportunities for gender equality protagonists. However, she also points to patchy results, indicating that this potential is accompanied by dangers.

Finally, in chapter 10, Fiona Beveridge and Samantha Velluti offer some observations and conclusions drawn from the preceding chapters and the collection as a whole. Returning to the themes identified in chapter 2, they draw together the evidence from chapters 3 to 9, which offers a range of challenging, sometimes contradictory, findings about the OMC as a promoter of gender equality. Some of the issues raised, such as the need for clearer objectives and clearer reporting standards, have implications for the OMC generally as a mode of governance. Other issues relate more specifically to the problems faced where the flexible and experimental OMC processes interact with values such as gender equality which are supposed to be 'core' values of the EU. Beveridge and Velluti conclude that there is a need for a clearer, over-arching vision for EU gender equality policy and a need for this to provide some orientation for OMC processes, where the two intersect.

References

Beveridge, F. and Nott, S. (2002), 'Mainstreaming: A Case for Optimism and Cynicism', *Feminist Legal Studies* 10: 299.

Beveridge, F. (2007), 'Building Against the Past: The Impact of Mainstreaming on EU Gender Law and Policy', *European Law Review* 32: 193-212.

Commission of the European Communities (1998) *Progress report from the Commission on the follow-up of the Communication: "Incorporating equal opportunities for women and men into all Community policies and activities."* COM (98) 122 final of 04 March 1998.

Council of Europe (1998), *Gender Mainstreaming: Conceptual Framework, Methodology and Presentation of Good Practices, Final Report of the activities of the Group of Specialists on Mainstreaming*, EG-S-MS(98)2, Strasbourg, Council of Europe.

European Commission (2006), *Roadmap for Equality Between Women and Men for the Period 2006-2010*, COM(2006) 92 final of March 1, 2006.

European Council (1997), *Guidelines for Member States Employment Policies for 1998* of 15 December 1997.

European Council (2000), *Presidency Conclusions*, Lisbon, 23 and 24 March 2000.

Fredman, S. (2005), 'Changing the Norm: Positive Duties in Equal Treatment Legislation', *Maastricht Journal of European and Comparative Law* 12(4): 369-397.

Jacobsson, K. (2004), 'Soft Regulation and the Subtle Transformation of States: The Case of EU Employment Policy', *Journal of European Social Policy* 14(4): 355-370.

Mosher, J.S. and Trubeck, D.M. (2003), 'Alternative Approaches to Governance in the EU: EU Social Policy and the European Employment Strategy', *Journal of Common Market Studies* 41: 63-88.

Rai, S. (2003), *Mainstreaming Gender, Democratising the State? Institutional Mechanisms for the Advancement of Women* (Manchester: Manchester University Press).

Rubery, J. (2005), 'Gender Mainstreaming and the OMC. Is the Open Method Too Open for Gender Equality Policy?' in Zeitlin, J. and Pochet, P. (eds) with Magnusson, L. *The Open Method of Coordination in Action. The European Employment and Social Inclusion Strategies* (Brussels: PIE-Peter Lang).

Shaw, J. (2005), 'Mainstreaming Equality and Diversity in European Union Law and Policy', *Current Legal Problems* 58: 255.

Squires, J. (2005), 'Is Mainstreaming Transformative? Theorizing Mainstreaming in the Context of Diversity and Deliberation', *Social Politics* 12: 344.

Velluti, S. (2003), 'Towards the Constitutionalisation of New Forms of Governance: A Revised Institutional Framework for the European Employment Strategy', *Yearbook of European Law* 22: 353.

Velluti, S. (2005), 'Implementing Gender Equality and Mainstreaming in an Enlarged European Union: Some Thoughts on Prospects and Challenges for Central Eastern Europe', *Journal of Social Welfare and Family Law* 27: 213.

Verloo, M. (2005), 'Displacement and Empowerment: Reflections on the Concept and Practice of the Council of Europe Approach to Gender Mainstreaming and Gender Equality' *Social Politics* 12(3): 344-366.

Chapter 2

Implementing Gender Equality and Mainstreaming in an Enlarged European Union: Prospects and Challenges

Fiona Beveridge

This chapter introduces the two central issues considered in this collection, EU gender equality policy and the Open Method of Co-ordination (OMC), providing an overview of each and identifying key characteristics. The emergence of gender mainstreaming as a strategy and its resonance and disconnects with OMC are noted and discussed. Finally this chapter identifies key themes which recur throughout the collection and offers some thoughts on how these should be approached. They are:

- Gender and the Nation State;
- Visions of Gender Equality;
- Strengths and Limitations of 'soft' approaches;
- Actors.

These key themes serve as a conceptual framework for analysing gender in the OMC, and are reflected in various ways in Chapters 3 to 9. In Chapter 10 these key themes are taken up again to reflect on the contributions to this volume and the prospects for the future.

Gender Equality in the European Union

The history and development of EU gender equality law and policy is well known and it is not the intention here to provide any systematic overview. The concern of this collection of chapters is with the present and future of gender equality policy, and with the possibilities offered by OMC processes to contribute to this. This chapter therefore seeks to identify key characteristics of current gender equality policy which are relevant to this debate. These are as follows: the progressive development of a rights-based set of legal obligations to address discriminatory practices which serve to maintain gender inequality (the traditional *acquis communautaire*); the use of 'soft' policy measures as an agenda-setting tool (policy setting measures); and a more recent turn towards new governance tools to complement the traditional approach both within the Community institutions (through mainstreaming activities) and *vis-à-vis* the Member States (such as the imposition of an obligation on public bodies to take a more proactive stance towards gender equality in their operations (the gender duty)).

The 'Acquis Communautaire'

The gender *acquis* began with Article 119, now Article 141 EC, and was initially supplemented with equal pay and equal treatment directives and with measures seeking to eliminate sex discrimination in social security systems.[1] More recent provisions extend this anti-discrimination approach to the provision of services.[2] A further set of provisions, introduced from the 1990s onwards, tackle issues affecting the reconciliation of work and family life, such as parental leave, the protection of pregnant women, and the protection of part-time employees.[3] Provisions on the protection from sexual harassment in employment, and on the burden of proof in discrimination proceedings are also included.[4] Directive 2000/78/EC adds *inter alia* a prohibition on sexual orientation discrimination in employment. The equal opportunities *acquis* did not remain static but was subject to legislative amendment and to further development through interpretation by the European Court of Justice. Many of these developments are reflected in the Recast Directive which, as Burrows and Robison (2007) point out, makes only minor changes to the law but simplifies it principally through consolidation.

Directive 2002/73 also introduces for the first time a requirement for Member States to maintain or establish a body or bodies to 'promote, analyse, monitor and support equality of treatment between women and men.' It also imposes on Member

1 Directive 75/117 implemented the principle of equal pay. Benefits paid in the context of occupational social security schemes also constitute pay within the meaning of Article 141, and Directives 86/378 and 96/97 implemented the principle of equal pay in this area. Directive 76/207, as amended by Directive 2002/73, implemented the principle of equal treatment as regards access to employment, self-employment and occupation, including working conditions, and vocational training. The Recast Directive, Directive 2006/54, consolidates the directives on employment and occupation and equal pay (including occupational social security), and codifies elements of the Court's case law: Directive 2006/54 on the implementation of the principle of equal opportunities and equal treatment of men and women in matters of employment and occupation (recast), 2006/54/EC, of 5 July 2006, cf. Burrows and Robison (2007).

2 Directive 2004/113/EC of 13 December 2004 implementing the principle of equal treatment between men and women in the access to and supply of goods and services.

3 Directive 92/85/EEC deals with the protection of health and safety of pregnant workers and workers who have recently given birth or are breastfeeding. It also addresses maternity leave and discrimination in the work place. Discrimination on grounds of pregnancy is also covered by the equal treatment legislation. Directive 96/34 sets out minimum requirements on (unpaid) parental leave for male and female workers giving universal effect to a collective agreement made under the Social Policy Protocol and later extended to the UK by Directive 97/75. Directive 97/81/EC provides for the removal of discrimination against part-time workers and seeks to facilitate the development of more flexible working arrangements, giving universal effect to a collective agreement made under the Social Policy Protocol and later extended to the UK by Directive 98/23/EC.

4 On harassment, see now Art. 2(2) of Directive 76/207, as amended. On burden of proof see Directive 97/80 on Burden of Proof in sex discrimination cases.

States a duty to 'actively take into account the objective of equality between men and women when formulating and implementing laws, regulations, administrative provisions, policies and activities',[5] a mainstreaming duty.

These hard law measures have been enforced in the 'old' (pre-2004) Member States, where necessary through a mixture of Community and private enforcement. The Commission has launched enforcement proceedings in the European Court of Justice (ECJ) against many states over the years for failings in the transposition of the provisions of these Directives into national law. Individual litigation through the national courts of the Member States, sometimes including a referral of the case to the Court of Justice for guidance, has also been pursued to a significant degree though as Alter and Vargas (2000) noted, rates of litigation vary significantly between different Member States. In general, however, in these states, levels of compliance with the formal requirements of Community law are high, though some states appeared to be dragging their feet over Directive 2002/73 and all new measures seem to raise some compliance issues in some states (cf. Network of Legal Experts 2007).[6]

In 'new' states which acceded in 2004 and 2007, the accession process is still very recent. The pre-accession agreements required these states to put in place measures to implement the existing *acquis* and by and large this was done (Sloat 2004). Post-accession, however, this obligation is supplemented by the obligation to ensure effective application and this depends in turn on much deeper cultural change in the legal system and in wider society (EPLC). Progress in bringing these provisions to life through litigation and court rulings has generally been slow. A variety of explanations can be offered for this. One is that new provisions were often in effect a 'transplant' from an existing Member State which is now proving to be an awkward fit with existing legal provisions. Another is the hangover of a judicial attachment to legal formalism which makes it unlikely that Courts will give the broader, more teleological rulings required if legislation is to be interpreted in line with the approach taken by the Court of Justice (Rodin 2007; Havelková 2007). Finally there is often a low level of awareness of the requirements of the new legislation which was generally passed through the national parliament by a fast-track process designed to ease preparations for accession, with the result that there was very little political input e.g. by national parliaments and equality activists at that stage, and very little public debate about particular provisions. Thus the levels of effective implementation of the *acquis* and patterns of compliance with it vary substantially across the EU as does the existence of effective mechanisms for promotion and enforcement of its provisions.

The existing *acquis* has focussed historically on the protection of substantive workplace rights, with the emphasis shifting over time from a non-discrimination (equal treatment) standard towards an equality of opportunity (equal outcome) standard, the latter serving as justification for the raft of measures on reconciliation of work and family life. More recently the scope of application has broadened to create a non-discrimination standard in relation to the provision of goods and

---

5 Art. 8a, Directive 76/207/EEC, as amended.

6 Enforcement proceedings have since been concluded in all but one case, as at February 2008.

services. However it is notable that there is little recognition in hard law of the concept of gender equality as a human rights obligation. Burrows and Robison (2007) comment that the Recast Directive was a missed opportunity in this respect, comparing it unfavourably to Directive 2004/38 on citizenship in this respect, and lamenting in particular that it failed to incorporate any reference to CEDAW in its preamble. The case of *Mangold*[7] suggests that this failure may be corrected at an early opportunity by the ECJ, given the opportunity, while a successful conclusion of the ratification process of the Draft Treaty of Lisbon (2007) would strengthen a human rights approach to gender equality through the incorporation of the Charter. What is already clear from the jurisprudence of the ECJ is that protection from sex discrimination is regarded as a fundamental right and one which pervades all areas of Community activity falling within the EC pillar.[8] In addition the mainstreaming duty, a duty positively to promote gender equality, is an important normative ideal.

These horizontal provisions are important as they serve as constraints on both the EU institutions and the Member States in all activities falling within the scope of the EC Treaty. However in the current context they have two important limitations. First, the mainstreaming duty is rather vaguely drafted and in practice has few teeth (Beveridge 2007). Secondly, the OMC, as a 'soft' law process, lies largely beyond effective legal control (see below).

Soft Law in EU gender policy

The use of 'soft law' as a policy-making approach in gender equality policy has a long history. Developments in the *acquis communautaire* have always emerged in parallel with developments in 'soft' policy initiatives with which they interrelate in a variety of ways. Sometimes 'Recommendations' have served to explicate normative agendas, raise the profile of hitherto un-regulated issues and/or test the ground in Member States for the introduction of binding measures in the future: thus, for example, recommendations on (e.g. Code of practice on sexual harassment at work) preceded any 'hard law' measures on the subject.[9] At other times soft law was used to enable progress to be made on issues even in the absence of legal competence, such as on childcare which lay outside the scope of Art 119 (now 141).[10] Measures such as Action Programmes also enabled the Commission to build up a constituency of interested parties, widening its policy agenda and supporting the case for greater competences to be conferred on it. These methods also meant that in periods when the Council lacked the political will to move forward on equality issues, the Commission could continue to push forward under the horizon (Hoskyns 1996; Mazey 1995; Mazey 2000).

---

7 Case C-144/04 Mangold v Helm [2006] All ER (EC) 383 (ECJ).

8 Case C-25/02 Katharina Rinke v Ärztekammer Hamburg [2003] ECR I-8349.

9 Harassment is now dealt with in Art. 2(2) of Directive 76/207, as amended by Directive 2002/73.

10 See for example the Recommendation on Childcare, 1992. This remains true today – childcare targets and recommendations are issued in the context of the EES and are non-binding.

The use of soft law for agenda-setting continues in the present day, with the Framework Strategy (European Commission 2000) and the Roadmap (European Commission 2006) as notable examples. In addition, though, the Member States have adopted a soft 'agenda' in the form of the Gender Pact (European Council 2006) Internally the quality of soft instruments has also evolved as self-monitoring and self-evaluation have become the norm (see below). Thus soft law remains an important feature of EU gender policy and its importance should not be overlooked.

New Governance for Gender Equality

Until the 1990s, equality activities in the European Commission were largely confined to the Equal Opportunities Unit, located within the Directorate-General for Employment and Social Affairs. The turn towards mainstreaming, first introduced in the Third Action Programme and fully endorsed in the Fourth in 1996, heralded both a broader approach extending across many more areas of activity and, in time, a broader range of tools (Beveridge 2007). Indeed many aspects of the programmes developed for the implementation of gender mainstreaming, such as annual target setting, reporting, and the use of a 'scoreboard', closely parallel those used under OMC processes.

Consequently it is not possible to draw a clear distinction between OMC processes and mainstreaming processes in a general or categorical way, since there has clearly been much borrowing and mimicking of policy initiatives across the Commission as a whole. This is clear whether one looks at gender mainstreaming generally (Beveridge 2007) or at a particular policy area. This can be illustrated with reference to the Structural Funds, one of the flagship or pioneer areas for gender mainstreaming in the EU.

In 1996 the Commission referred in the guidelines for the Structural Funds to equal opportunities as a 'horizontal priority', requiring that this dimension be addressed throughout Objective 2 activities. This was followed by the adoption of a resolution on mainstreaming equal opportunities throughout the structural funds (Council 1996), and the adoption of guidelines incorporating this requirement into Objective 1, 5b and 6 activities. As Braithwaite comments, this resolution "had come too late to influence more than superficially the adjustment of Structural Funds programmes for the final period 1997-1999" (Braithwaite 2000). However, following a period of consultation and development, a new regulation in 1999 made gender mainstreaming a requirement across all aspects of the Structural Funds (Regulation 1260/1999). It was possible, on this occasion, to address equal opportunities issues throughout the revision and drafting process on the new regulations, so that equal opportunities' requirements were integrated across a wide range of activities. Surprisingly, perhaps, the Member States broadly accepted this approach, which was also in line with the new commitment to gender mainstreaming inserted as Article 3(2) of EC Treaty by the Treaty of Amsterdam. Gender equality is explicitly mentioned in 10 of the 56 articles of the 1999 regulation, which clearly embraces the dual strategy of combining gender mainstreaming with specific actions on equal opportunities.

Pollack and Hafner-Burton note that the acceptance of the concept of gender mainstreaming in the Structural Funds context was achieved by the strategic framing of mainstreaming as a question of economic efficiency; that is, by suggesting that the Structural Funds would fail in their task of reducing long-term economic and social disparities between the European regions if structural inequalities between men and women were not addressed (Pollack and Hafner-Burton 2000: 441). The introduction of a gender mainstreaming approach thus built on a developing understanding that previous rounds of Structural Funds programmes had failed in this respect (Braithwaite 2000). This analysis is carried through into the 1999 revisions, and formed the starting point for evaluation of progress under the new regulation: "until now, the Funds have mainly supported specific measures for women or pilot projects. These are important but cannot remedy structural inequalities." (Commission 2002: 3)

Braithwaite draws attention to activities organized by the Commission to support the introduction of a gender mainstreaming approach to the Structural Funds. European conferences in 1996 and 1998 sought to disseminate this approach to officials within Member States carrying responsibilities for equal opportunities: this in turn may have served to empower these people within their own policymaking circles. Good practice was disseminated and recommendations drafted. The Commission has also conducted work on instruments and indicators which can be used to measure and monitor the gender impacts of Community-funded interventions. A final role played by the Commission itself is as advocate, encouraging Member States to develop good practice, to adopt particular approaches recommended by the Commission and generally, to give the issue of gender high priority in Structural Funds activities. While this prioritization is required to some extent under the Regulations, the Commission is able, through its co-operative activities with Member States to encourage states to go above and beyond the paper requirements.

Over time, these activities intensified. A number of weaknesses were identified in the approach to gender equality which had been pursued in the period 1994-1999. One was that gender equality was mostly addressed through specific measures of support for women, or pilot projects, neither of which tackled structural inequalities in the labour market. Another was that gender equality was largely seen as relevant to the ESF, rather than the Structural Funds more generally, though some success was noted in the New Opportunities for Women initiative, particularly relating to women's entrepreneurship and initiatives to reduce segregation in the labour market.

The 1999 regulation governing the period 2000-2006 broadened the gender equality dimension and incorporated this into the methodological working papers. Gender requirements were incorporated in relation to programming, ex-ante evaluation, monitoring and evaluation. In addition a technical paper was produced by the Commission, detailing the practical arrangements for mainstreaming gender (Commission 2000). In 2002 the Commission produced a report on implementation of gender mainstreaming in Structural Funds programming for 2000-2006 (Commission 2002). This report yielded a number of important conclusions:

> Gender equality activity was concentrated in the field of employment and human resource development and funded to a large extent by the ESF: it was neglected in areas such as environment, transport, rural development and research and development. (European Commission 2002: 4)

It was also noted that measures which reinforced existing gender patterns and labour force segregation were more common than measures to reduce gender segregation, reduce the gender pay gap or promote women in decision-making. This was particularly noticeable in growth sectors such as information technology. This suggested the need for further development of the mainstreaming approach. The most recent revisions to Structural Funds Regulations demonstrate further intensification of the gender mainstreaming approach and the particular requirements associated with this, with a horizontal mainstreaming article in the General Regulation (Council 2006: Art. 16) supplemented by more detailed provisions in the new ESF Regulation (Regulation 1081/2006: Art. 2(2); Art. 3(1)(b)(iii); Art. 4(5); Art. 6; Art. 10) and by supporting instruments (c.f. Commission 2006). The approach is a dual one, of cross-cutting mainstreaming, supplemented with positive action in specific areas, and the documentation ties the new phase of structural funds closely to the Lisbon agenda. Attention is paid also to implementation:

> The programming strategy of a Member State should integrate gender mainstreaming into every step of policy processes, and should be applied as a cross-cutting horizontal principle, incorporating the gender dimension to all stages of programming, implementation, and evaluation process. (Commission, 2006; Regulation 1081/2006, Art. 6)

Moreover, representation of women in the governance of programmes is also subject to scrutiny, with Member States required to promote balanced participation in the management of programmes at local, regional and national levels (Regulation 1081/2006: Art. 6). This outline of the introduction of gender mainstreaming into the Structural Funds – not an OMC area – suffices to demonstrate the processes by which gender mainstreaming has been implemented into particular policy areas. It is noteworthy that the tools developed display cyclical processes of evaluation, policy learning, target-setting and monitoring – the constituents of a virtuous circle which is also often seen as the hallmark of OMC processes.

This brief consideration of the Structural Funds demonstrates, in conclusion, that no clear line can be drawn between 'OMC' and 'non-OMC' processes or policy areas in terms of the tools and techniques used. Against this background analysing the interplay between OMC and EU gender equality law is fraught with difficulty.

The Creation of the OMC

As noted in chapter 1, the OMC first emerged in conjunction with the development of the EES in 1997. It is often presented as a compromise between two competing demands: one, that the Member States develop a coordinated approach to employment to stimulate competitiveness and growth; and the other that control of employment policy remain with the Member States. Addressing a wide range of economic situations in different Member States, set to increase with pending enlargement, was another significant factor. Under the strategy agreed, general policy goals are agreed by consensus, with the Council agreeing general guidelines on the basis of reports drawn up analysing the problem. These general guidelines are then addressed to individual Member States along with tailored recommendations, and the states in turn produced national action plans. Implementation of these plans is supplemented by exchanges of information and good practice between states and periodic review mechanisms are created to help build up a detailed picture of the results. These are then followed up by mutual evaluation, peer review and the subsequent instigation of a new cycle. OMC now exists in various forms in a plethora of policy areas (Szcszyzak 2007) and in each it has evolved over time so that no particular version ever seems to crystallize.

There are many aspects of OMC which raise challenges for scholars: the range and diverse forms of the OMC processes, the variable relationships between these processes and 'harder' processes in different policy domains, its relatively porous nature, with ideas feeding into and emerging from OMC processes in a multitude of ways and directions, and the general difficulty of attributing any causal links between OMC activity and national policy change. Though some commentators stress that the OMC is not new at all, but rather a continuation of older forms of policy-making (Hatzopoulos 2007), it has been read by scholars as presenting new challenges. The multi-level nature of the process, its apparently iterative style, and its heavy reliance on 'soft' mechanisms may mean that many of the analytical tools associated with European policy studies are harder to deploy here: compliance-centred analyses, policy tracing methods and textual analyses all appear rather problematic, though the more encompassing but rather open-ended Europeanization-centred enquiries may better capture the OMC processes.

The chapters in this collection focus mainly on two OMC areas, the EES and the Social Exclusion Strategy, both central to the effective promotion of gender equality. The development of a Community dimension in Member State employment policies came about as a result of the incorporation of a new 'Employment' chapter in the EC Treaty by the Treaty of Amsterdam in 1997 and, as O'Connor and Aybars both document, the promotion of gender equality in employment has been a central concern. Target-setting has been particularly clear in this area, with the Lisbon strategy establishing clear targets for the female employment rate in all states of 57 per cent by 2005 and over 60 per cent by 2010 and the Barcelona Council in 2002 setting targets for the provision of childcare for 90 per cent of children between 3 years old and the mandatory school starting age and for 33 per cent of children under 3 (European Council 2000; 2002).

The concept of the social policy agenda emerged from the Lisbon Ministerial Council in 2000, as a key pillar of the EU's new 'integrated' approach towards economic and social renewal. The adoption of a social policy agenda was an act both of continuity and of change: continuity, because it recognized the previous contribution and on-going importance of the European 'social model' to the project of European integration; and change, because it marked the beginning of a reorientation or refocusing of the 'social' aspects of the EU project to support the economic goals adopted at the Lisbon summit.

The EU's new strategic goal for the period 2000-2010 was to become "the most competitive and dynamic knowledge-based economy capable of sustainable economic growth with more and better jobs and greater social cohesion" (European Council 2000a). Within this context, the stated role of the Social Policy Agenda was "to strengthen the role of social policy as a productive factor" (European

Commission 2000). Thus, in the wake of a period where there was great focus on the need to reduce public expenditure to meet the convergence criteria established in relation to Economic and Monetary Union (EMU), there was now a rather different message from the EU: according to the Social Exclusion Strategy "[Most] social expenditure on health and education represents an investment in human resources, with positive economic effects...there can be a positive correlation between the scale of such expenditure and the level of productivity in the countries concerned." Also stated clearly is that the new Social Policy Agenda "does not seek to harmonize social policies." Working towards the Lisbon objectives, with increased coordination of social policy where appropriate, greater efficiency and better focus towards investment in people are the key strategies of social policy.

The Social Policy Agenda was to be pursued by an OMC process, but the role of legislation, social dialogue and the Structural Funds were also emphasized. The tool of mainstreaming was to be further strengthened and developed and the close relationship between the employment policies and the Social Policy Agenda was stressed at many points. Given this acknowledged relationship and the failure of many states to deal with particular issues such as reconciliation of work and family life across the two processes in a cohesive manner (see O'Connor, Koldinská, in this volume) the 2008 synchronization of the EES and the Social Policy Agenda was perhaps inevitable.

Gender equality is one of the key areas of focus within the Social Policy Agenda. Equality of opportunity is seen as central both to the employment dimension (to both the goal of full employment and the goal of improving quality at work) and to the social dimension (to both promoting social cohesion and addressing social quality). While gender inequality in particular, is addressed at many points in the documentation, there is an accompanying concern that all socially excluded groups require assistance. In detailing the objections and actions proposed to meet those objectives, the Commission focuses on gender equality in the following ways:

- on "more and better jobs" – to raise employment levels generally, and particularly to meet the target of 60 per cent of women in work by 2010, gender segregation and low skill and low wage employment need to tackled;
- on "exploiting the opportunities of the knowledge-based economy" – to accelerate the development of the knowledge based society, there is a need to close the gender and skills gaps, to promote the employability and access of women to ICT and other scientific and technological jobs, particularly through education and training;
- on "promoting social inclusion" – to tackle poverty and promote economic and social integration, an integrated and comprehensive approach is required which includes a gender perspective;
- on "reinforcing fundamental rights and combating discrimination" – the need for direct involvement of all key actors "in particular non governmental organisations and grassroots organisations" is stressed. Dialogue between the Commission and social NGOs, and co-operation between the social partners and NGOs are identified as key strategies;

- on "preparing for enlargement" – the need to mainstream gender equality in the pre-accession strategy is recognized.

Besides these specific items, there are many other areas of the Social Policy Agenda outlined by the Commission where gender equality considerations would generally be regarded as central to effective policy-making and where, therefore it might be expected that the institutions and the Member States would elaborate further in due course. This means, in effect, that the social policy process has become a highly significant context for the future development of gender equality issues in the European Union. Besides positioning gender equality firmly at the core of the EU project, the embrace of social policy as part of the Lisbon strategy raised its importance and its profile as an EU policy. It set in motion a process of monitoring and revision with the potential to give gender equality policy an unprecedented push. Writing about traditional gender equality policy Ostner and Lewis (1995) identified the need to negotiate new policy developments through the two 'needles' eyes' of the EU and the Member State polities. A key question for this collection is whether that process has become easier as a result of the development of OMC processes around the EES and the social policy agenda, both of which appear to strongly embrace a gender equality ambition.

The following emerged as key themes of the papers.

Gender and the Nation State

One of the key issues which arises in relation to gender equality and the OMC is the question of whether and how OMC processes reflect, respond to and take account of diversity between the Member States. This question arises in relation to both hard and soft policy-making processes, so the question in reality is whether and to what extent the soft OMC processes take greater account of diversity.

Hard law methods take account of diversity in a range of ways. First, in areas of shared or complementary competence at least, the principles of subsidiarity and proportionality restrain the Community institutions from action at all, except where the objectives cannot be achieved sufficiently well by the Member States themselves, and confine Community action to that which is necessary to achieve the objective in question (Article 5 EC). The Protocol on the Application of the Principles of Subsidiarity and Proportionality, added by the Treaty of Amsterdam, reiterates earlier understandings too that forms of legislation leaving more scope to Member States in the implementation process should be preferred where possible (e.g. Directives over Regulations) and that well-established national arrangements and legal systems should be respected. Openness and consultation in the preparatory phases are also promoted in this Protocol.

Hard law can also take account of diversity between nations in its substantive provisions which can leave room for higher national standards on the part of some states, or included 'not-lowering-standards' provisions,[11] or allow opt-outs for

11 In Mangold, supra note 7, the ECJ noted that implementation of a measure could not in itself serve as justification for lowering standards, but noted that such provisions did not

certain states and/or on certain issues. Even where hard law appears to promote a universal solution to a particular problem, studies reveal that the way in which these rules actually operate in the context of differing national legal systems will vary enormously: a substantial body of literature on legal transplants now testifies to this.

Despite these formal and empirical accommodations of diversity it can be argued that hard law generally possesses a hegemonic character and, on paper at least, proposes a unity of outcomes, or of minimum standards at least, for the Member States. Formally the same rules apply to all and, in an abstract sense at least, all must take the same or similar steps to comply, though in reality this will impose a greater burden on some than others.

OMC methods, by contrast, operate differently. Although policy goals are collectively determined and there is therefore unity of purpose in a sense, these are meta-goals for the EU as a whole and there is no expectation that this will translate into equal demands on all states even formally. The EES exemplifies this well, with general recommendations directed towards all states, coupled with individually-tailored recommendations directed to each Member State. On the face of things, therefore, diversity can be more fully accommodated in the OMC processes than is typical in the traditional hard law Community processes.

In respect of gender equality which, as was discussed above, is a fundamental right and a 'core value' of the European Union, the question arises of how much diversity in levels of protection can or should be permitted. At what point does respect for diversity between different states tip over into acceptance of inequality? This question cannot be answered in the abstract – it is necessary to know in greater detail what the duty to eliminate discrimination and the duty to promote equality entail, both in substance and in scope. When this is clarified it is clearly then one thing to accept that different states will take longer to reach an agreed common goal, and hence that lower targets are currently justified, and another to allow national autonomy or political choices to undermine that common goal.

This analysis must underpin an examination of diversity in OMC processes from a gender equality perspective. It should be asked whether there is clear evidence in the OMC processes examined of policy diversity from a gender equality perspective. If there is, is the accommodation of policy diversity treated merely as a starting point – i.e. supporting the advocacy of different solutions to bring the parties from their divergent positions to points closer together – or is diversity also treated as a valid and desirable outcome – i.e. supporting the preservation of national cultures, social and political attitudes and systems as an end in itself? If it seems that divergences in gender regimes are seen as valid outcomes, what in turn does this suggest about the conceptualization of gender equality and the duty to promote gender equality at EU level?

In the OMC this is critical to an analysis of how the identification and sharing of good practice operates and is managed: the degree to which some states seek to evangelize, promoting their solutions as models for others to copy. The issue of diversity therefore raises both normative and empirical questions: normative questions about the extent to which diversity should be preserved, encouraged and/

---

guarantee against the lowering of standards for other unconnected reasons.

or promoted; and empirical questions about the extent to which OMC, as compared to traditional Community processes succeeds or fails in these objectives.

The study of diversity raises difficult methodological questions about comparative technique and about the use of 'models' as standards against which to measure change. Annesley (2007), following the conceptual categories established by Lewis (2001), identifies the Adult Worker Model as a central goal of the EES, arguing further that the EES has supported a turn to a 'supported' rather than 'unsupported' Adult Worker Model in ways which are potentially very significant from a gender perspective, particularly in providing a normative justification for policies aimed at easing the reconciliation of work and family life. The use in this way of a substantive policy model as a 'benchmark' for the EES has clear potential. Such models may serve as a barometer against which improving and deteriorating state performances might be measured and as a counterpoint to the absence of a clear vision of gender equality (see below).

Within this volume both Aybars and Velluti rely on Esping-Andersen's typology of welfare states and deliberately choose for their case studies states which fall into different categories within that typology, Aybars supplementing it to take account of the Southern enlargement of the EU to encompass Spain, Portugal and Greece. However, for the future, the 2004 and 2007 EU enlargements invite the development of a further category or categories, though it is not yet clear what that might be. In addition, the use by Aybars of France rather than Germany as an example of a conservative welfare regime raises interesting questions about the utility of the Esping-Andersen typology where gender policy is concerned since those two states present very different problems from a gender/family policy perspective, as Aybars makes clear. The focus in this volume on the OMC and gender can contribute to future debates about a welfare state typology, as the practice of tailoring policy recommendations to each individual state, based on empirical evidence generated through the monitoring and benchmarking processes, invites a fresh look 'behind the labels' of such models.

As noted, a future challenge arises from the 2004 and 2007 enlargements, which have brought into the European Union new states who cannot be readily 'inserted' into Esping-Andersen's existing typology and which suggest the need for further categories, if this typology is to remain useful in the EU context. Koldinská selects five states for examination, the Czech Republic, Slovakia, Slovenia, Estonia and Poland, all of which present slightly different welfare state models, raising questions about how such further categories could be defined.

Another possible model revolves around the concept of gender. Aybars, in earlier work, refers to the substantial body of French-language literature on gender contracts (Aybars 2007). Elsewhere Walby (2004) uses the concept of a multi-variant gender regime and suggests that the EU is in the process of creating a new model of gender regime through its articulation of policies across a broad range of policy domains. This would seem to be promising territory for the future: a key challenge for such models is to capture the gender characteristics and differences of States across a broad range of policy areas in ways which will enable the complementary mapping and evaluation of gender mainstreaming strategies and policies.

One key theme to emerge in this collection is the significance and influence of diversity among Member States in relation to gender equality. OMC accommodates this diversity in two distinct ways. First, as a 'soft' process it leaves room for states to negotiate their 'compliance' with the stated targets or policies in ways which differentiate it from hard law options: it is, as O'Connor identifies, a 'two-level' game. Secondly, it allows for a differentiated approach with different targets and policy changes being set for different states. Thus it does not seek to homogenize Member State approaches to the same extent as harder policy-making approaches and, indeed, could be used to promote increased diversification on some issues if that is what the overall policy objective appeared to require.

However, this diversity raises further issues. As with hard law processes, questions arise about which states have the stronger influence on the development of policies i.e. which are net importers and which net exporters of policy. In the development of hard law proposals negotiations are mediated through the arrangements for the adoption of legislation and the process is, on the whole, open and transparent involving, in most cases, the Commission (as drafter) and the Council and the Parliament (as legislator and depending on the precise legislative method specified) and also including in many instances opportunities for consultation with other institutions such as ECOSOC and/or the Social Partners and/or other non-governmental bodies. OMC, on the other hand, depends on different processes in which (typically) the Commission will have fairly strong powers to assess the progress of each Member State and to propose recommendations which will then be adopted by the European Council, widely acknowledged to be the least transparent of the institutions. Against this background it may be difficult to detect the direction and flow of policy transfer, particularly in light of the discursive aspects of the OMC process.

Yet from an analytical point of view it is important to remain sensitive to this phenomenon, as a key structural element of the OMC. Laid bare for a short period, perhaps, during the process leading to the 2004 accession, 'mutual learning' can in fact translate into a one-way process (Fuszara in this volume), just as the accommodation of the *acquis communitaire* is not subject to negotiation in the accession context. The apparent 'soft' and consensual form of the OMC should not blind commentators to this possibility.

Visions of Gender Equality

A recurrent theme in the chapters of this book is the question of what sort of equality can or should be promoted at EU level, and what vision of equality underpins current OMC initiatives. A number of developments make this question particularly pertinent at this time. Gender mainstreaming has developed, as I have argued elsewhere, as a response to perceptions that previous equal opportunities policies and laws have failed to deliver equality. This in itself raises the question about what 'success' and 'failure' look like, and how gender mainstreaming can offer more promise than those previous policies. Moreover, the turn to gender mainstreaming has expanded the scope of community gender policy to cover new areas, such as violence against women and health, raising questions about whether, in any case, the concept of equality pursued in those areas should reflect past approaches or whether new policy areas require new thinking. In tandem to this, OMC has developed, as noted above, in areas not susceptible to regulation under the Community method for reasons of competence and/or political expedience. Thus it too operates in areas which are 'new' to the EU and in which ideas about gender equality are open to negotiation.

Moreover many of the areas covered by OMC processes – social exclusion, employment policy, health care and pensions – are areas in which the boundary between the public policy arena and the private or family sphere is very much open to contestation. Policies in these areas help to shape the public/private divide which feminist commentators have identified as central to the maintenance of gender inequalities in society, and have the capacity to address key elements of the 'organisation of intimacy' (Verloo 2005; Verloo and Lombardo 2007) within what might generally be labelled the 'domestic' sphere.

Despite this, it is a commonly-raised concern about the OMC areas above, and of community gender equality law and policy more generally, that EU initiatives in these areas are not grounded in any clear articulation of gender objectives (Beveridge 2007; Daly 2005; Lombardo and Meier 2007; Rubery and Fagan 2000). Indeed while feminist commentators have increasingly articulated the need for the EU's gender equality policy and mainstreaming initiatives to pursue 'transformative' goals (Rees 1998; Squires 2005; Walby 2005), in essence seeking to re-write the gender contract, it is also widely noted that in OMC areas gender equality issues are consistently framed as efficiency concerns and subjugated to the meta-goals of the OMC process in question (Beveridge 2007; Fredman 2006; Rubery 2002). Thus in EES and the Social Policy Agenda gender equality is a means for improving the success rate and hence advancing the 'Lisbon' agenda. In pensions, addressing the issues of female poverty linked to contributions-based pensions systems is an essential component of the 'adequacy' pillar which focuses on preventing social exclusion in old age, allowing people to maintain their living standards in retirement, and promoting inter-generational solidarity. Meanwhile in health the gender dimension of health, though recognized and promoted by the European Parliament, has received little attention.

An argument advanced by Rubery (2003) is that the OMC is in fact too 'open' in this respect, leaving Member States too much freedom to assert that their policies promote gender equality, with no effective criteria against which such claims can be assessed. She cites the example of states being able to define 'unemployment' for themselves, rendering the requirement that activation policies involve women and men in proportion to their relative unemployment rates meaningless since this enabled some states to discount women who were ineligible for unemployment benefits.

This problem is not, however, confined to the areas dealt with by OMC processes but a central problem in EU gender law and policy. The MAGEEQ and QUING projects[12] have demonstrated the way in which gender mainstreaming initiatives undergo meaning shifts as they are framed to 'fit' into different policy areas (Verloo 2007), and similar arguments have been raised about mainstreaming in asylum policy (Bell 2001), family policy (Lombardo and Meier 2007) and more generally (Pollack and Hafner-Burton 2000). This raises the more fundamental question of what sort of vision of equality the EU can and should pursue, and how this should

12 www.mageeq.net and www.quing.eu.

be linked to debates about governance. This, in turn, would seem to straddle debates about the constitutional reform of the European Union, and the place of equality in those reforms, and debates about the European Social Model.

The first of these questions is dealt with by Shaw, who considers whether the (then) Constitutional Treaty (see now the Draft Treaty of Lisbon) "offer(s) the possibility of a more comprehensive and comprehensible policy of mainstreaming equality and diversity within the law and policy-making practices of the EU" (Shaw 2005). Shaw argues that while the likely treaty revisions focus mainly on the traditional law-making methods of the EU, the provisions on equality and diversity need to go beyond this and into the realms of 'new governance' to deliver effectively. Additionally she argues that mainstreaming demands a new culture of governance, with greater opportunities for participation, concluding that the revised Treaty contains "important proposed changes, which could set the frame for a different type of politics of equality and diversity in a future European Union." Key to this is the way in which gender mainstreaming in turn is conceptualized and hence, in Shaw's account, the goal and the tools are inescapably interlinked, indeed deeply entwined with each other, within wider debates about governance. In this she echoes Squires (2005) who similarly highlights the links between the processes of decision-making and the outcomes, linking the development of mainstreaming to discussions of democratic deliberation and legitimacy. Verloo *et al.* (2007) focus on participation, particularly by civil society, as a strategy of empowerment, creating space for alternative non-hegemonic voices to be heard, including within feminism. Both carry implications for this collection of chapters in highlighting the inter-relationships between processes and outcomes and pointing to the impossibility of providing an adequate account of gender in OMC processes without examining these two elements together. The focus on deliberative democracy is particularly salient in discussions of OMC processes since improved transparency and democratic participation are held up as key potential benefits of the OMC mode of governance (De la Porte and Nanz 2004).

From a slightly different tack, a number of commentators approach the OMC as a mode of governance which offers potential for the development and embedding of a new European Social Model (e.g. Pochet 2005; Jepsen and Serrano Pascual 2005), and it is possible to approach the issue of gender in the OMC from this perspective (Scharpf 2002; Esping-Andersen 2002). This maps well onto the key OMC policy areas of EES and Social Exclusion as well as offering a good fit with the view of gender mainstreaming as a horizontal strategy operating across a range of policy areas. Indeed as Annesley (2007) demonstrates, introducing gender into debates about the European Social Model opens up key questions about the model and highlights that it is far from uncontested as a vision for Europe.

Both of these approaches raise very challenging questions about how gender equality 'fits' into the core values of the EU, and its place in future EU activities.

Strengths and Limitations of 'Soft' Approaches

What can we learn about this from OMC practices? From gender mainstreaming practices? How does the choice of hard/soft relate to EU political commitment on the one hand and Member State acceptance/compliance on the other?

The introduction and formal recognition of OMC as a mode of governance in the EU has rekindled interest in debates about 'hard' and 'soft' law and issues of compliance. 'The labels 'hard' and 'soft' have their origins in a positivist legal mind-set which rests on a dichotomous distinction between 'law' and 'non-law', in which 'soft' law possesses some, but not all, of the characteristics of law. Typically, soft law will lack the formal characteristics of law i.e. it will not have recognized binding force, but will nonetheless impact on certain parties – i.e. cause them to modify their behaviour – as if it were law in a formal sense. Often attention focuses too, on the absence of legal sanctions in relation to soft law measures, despite the fact that in many contexts legal obligations can be said to have 'binding force' even in the absence of sanctions.

This form of discourse about hard and soft law fits well with the EU which has a strongly defined and well-delimited legal order. Formal legal measures are recognized as having binding force, variously on the institutions, the Member States and on natural and legal persons who are operating in the territory of the Member States, who possess the nationality of a Member State or who are otherwise determined by legal process to fall under the scope of operation of EU law. Generally sanctions exist for breaches of EU law, notwithstanding that in some areas take-up of litigation is very low or nearly non-existent. Moreover there are rarely disputes about whether a particular measure has binding legal force or not – the identification of 'legal acts' in Article 249(EC),[13] together with the principle of attributed powers (Article 5), mean that beyond challenges to the validity of some acts, legal debates tend to focus instead on the reach of particular provisions, for instance on the direct or incidental effects of a Directive in private law contexts.

Under the traditional Community method, therefore, Regulations and Directives and Decisions always have binding force, as do certain treaties, whereas Recommendations and Commission Communications never do. Attention has therefore focussed, in this binding/non-binding debate, on other ways in which recommendations and Commission Communications may influence the determination of the legal position or the future behaviour of parties.

It is at this point that terminological confusion enters the discussion. In the positivist law/non-law dichotomy, the term 'soft law' is generally confined to acts which, though not formally legally binding, do possess some characteristic which is law-like *and which distinguishes those acts from other 'soft' instruments.* In other words, legal positivism focuses on the law-like elements of 'soft law' measures, in turn distinguishing soft law measures from other 'mere' policy measures. By contrast more empirically-grounded or policy-based discourses tend to focus not on any essential characteristics of measures but on their impact. From this perspective there is a tendency to lump together all non-binding policy measures which appear to have visible impact on the future behaviour of parties as 'soft law.'

---

13 Similar provisions exist in the TEU, though there is less cohesion: see e.g. Arts. 12, 14, 15, and 34. The legal acts of the European Central Bank, by contrast are clearly defined in Art.34 of the Protocol on the Statute of the European System of Central Banks and of the European Central Bank.

This definitional confusion pervades accounts of the OMC which is frequently described as a 'soft law' approach with little or no explanation of that term, or of how OMC measures satisfy any definitional criteria. This is problematic in the context of a comparative discussion of the advantages of traditional Community method and OMC, since such discussions often proceed on the basis of unspecified assumptions: first, that Community method is based entirely on the production of 'hard law' measures (ignoring the significant role, in gender equality policy, for instance, of 'soft measures'); and secondly, because it often fails to recognize that measures which are 'hard' from a positivist perspective i.e. which have formal binding force, will have hugely different rates of implementation, observance, compliance and enforcement from an empirical perspective i.e. hard law may not have the presumed impact on the behaviour of actors which lies behind its labelling as 'hard' in many accounts. In reality there is no strict correlation between these elements and the hard/soft dichotomy – 'soft' measures may at times produce greater impact than 'hard' measures, for example if they give rise to 'pro-active' measures to combat inequality, rather than a (negative) injunction not to discriminate.

OMC can be seen to suggest the use of a broad range of policy tools within states, both 'hard' and 'soft.' Its discursive nature and its focus on outcomes invite states to report on both central and flanking policies in each area, reporting on initiatives ranging from new legislation to research studies and training programmes. This is clearly different from the situation under the 'community method', whereby the EU institutions have a clear interest in the transposition of hard law rules into the legal orders of the Member States, and otherwise rely largely on litigation to expose weaknesses in compliance and enforcement. The widening of the lens under OMC to take notice of a broader range of measures might be expected to have the effect of legitimising 'soft' measures within Member States which are portrayed as contributing to Community policy.

Actors

Who are the actors who participate in OMC (and who doesn't)? Why? What does it matter? A number of the chapters in this book raise issues about the actors who participate in OMC processes, about the effectiveness of their participation, and about those who are excluded or sidelined. Both empirical and normative questions arise.

Empirical approaches might question who the actors are who are currently engaged in OMC processes, what their respective roles are, how effective that engagement is and how the constellation of actors here differs from those active under traditional EU law – and policy-making processes. In this connection much is made of the fact that OMC is, by its nature, a multilevel process, on the one hand, and that it requires the involvement of the Social Partners, on the other. However, both of these observations are also true of traditional social law and policy in the EU, and there is a danger that these elements are over-emphasized in the OMC literature.

To begin with, then, some trite observations can be made about the differences between the roles of the institutions and key players in OMC by comparison with traditional social policy:

- The Commission's role is different and probably enhanced in OMC, though it still performs its familiar functions of policy development and monitoring, and it is probably subject to less direct scrutiny by the Parliament. Hodson and Maher (2001: 729) argued that "[t]he Commission's role of analysis, neutrality and synopsis is different from under the classic Monnet method and arguably weakened with its usual agenda-setting function reduced." However they also suggested that it might regain influence over time, given, in particular, its considerable secretariat role and intellectual resources and this may well have happened.
- The Parliament's role is reduced which may be of significance first, because it is widely taken to inject greater democratic input into EU affairs; and second, because it has quite a strong record, historically, on gender equality issues.
- The Council's role is enhanced, not least because the need to find consensus is tempered by the ability to adopt different guidelines for different states, but also because the process is inter-governmental rather than supra-national and subject to far less external scrutiny. Two factors may explain this: first, that in this policy-setting role the Council has historically had an extensive freedom and autonomy which is merely continued in OMC processes; and secondly, that the obligations are non-binding and hence non-justiciable. Notably it seems to make little difference whether the OMC in question involves the European Council or the Council of Ministers – the result is the same.
- The Court of Justice appears to have very little role in this area, due to its soft nature. On the one hand, it is only where OMC processes lead to recommendations for hard law measures can the Court have much role, since the Court will only exercise its jurisdiction to review the legality of acts of the institutions where those acts are intended to have legal effects.[14] On the other hand, since most OMCs have developed in areas where Community competences are absent or weak, there is in fact little overlap (but see further below).

Further parties involved in OMC processes include the Social Partners, whose formal involvement in social affairs dates back to the Treaty of Maastricht and whose involvement is an extension of the long-standing European Social Dialogue. Velluti (in this book) explores the involvement of the Social Partners in OMC processes. As with gender mainstreaming, however, it is difficult to separate OMC and non-OMC processes. One reason is that the Social Partners are guaranteed roles both in traditional and non-traditional modes of governance: indeed recognition of the role of the Social Partners is confirmed in the text of the Draft Treaty of Lisbon (2007: Srt. 136a). The other is that they are active over a wide range of issues straddling

14 Case 22/70 Commission v Council [1971] ECR 263; Case C-57/95 France v Commission.

OMC and non-OMC areas of activity, such as the promotion of better employment practices to combat discrimination in recruitment and promotion, the adoption of policies to encourage the introduction and take-up of reconciliation measures, and the raising of awareness of career options for girls (c.f. ETUC *et al.* 2007).

It is clear that the OMC also implicates a different and potentially wider range of actors in the implementation of recommendations than might generally be involved formally at least in the implementation of legal norms. The category might include the social partners but also extends to many governmental and non-governmental bodies: in the EES, for example, it might include public and private bodies involved in employment activation and training initiatives, education, childcare provision and regeneration agencies. The question of which actors are involved is linked in the literature on OMC to the question of effectiveness: since the OMC is an iterative, policy learning process, the involvement of a broad range of key actors, and their 'socialisation' through the OMC process, is regarded as key to its success (Atkinson 2002).

Two key questions, therefore, are whether that involvement is evident in practice and, if so, whether it makes the assumed contribution to the effectiveness of OMC policies. The first is raised in a number of the contributions to this chapter while the second, by its nature, is much more difficult to assess. Normative questions also arise. One derives from the description of OMC as a form of 'competence creep' (Szcszyzak 2006) whereby the EU is developing or intensifying its policy competence in areas where no or only weak competences have been formally conferred. However this is contested with others seeing the development of OMC processes as a form of repatriation of power to the Member States: under this view the fact that the recommendations are 'soft' demonstrates that no transfer of competence has occurred and the argument suggests that the inter-governmental nature of the process has reinvigorated Member State activity in areas where policy development and/or coordination was previously weak. Szyszczak, for instance, gives the example of the healthcare OMC which was designed in part "to handle the erosion of the Member States' sovereignty in the area of providing medical services as a result of the increasing opportunistic litigation before the Court of Justice" (Szyszczak 2006: 494).

A second perspective focuses on OMC as a potential source of 'reverse competence creep.' Here the argument starts from the premise that there are spillovers from OMC policy areas e.g. from EES into social policy, including equality, or from the Broad Economic Policy Guidelines into Economic and Monetary Union, and that the possibility of 'reverse competence creep' arises where OMC processes and associated 'soft' measures are utilized in place of the hard measures which might have been adopted under Community competences (Hatzopoulos 2007). There seems to be no legal safeguard against this: indeed the Draft Treaty of Lisbon (2007: Art. 249D) seems to confirm that the Council can adopt Recommendations in any area, and regardless of the existing competences laid down elsewhere in the treaties.

Both these perspectives centre on issues of legitimacy, an issue which is high on the agenda of many commentators. In relation to 'competence creep' the issue is the long-running question of whether, in running ahead of reforms of the treaties and the debates over a new constitutional settlement OMC represents a threat to whatever fragile consensus might have been reached over the division of competences between the Member States and the EU institutions. The latter, by contrast, raises the suggestion that powerful OMC processes which have the support of the Member States could have the effect of 'hollowing out' the competences of the institutions derived from the Treaty and hence could jeopardize what is assumed to be an inter-institutional (and Community – Member State) balance with some claim to legitimacy. On a more practical level Hatzopoulos (2007) adds to this that the Commission's strong involvement in the OMC runs the risk that it will have to reign in its other functions, threatening the efficiency of the EU and the rule of law and protection of individuals.

Each perspective raises a plethora of questions about the actors included in or excluded from OMC processes and the grounds on which such inclusions and exclusions are based. Again there is no easy basis for comparison of OMC processes in this regard to other processes as the 'traditional' policy-making processes present a very wide variety of configurations for the formal involvement or less formal consultation of a broad array of actors and interest groups.

In mainstreaming literature the question of actors is relevant to the issue of how participatory mainstreaming practices are, and the extent to which mainstreaming can be conceived as a form of deliberative democracy, as discussed above, and similar issues have been raised about OMC (Scott and Trubeck 2002). These arguments approach the question of actors within a legitimacy frame, and as a critique of existing arrangements. Benz, writing about the OMC, challenges the idea that widening participation might improve legitimacy by raising issues of accountability and arguing that 'soft' processes like OMC might simply 'facilitate the blame game' (Benz 2007). Clearly there are important issues here, though it is open to debate from a gender perspective how 'new' and' traditional' forms of accountability can best be developed and co-opted to improve gender outcomes.

Conclusion

This chapter has set out the background to the issues raised in the following seven chapters by setting out in a brief form the development of EU gender equality policy on the one hand and OMC on the other. It has also introduced and offered some reflective comment on four key themes which seem to underpin the chapters which follow. It can be seen that the task of this volume, to examine the contribution which OMC might make to the furtherance of gender equality policy, presents considerable challenges for researchers. OMC offers considerable potential, as well as raising a host of concerns from a wide range of perspectives: these included issues about effectiveness, legitimacy and good governance. In Chapter 10, Beveridge and Velluti return to these themes to draw together some of the evidence which emerges from the intervening chapters, and to consider what light, if any, they shed on the many questions raised here.

References

Alter, K.J. and Vargas, J. (2000), 'Explaining Variation in the Use of European Litigation Strategies: European Community Law and British Gender Equality Policy' *Comparative Political Studies* 33: 452-82.

Annesley, C. (2007), 'Lisbon and Social Europe: Towards a European 'Adult Worker Model' Welfare System' *Journal of European Social Policy* 17: 195-205.

Atkinson, T. (2002), 'Social Inclusion and the European Union' *Journal of Common Market Studies* 40(4): 625-43.

Aybars, A.I. (2007), 'Patterns of Europeanisation across Welfare Regimes: Gender Equality in Employment From the Treaty of Rome to the Open Method of Coordination' Ph.D. thesis, University of Ulster.

Bell, M. (2001), 'Mainstreaming Equality Norms into European Union Asylum Law' *European Law Review* 26: 20-59.

Benz, A. (2007), 'Accountable Multilevel Governance by the Open Method of Coordination?' *European Law Journal* 13(4): 505-522.

Beveridge, F. (2007), 'Building Against the Past: The Impact of Mainstreaming on EU Gender Law and Policy' *European Law Review* 32: 193-212.

Braithwaite, M. (2000), 'Mainstreaming Gender in European Structural Funds' Paper prepared for the Mainstreaming Gender in European Public Policy Workshop, University of Wisconsin-Madison, Oct 14-15, 2000.

Burrows, N. and Robison, M. (2007), 'An Assessment of the Recast of Community Equality Laws' *European Law Journal* 13(2): 186-203.

Commission of the European Communities (2000b), Communication from the Commission to the Council, the European Parliament, the Economic and Social Committee and the Committee of the Regions, *Social Policy Agenda*, COM (2000) 379 final of 28 June 2000.

Council of the European Union (1996), Council Resolution on Mainstreaming Equal Opportunities for Men and Women into the European Structural Funds of 2 December 1996.

Council of the European Union (2006), Regulation (EC) No. 1083/2006, OJ L210/25 of 31 July 2006.

Daly, M. (2005), 'Gender Mainstreaming in Theory and Practice' *Social Politics* 12: 433-450.

De la Porte, C. and Nanz, P. (2004), 'The OMC – A Deliberative-democratic Mode of Governance? The Cases of Employment and Pensions' *Journal of European Public Policy* 11(2): 267-288.

Draft Treaty of Lisbon (2007), Cm 72944 of 2007, London, HMSO.

EGG (2004), *Enlargement, Gender and Governance: The Civic and Political Participation and Representation of Women in the EU Candidate Countries: Comparative Report* (Belfast, CAWP).

Esping-Andersen, G. (2002), *Why we Need a New Welfare State* (Oxford, OUP).

ETUC, BusinessEurope, UEAPME and CEEP (2007) *Framework of Actions on Gender Equality: Second Follow-up Report*, http://ec.europa.eu/employment_social/social_dialogue/docs/fram_actions_gender_2ndreport07_en.pdf.

European Commission (2000), Technical Paper 3, *Mainstreaming Equal Opportunities for Women and Men in Structural Fund Programmes and Projects* March 2000.

European Commission (2000), *Towards a Community Framework Strategy on Gender Equality (2001-2005)* COM (2000) 335 final of 7 June 2000.

European Commission (2002), Communication from the Commission to the Council, the European Parliament, the European Economic and Social Committee and the Committee of the Regions, *Implementation of gender mainstreaming in the Structural Funds programming documents 2000-2006,* COM(2002) 748 final of 20 December 2002.

European Commission (2006), *European Social Fund (2007-2013) support Gender Equality* (Brussels, European Commission).

European Commission (2006), *Roadmap for Equality between Women and Men for the Period 2006-2010* COM (2006) 92 final of 1 March 2006.

European Council (2000), *Lisbon European Council, Conclusions of the Presidency, March 23-24, 2000.*

European Council (2002), *Barcelona European Council, Conclusions of the Presidency.*

European Council (2006), *European Pact for Gender Equality* Annex II, Conclusions of the Presidency, 2/15 Bulletin of the European Union 3-2006.

European Public Law Center (EPLC) (undated), *The Institutions in Candidate Countries Defending Gender Related Issues – Capacity to Implement and Control Equality*, Report by the EPLC on behalf of the European Parliament.

Fredman, S. (2006), 'Transformation or Dilution: Fundamental Rights in the EU Social Space' *European Law Journal* 12(1): 41-60.

Hatzopoulos, V. (2007), 'Why the Open Method of Coordination is Bad For You: A Letter to the EU' *European Law Journal* 13(3): 309-342.

Havelková, B. (2007), 'Burden of Proof and Positive Action in the Czech and Slovak Constitutional Courts – Milestones of Milestones in Implementing EC Equality Law' *European Law Review* 32(5): 686-704.

Hodson, D. and Maher, I. (2001), 'The Open Method as a New Mode of Governance: The Case of Soft Economic Policy Co-ordination' *Journal of Common Market Studies* 39: 719-46.

Hoskyns, C. (1996), *Integrating Gender: Women, Law and Politics in the European Union* (London, Verso).

Jepsen, M. and Serrano Pascual, A. (2005), 'The European Social Model: An Exercise in Deconstruction' *Journal of European Social Policy* 15(3): 231-45.

Lewis, J. (2001), 'The Decline of the Male Breadwinner Model: Implications for Work and Care' *Social Politics* 8: 52-70.

Lombardo, E. and Meier, P. (2006), 'Gender Mainstreaming in the EU: Incorporating a Feminist Reading?' *European Journal of Women's Studies* 13: 151-166.

Lombardo, E. and Meier, P. (2007), 'European Union Gender Policy Since Beijing: Shifting Concepts and Agendas' in Verloo M. (2007), (ed.) *Multiple Meanings of Gender Equality: A Critical Frame Analysis of Gender Politics in Europe* (Budapest, CPS Books), pp. 51-75.

Mazey, S. (1995), 'The Development of EU Equality Policies: Bureaucratic Expansion on Behalf of Women?' *Public Administration* 73(4): 591-610.

Mazey, S. (2000), 'The Emergence of Gender Mainstreaming in the EU: Policy Succession in Hard Times' presented at Mainstreaming Gender in European Union Public Policy: A Workshop at the University of Wisconsin-Madison, October 2000.

Network of Legal Experts in the fields of employment, social affairs and equality between men and women (2007), *General Report on Developments in EU Gender Equality Law, June 2006-May 2007*, Brussels, European Commission, http://ec.europa.eu/employment_social/gender_equality/docs/2007/genrep_06_07_en.pdf.

Ostner, I. and Lewis, J. (1995), 'Gender and the Evolution of European Social Policies' in Leibfried S. and Pearson P. (eds.) *European Social Policy: Between Fragmentation and Integration* (Washington, DC: Brookings Institution), pp. 159-93.

Pochet, P. (2005), 'The Open Method of Coordination and the Construction of Social Europe: A Historical Perspective' in Zeitlin, J and Pochet, P. (eds.) *The Open Method of Coordination in Action* (Brussels, Peter Lang), pp. 37-82.

Pollack, M and Hafner-Burton, E. (2000), 'Mainstreaming Gender in the European Union' *Journal of European Public Policy* 7(3): 432-56.

Rees, T. (1998), *Mainstreaming Equality in the European Union, Education, Training and Labour Market Policies* (London, Routledge).

Regulation (EC) No. 1260/1999 laying down general provisions on the Structural Funds, OJ L161 of 26/6/1999.

Regulation (EC) No. 1081/2006 on the European Social Fund, OJ L210/12 of 31/7/2006.

Rodin, S. (2005), 'Discourse, Authority and Making of the Constitution for Europe' in Curtin D. Kellermann A.E. and Blockmans S. (eds.) *EU Constitution: The Best Way Forward?* (Hague: Asser Press), pp. 145-163.

Rubery, J. and Fagan, C. (2000), *Gender Impact Assessment and European Employment Strategy* (Manchester, EWERC).

Rubery, J. (2002), 'Gender Mainstreaming and Gender Equality in the EU: The Impact of the EU Employment Strategy' *Industrial Relations Journal* 33(5): 500-522.

Rubery, J. (2003), 'Gender Mainstreaming and the Open Method of Coordination: Is the Open Method too Open for Gender Equality Policy?' in Zeitlin J. and Pochet P. (eds.) *The Open Method of Co-ordination in Action. The European Employment Strategy and Social Inclusion Strategies* (Brussels, Peter Lang), pp. 391-416.

Rubery, J. (2005), 'Gender Mainstreaming and the OMC: Is the Open Method Too Open for Gender Equality Policy?' in Zeitlin J. and Pochet P. (eds.) *The Open Method of Coordination in Action* (Brussels: Peter Lang), pp. 391-416.

Scharpf, F.W. (2002), 'The European Social Model: Coping with the Challenges of Diversity' *Journal of Common Market Studies* 40(4): 645-670.

Scott, J. and Trubeck, D. (2002), 'Mind the Gap: Law and New Approaches to Governance in the European Union' 8 *European Law Journal* 1-18.

Shaw, J. (2005), 'Mainstreaming Equality and Diversity in the European Union' *Current Legal Problems* 58: 255-312.

Snyder, F. (1993), 'The Effectiveness of European Community Law: Institutions, Processes, Tools and Techniques' *Modern Law Review* 56: 19-54.

Sloat, A. (2004), 'Legislating for Equality: The Implementation of the EU Equality *Acquis* in Central and Eastern Europe' *Jean Monnet Working Paper* New York, NYU School of Law.

Squires, J. (2005), 'Is Mainstreaming Transformative? Theorizing Mainstreaming in the Context of Diversity and Deliberation' *Social Politics* 12(3): 366-388.

Szcszyzak, E. (2006), 'Experimental Governance: The Open Method of Coordination' *European Law Journal* 12(4): 486-502.

Verloo, M. (2005), 'Displacement and Empowerment: Reflections on the Concept and Practice of the Council of Europe Approach to Gender Mainstreaming and Gender Equality' *Social Politics* 12(3): 344-366.

Verloo, M., Bustelo M and Lombardo, E. (2007), 'Conclusions on Framing Gender Inequality as a Policy Problem in Europe' in Verloo, M. (2007), (ed.) *Multiple Meanings of Gender Equality: A Critical Frame Analysis of Gender Politics in Europe* (Budapest, CPS Books), 281-301.

Verloo, M. and Lombardo, E. (2007), 'Contested Gender Equality and Policy Variety in Europe: Introducing a Critical Frame Analysis Approach' in Verloo, M. (2007), (ed.) *Multiple Meanings of Gender Equality: A Critical Frame Analysis of Gender Politics in Europe* (Budapest, CPS Books), 21-49.

Verloo, M. (2007), (ed.) *Multiple Meanings of Gender Equality: A Critical Frame Analysis of Gender Politics in Europe* (Budapest, CPS Books).

Walby, S. (2004), 'The European Union and Gender Equality: Emergent Varieties of Gender Regime' *Social Politics* 11: 4-29.

Walby, S. (2005), 'Gender Mainstreaming: Productive Tensions in Theory and Practice' *Social Politics* 12(3): 321-343.

Chapter 3

Employment Policy, Women's Labour Market Activation and Demographic Trends

Roberta Guerrina

Demographers' warnings of decreasing birth rates and an ageing population have finally entered the consciousness of European policy makers and political leaders. As a result, in recent years demographic trends and social indicators have become a hot topic of discussion. The interest in the current demographic transition, however, has to be understood within the context of welfare retrenchment and the impact of globalization on the long term future of the European Social Model. Predictions for the second half of the 21st century are not optimistic and if the current decline in birth rates persists, Europe will face a labour shortage as early as 2030. This trend will ultimately have repercussions for economic growth and the ability of the EU to compete in the global market. It is thus becoming increasingly clear that in order to tackle these challenges, EU Member States need to adopt a multidimensional approach to employment policy which takes into consideration current changes to family structures and social dynamics.

Given this background, the context of this chapter is twofold. Firstly, it is located within current debates about the population time-bomb in Europe. Secondly, it looks at recent policies aimed at increasing women's participation in the official labour market (i.e. activation policies). It seeks to bring together these two discourses by looking at the issue of work-life balance, as women's engagement with the labour market is dependent upon their ability to reconcile the demands of paid employment with those of care duties. Analysis of the European Employment Strategy (EES) seems pertinent within this framework, particularly given the target of 60 per cent female employment by 2010 and the call for improved childcare services.

The central question that underpins the analysis presented here is as follows: can the EES provide the right framework for the development of a multidimensional approach to gender equality that will encourage higher female participation in the official labour market, whilst challenging traditional power structures in the family? In order to answer this question the chapter will explore three interrelated issues: (1) Can employment policies be used to tackle gender power hierarchies in the family? (2) Do gender inequalities influence women's choices about mothering/motherhood? (3) Is there a link between the consolidation of the adult worker model and declining fertility rates?

Looking at current employment trends within the wider context of the demographic transition in Europe, it is important to ask whether this shift in the policy agenda is the result of increasing awareness about the gendered nature of women's choices or a reaction to the economic challenges facing the Single Market. By looking at the equal opportunities objectives entrenched within the EES, this chapter will unpack the values that define employment and family policies in Europe. In so doing, it asks whether policy-makers are seeking to advance women's rights/interests or are simply seeking to safeguard the interests of the state/market.

The chapter begins by looking at the impact of demographic trends (specifically, decreasing birth rates and ageing population) on policymaking choices in the area of equal opportunities and employment. It will then evaluate the current discourses in favour of family friendly policies and/or reconciliation between work and family life, focussing in particular on the displacement of the male breadwinner model by an 'adult worker model'. Looking at the overarching aims of reconciliation policies from a gender perspective, it will examine the biases and norms entrenched within this policy area. The chapter will discuss how this shift in focus came about and the impact it might have on social, economic and political structures in Europe. Next, the chapter will turn to look at women's employment, examining the link between the introduction of work-life balance as a policy principle and the current drive to expand women's participation in the official labour market at a time when declining birth-rates are threatening the long-term viability of the European Social Model. Two further sections then consider the relationship between demographic trends and policy, and the possible role for EES in addressing these issues. Finally, some conclusions are offered about the potential of EES to address demographic issues on the one hand, and gender equality issues on the other.

Demographic Trends in Europe – An Overview

It is a well documented fact that European population trends in the 20th century have been defined by low birth and death rates. In other words, Europeans are living longer and are having fewer children (Hilgeman and Butts 2004). The decline in birth rates over the last century is common to most developed countries, but the sharp down turn that has taken place in Europe since the end of the Second World War has been paralleled only in Japan. Although there is a degree of variation in birth and fertility rates amongst Member States of the EU, in 2003 the average for the EU as a whole was 1.47 children per woman. This figure includes a high of 1.88 children per woman in France and Ireland, and a low of 1.17 children per woman in the Czech Republic (European Commission 2004: 14). The decline in fertility rates has also been accompanied by an increase in life expectancy. The cumulative effect of these two trends is the EU's ageing population. Recent forecasts predict that by 2030 the population of over 65s will account, on average, for 22 per cent of the total population (European Commission 2004: 14, 38). Enlargement of the EU is also due to have a negative impact on current population trends within the EU. Although in the first instance it will help to reduce the median age, population decline in Central and Eastern Europe is also becoming cause for concern (European Commission 2004: 11).

This demographic transition, however, has not occurred in a vacuum. Rather, it has taken place within the context of changing social relations and economic structures. Particularly notable are the changes in family structures, such as the marked increase in births outside marriage, cohabitation and lone-parenting as well as the significant growth in women's employment rates (Babb et al. 2006; Eurostat 2005; European Commission 2004; Lewis 2001; Craig 2007). What these statistics point to is substantial changes in socio-political and economic relations in Europe, to the point that it has been argued that changes in women's expectations and educational achievement are starting to have a significant impact on the demographic make up of Europe (Eurostat 2006; Crompton 2001). As Lewis (2001: 156) explains, "it is now widely accepted that women will engage in paid work, and attitudinal surveys have shown consistent increases in acceptance by men and women of female employment at all stages of the life course". More specifically, there appears to be a reality-expectation gap, whereby social attitudes/norms about traditional gender roles/functions are coming into conflict with women's expectations, household economic needs for a dual income and the more general need of the European economy to increase the percentage of its working population. This gap and the inequitable distributions of labour within the household or family ultimately contribute to women's choice to have fewer children than they would deem to be ideal (Craig 2007).

Employment policies can help (albeit only in part) to address some of these dilemmas by easing current pressures on families and helping women to remain active within the official labour market during the childbearing years. The replacement of the male breadwinner model with the adult worker model in European welfare states highlights the complexity of current socio-economic interactions. Yet, it would be naïve to assume that this new model is either gender neutral and/or implicitly advances a more equitable distribution of care work within the family unit.

From the Male Breadwinner Model to the Adult Worker Model – Some Theoretical Considerations

The most important body of literature seeking to deal with the complexities that define the relationship between care work and employment come from the field of social policy. More specifically, the vast body of research looking at breadwinner models seeks to unpack the impact of gender power hierarchies and divisions of labour on welfare regimes. This section provides an overview of current debates dealing with the transition from male breadwinner model to adult worker module that is currently under way in Europe.

In the 1990s a wide body of work was published looking at the gender dimension of welfare regimes theories. Leading the way was Jane Lewis's (1992) pioneering work on the male breadwinner model, though many other scholars contributed to this literature by expanding the field of analysis to lone-parent families (Duncan 1995; Duncan and Edwards 1999; Daly 1994) and the diversity in gender divisions present in Europe (Sainsbury 1994). More recently, changes in the social policy agenda towards flexible employment structures forced a reconsideration of how gender is incorporated within policy and academic discourse. It is in this context that a shift occurred from discussions about the male breadwinner model to something that is in appearance more gender neutral, but which in fact fits within wider economic and power hierarchies. As Lewis (2006: 33) explains, "the [male breadwinner model] assumed full male employment and stable families', however economic changes driven by greater female participation in the employment market can potentially pose a challenge to the social fabric that underpins this model".

Lewis's assessment of gender hierarchies in the 1990s drew attention to the complex set of structures that have defined the social policy agenda of European states since the end of the Second World War. Her thesis developed as a critique of Esping-Andersen's (1990) welfare regime model, which she argued was gender-blind in as far as it failed to take into consideration the implicitly decommodified nature of women's work in the domestic sphere (Lewis 1992). She provides an alternative framework for the categorization of welfare states, based predominantly on gender relations and hierarchies in the family. She argued that "modern welfare regimes have all subscribed to some degree to the idea of a male-breadwinner model", though there has been substantial variation in the way in which such structures have been played out in practice (Lewis 1992: 162).

The basic premise of the male breadwinner model is a division of labour whereby men are the primary or sole breadwinners, and women are the primary carers. This division of labour reflects the assumption that the public and private spheres are distinct and independent. Lewis's work in the last fifteen years has sought to challenge this distinction. In the first instance, she has shown how social policies serve to constrain individual choices. Secondly, her assessment of welfare regimes help to stimulate debate on the power dynamics that support the social policy agenda, in as far as the male breadwinner model was based on three key factors: (1) women's economic dependence; (2) full male employment; and (3) the traditional family (Lewis 1992; Lewis 2003). Haas (2005: 495) develops this analysis further by spelling out something that is implicit in much of Lewis's work: gender divisions of labour that underpin the male breadwinner model are based on a narrow understanding of mothering which is tantamount to nurturing and caring.

Although the core assumptions at the heart of the male breadwinner model provide a starting point of analysis, it is important not to underestimate the wide variety of approaches in which these principles were put into effect. At one end of the spectrum we can find the Nordic states that have sought to encourage female participation in the official labour market, whereas Southern European states have sought to secure the long term viability of the familial welfare model. Moreover, as Lewis (2001: 153) points out,

> A pure male breadwinner model never existed; women always engaged in the labour market. [However] there has been an enormous behavioural change in the second half of the twentieth century, with increasing numbers of women entering the labour market. Indeed, this has become one point of convergence among EU Member States.

What a number of studies carried out in the last ten years have shown is that changes in social and economic dynamics that have led to increased female participation in the employment market are slowly challenging the very basis of the male breadwinner model (Lewis 2003; Craig 2007; Duncan 1995; Haas 2005; Crompton 2001). Lewis's (2001: 155) recent work in this area also concludes that 'the pattern of work between men and women in households is now much more difficult to predict, but patterns of unpaid work have not changed so much'.

Two issues/questions arise from this discussion: (1) There is a high level of uncertainty about the impact the current socio-economic transition will have on welfare provisions; (2) Changes in women's employment patterns have not led to a substantive reallocation of unpaid work within the family. As Lewis (2001: 158) explains, "female employment is now expected, although to what degree and for which groups of women remains unclear. This is not surprising given that the new assumptions may actually be running ahead of behavioural change".

Policy makers have thus turned towards the principle of activation in order to find a way forward in the context of an increasingly insecure labour market. The individual, rather than the family, has been the focus of this shift. In this context, women (and specifically women with care responsibilities) become the target of policy initiatives as their participation in the formal economy is seen as central to long term economic success. As Lewis and Bennett (2003: 43) explain, "As a set of processes, individualization has major implications for family formation, labour supply and gender equality". The picture that is emerging, however, is rather complex. These initiatives are coming up against other policies and social norms about gender hierarchies and divisions of labour (Lewis and Bennett 2003: 43).

Clearly, gender norms are important but are not the only issue that needs to be considered in this analysis. More general trends in welfare provision, specifically welfare retrenchment, are a particularly notable reason for encouraging wider female participation in the official labour market. Yet, the question of care remains unresolved (Lewis 2003: 178).

The question that follows is whether such a shift in policy denotes a wider change in attitudes and a move towards substantive equality (based on an equitable division of care work in the private sphere). The shift towards an adult worker model is based on two key principles: individuation and commodification. In order words, benefits are ascribed to individuals on the basis of their interactions with the employment market. Women's position in society is thus no longer solely defined by their role as carers; but they face increasing pressure to participate in the official labour market. Lewis's (2006) assessment of this transition is not entirely positive. Despite an increasing preference for long part-time hours (thus the adult worker model formulation), she raises some points of caution: (1) Women are over-represented in part-time employment; (2) Expectations of women's contributions to the family income remain unspecified. Ultimately, the basis for this shift in 'paradigm' (Lewis 2006: 34) is based on the commodification of care work, not a change in attitudes towards the importance and/or value of care. As she further points out, "limits on *paid working time* are necessary, but not sufficient to secure men in particular time to care" (Lewis 2006: 35). The move towards the establishment of the adult worker model should, therefore, not be seen as unproblematic. Social and economic structures that defined power relations in the public and the private sphere under the male breadwinner models have changed but have not been removed (Lewis 2003: 180).

Although it is tempting to talk about the adult worker model as a monolithic approach to increasing female employment rates, Lewis (2001) identified at least four dual breadwinner family types ranging from a division of labour more closely associated with the male breadwinner model (male partner in full time employment, female partner working short part time hours) to one centred around full economic activation of both partners (dual career family). Haas (2005) also provides a detailed breakdown of different types of breadwinner models that are becoming established. Haas's typology allows for greater variety of family types and arrangements. Building on Lewis's (1992) earlier work, she includes the *traditional breadwinner model* and the *modified breadwinner model* (male partner in full time employment, female partner in part time employment). This contrasts with the *egalitarian employment model* in which 'gainful employment is universalized, but care and housework are not. It is mainly the woman who carries out private unpaid work in the household' Haas (2005: 496). Her last two models, however, are the most radical. Under the *universal carer model* both men and women are both workers and carers, thus allowing the family to continue to take the lion's share in the social function of care, but challenging gender divisions of labour in the private sphere. Finally, under the *role reversal model* the female partner takes on the role of breadwinner. This model is the least likely to take root, she argues, partly because it challenges deeply rooted assumptions about gender roles and the individual's relationship with the market and welfare structures.

The problem with this shift in policy is that women's activation continues to be constrained by social norms about care and women's role in the family. In other words, according to Lewis (2001: 161) it assumes a level of economic independence that has not been achieved by the vast majority of women. Crompton's (2001: 268-9) analysis of this transition supports this assessment, adding that a shift in favour of women's full time employment is more likely to challenge gender hierarchies and divisions of labour upon which the traditional male breadwinner model is based. Although increased participation will inevitably have an impact on arrangements in the private sphere, without a substantive change in attitudes towards the social function of caring this model rests on women continuing to take on the double burden of care and paid employment.

A number of interlinked questions arise from the analysis of changing care-work patterns presented here: (1) Is the introduction of the adult worker model tantamount to substantive equality? (2) Can a policy shift towards supporting a dual breadwinner family help to reverse the current decline in birth rates? (3) Will the establishment of the adult worker model neutralize the impact of gender power hierarchies? Although a policy shift in favour of activation and individualization of rights is increasingly being accepted as the norm, "it is, in essence, the gendered divisions of unpaid work in the home as well as in the workplace that lie behind the problems posed by this shift towards an adult worker model family" (Lewis 2006: 34). Policy blindness towards the contradictory interests of employment and care only contribute to forestalling the reorganization of employment structures necessary for the establishment of gender sensitive work-care structures (Crompton 2001: 283).

In terms of the questions outlined above, it is worth noting that much of current policy action in this field is premised on the acceptance of the commodification of care work. This results from a narrow focus on activation and thus an implicit blindness to gender hierarchies in the private sphere (Lewis 2006: 34; Lewis 2003: 180). As Lewis (2006: 53) further points out, "it is particularly hard to devise policies that encourage men to change their behaviour; compulsion is antithetical to both the idea of genuine choice and to the ethics of care". And again, "it is difficult for policies designed to reconcile work and family responsibilities to actually strike a balance in terms of the incentives for both men and women to work and care" (Lewis 2006: 36).

This recognition is important in the context of European social policy and the EES in particular. As the analysis presented here has shown, "'employment-anchored' social policy, is not likely to effectively address the issue of gender equality" (Lewis 2006: 37). Clearly, activation policies and increased labour market participation are the easiest way for the EU and its Member States to maintain a competitive labour market in the global economy. Yet these policies are neither constructed in a social vacuum nor gender neutral (Lewis 2001). The long term implications of increasing female labour market participation without consideration for gender hierarchies and divisions of labour may not be felt in the immediate future but may nevertheless have long term repercussions on the demographic make up of Europe.

This section has sought to provide a conceptual framework for the analysis of current changes in European labour market trends. The shift from the male breadwinner model to the adult worker model inevitably poses important questions about the relationship between employment policies and the social function of care. More importantly, it highlights the implicit tension between welfare retrenchment leading to the family taking an even greater share of the care burden and the need for some commodification of care in order to implement the overall aims of employment policies based on individualization and activation. The next section of this chapter will look at female employment trends and seek to unpack the complex web that informs women's choices about work and childbearing.

Women's Employment and Participation in the Official Labour Market

Changes in the socio-economic position of women in Europe since the end of the Second World War have been widely documented.[1] Increased female participation in the official labour market and the political arena are only two of the key areas in which women's presence has become more noticeable. Recent surveys highlight how deeply rooted this transition has become in the consciousness of European women (Cousins 1999; Muehlberger 2000; Rubery et al, 1999; Lewis 2001; Crompton 2001). Women's expectations seem to have changed with an increased focus on

1 For details on women's employment rates in the first half of the 20th century, see Bock and Thane 1994; Stier et al 2001.

the public sphere and particularly the employment sector. This section will look at current trends in women's employment and the structural impediments that women have to contend with when negotiating work and family responsibilities. In order to do this, I will assess the relationship between employment policies, life choices (such as mothering), and social/welfare models outlined in the previous section of this chapter.

A number of factors can help to explain how this transition has occurred. Firstly, changes in employment law and increased awareness of equal opportunities have facilitated women's entry into the labour force. Secondly, women have surpassed men in terms of educational attainment. For instance, in 2003 women accounted for 54.6 per cent of all students enrolled in higher education. Despite the persistence of gender segregation in terms of chosen disciplines, these trends highlight a greater involvement of young women in the public sphere and hence higher expectations of employment following the end of this period of study. Yet, women's success in education has not automatically converted into greater success in the employment market. It is interesting to note that there is a high proportion of highly skilled and educated women working short/part time hours (Eurostats 2006; Rubery et al 2001; Del Boca et al 2004). Given these statistics, it is important to look beyond factors such as education and training to explain gender inequalities in the labour market.

Women's role in the social function of reproduction has been put forward by many scholars (Guerrina 2005; Craig 2007) as the main reason why women still lag behind men in the area of employment. It is interesting to note that there is little difference in employment rates and/or the number of hours worked by single men and women. However, women's participation in the official labour market declines sharply following the arrival of children. And, the higher the number of children present in a household, the less likely is the mother to engage in paid employment (Aliaga 2005). This trend is particularly important as it highlights welfare states' continued reliance on women fulfilling the social function of care. In this context, wage differentials between men and women, as well as socio-economic hierarchies in the labour market, ultimately ensure that childbearing has a direct impact on women's and/or families' choices about employment.

Yet, women's participation in the official labour market is increasingly being advanced as central to finding a solution to Europe's impending labour shortage, as well as to promote competition and economic growth. As a matter of fact, the Lisbon strategy established a target of 60 per cent female employment by 2010 (Del Boca 2004; Lewis 2006). Achievement of this objective has been sought through the implementation of active labour market policies, which reinforce the current trends towards the establishment of the adult worker model in Europe. Unfortunately, structural issues that underpin inequality and gender power hierarchies were largely ignored during the negotiations, despite the high profile of the equal opportunities pillar in this process. As Fagan et al. (2005: 569) explain, "attention to the quality of women's jobs (e.g. pay, segregation, working time) were largely neglected even though reductions in the gender pay gap was identified as a policy target and included as a structural indicator in the Broad Economic Policy Guidelines". In terms of the analysis presented here, it is interesting to note that the provision of childcare did acquire a more prominent status and was included in the 2002 Barcelona targets.

This harks back to Lewis's (2006) analysis about the commodification of care. As families (i.e. women) become more engaged in the official labour market they are less able to fulfil the social function of care. What emerges is a shift in favour of outsourcing care responsibilities to the public sphere, rather than a reallocation of care time between partners in the traditional family (Lewis 2006; Fagan et al. 2005).

This discussion raises some important issues that will be considered in more detail later in this chapter regarding the ability of the EES to provide the necessary framework for the development of a multidimensional approach to equality. For now, it is worth noting that the inclusion of childcare within this process is not the result of increased awareness of the role that social and economic policies play in reinforcing gender power hierarchies. Rather, it reflects a simple acknowledgement that in order for women to be able to enter the official labour market, the issue of care needs to be addressed. Improvements in the provision of childcare are an economic and/or strategic objective, rather than a way to promote substantive equality.

This discussion takes on a whole new dimension within the context of the debate about declining fertility rates. There are some very interesting research results coming to the fore in this particular area. Hilgeman and Butts (2004: 6-7) found that there is a negative correlation between female educational attainment and fertility rates. They forecast that as women seek to expand their participation in the official labour market on the back of their increased educational attainment, fertility rates will continue to decline (Hilgeman and Butts 2004: 20). Still focusing on women's education and training as a variable, Rubery et al. (2001: 37-41) found that this variable only marginally improves the likelihood of employment following the birth of children. These studies support the conclusions arrived at by Craig (2007) and Del Boca et al (2004) that mothering has a negative impact on women's participation in the official labour market.

In order to explain these trends, our first port of call has to be the persistent inequalities and power hierarchies that underpin employment and social structures in the EU. For instance, women's unemployment rates continue to be higher than men's (9.6 per cent against 7.6 per cent), which includes striking disparities between Member States. At present Ireland has the lowest rate of women's unemployment (3.8 per cent) whereas Poland has reported the highest at 19.1 per cent (Eurostat 2006). These statistics highlight persistent problems with access to the labour market for women. EU employment statistics for 2005 put men and women's employment rates as follows: 56 per cent of women compared to 71 per cent of men are in paid employment, and, on average 1/3 of women are employed part-time, with a high of 75 per cent of all employed women working part-time in the Netherlands (Eurostat 2006).

These problems are further exacerbated by the persistent gender pay gap, currently reported at 15 per cent, and the gender segregation of the labour market, whereby women tend to be concentrated in part-time employment and the service sector (Eurostat 2006). These are some of the realities that women are faced with when seeking to reconcile the demands of work in the official labour market with the responsibilities of care in the private sphere. EU statistics point to the persistence of gender divisions of labour and time allocation within the family (Eurostat 2006).

These findings are supported by more qualitative studies which look at the impact of family structures on labour market participation. Kay (2003: 236) in particular found that the extent to which the burden of reconciling demands on the household falls upon women is a constant theme in accounts of family life. Findings from interviews are in line with Eurostat data, which show strong inequality in the distribution of domestic tasks. More importantly, she draws attention to the disparity between policy areas: "the widespread encouragement for women to further their education and training and equip themselves for employment has not been matched by the necessary infrastructure to support increased labour market activity by parents. Formal childcare is frequently inadequate" (Kay 2003: 236). As Duncan (2000: 309-10) further explains, the structures that underpin the male breadwinner model upon which European welfare states have become reliant for the provision of care are unable to support women's entry into the official labour market. However, a shift towards the dual breadwinner family or the adult worker model provides only a temporary solution. As discussed in the previous section, more work needs to be done to assess the adverse effects of activation policies and the establishment of the adult worker model on women's double burden.

This evidence led Hilgeman and Butts (2004) as well as McDonald (2000) to conclude that declining fertility rates result from a mismatch between women's expectations on the one hand and socio-economic structures for the promotion of gender equality on the other. More specifically, McDonald (2000) found that those countries with social structures most aligned with the male-breadwinner model are those that have experienced the most substantial drop in birth rates in the last thirty years. The assumption that women will continue to fulfil the primary function of care is set against the demands of the employment market and women's expectations of their potential contributions to the public sphere and household income. In this context, it is interesting to note Del Boca's et al. (2004) assessment of the current state of affairs in Mediterranean states. They come to the conclusion that it is possible to draw a correlation between declining birth rates on the one hand and conflict between women's roles as carers and workers on the other.

What is interesting to note is that both studies point to policies for the reconciliation between work and family life as a possible avenue to resolve this conflict. In particular, Hilgeman and Butts (2004: 20) argue that widely available, good quality, flexible and affordable childcare, rather than parental leave arrangements, would have the greatest impact on fertility rates. These findings are interesting as they draw attention to the norms that define employment patterns. In short, the provision of childcare, unlike leave arrangements, does not challenge traditional assumptions about care. The commodification of care allows women to reconcile work and family life, but does not challenge gender divisions of labour in the family. The focus on care provisions thus highlights the very bias at the heart of work-life balance policies: despite the gender neutrality of the language they are addressed to women workers.

These findings thus seem to support current thinking at European level which has sought to foster a shift from the traditional male breadwinner model to the adult worker model (Lewis 2001). As discussed in the previous section, the assumption that underpins this new model of employment and welfare is that "all adults should take employment, and that in families there will be two earners, but this could be on a full or part time basis" (Annesley 2006: 6). The focus of this policy shift is in favour of women's activation; however, it does not challenge the norms that define/underpin gender power hierarchies in the public and private sphere. This will ultimately turn out to be the most significant shortcoming of the EES and its associated targets.

Demographic Trends and Policy Making Choices

Women's entry in the official labour market has been advanced as one of the main reasons for declining birth rates. Concern over the longer term repercussions this shift entails, particularly in terms of demographic trends and traditional family structures has implicitly underpinned employment policies for a number of years (Hakim 2003). Duncan (2000) goes as far as arguing that this is a key area of concern that has helped to define European equal rights policies. National family policies are increasingly incorporating pronatalist elements such as economic incentives and extended leave. However, recent studies suggest that family policy has only a limited impact on increasing birth rates. The extent to which Member States have incorporated the family friendly/work-life balance agenda within their policy structures seems to have a much greater impact on birth rate differentials (Duncan 2000; European Commission 2004: 14). As Hilgeman and Butts (2004: 10) explain, economic incentives and leave alone have only limited impact on family choices. As they further point out, "pronatalist norms create the expectation that most people have [or] should have children. Such norms tend to have a particularly strong impact on women as the responsibility of childrearing has fallen disproportionately on them" (Hilgeman and Butts 2004: 4). This is the reason why it is important to consider the relationship between family friendly policies and family life and substantive equality.

Reconciliation between work and family life is now a key pillar of EU employment policies. EU institutions have recognized that in order to promote women's participation in the official labour market, employment structures and policies need to tackle the issue of care. The Lisbon strategy, in particular, presents work-life as essential in tackling gender inequalities in Europe (Guerrina 2003; Paraskeva 2003). Thus far, EU policies have sought to promote a flexible approach to reconciliation between work and family life, with a particular focus on paid and un-paid leave (Guerrina 2005; Guerrina 2003; Paraskeva 2003).[2] Despite acknowledging the importance of structural impediments to women's participation in the official labour market, EU strategy has focused on policies that shift the burden of implementation onto employers, rather than tackling structural impediments to reconciliation between work and family life such as the chronic absence of affordable and good quality child-care in many Member States and the unequal distribution of care work in the family (Paraskeva 2003).

Over the last five years there have been a number of statements that sought to acknowledge the impact of socio-economic structures to women's participation in

2 For instance, see the Pregnant Workers Directive (92/85/EC), the Parental Leave Directive (96/34/EC), and the Part-Time Workers Directive (97/81/EC).

the official labour market. Paraskeva (2003: 4) for instance claims that in March 2002 the European Council went one step further and set targets for the supply of childcare facilities. By 2010, Member States should provide childcare for at least 33 per cent of children under 3 years of age, and 90 per cent of children aged between 3 and mandatory school age. Already in their Employment Plans for 2002, several Member States reported new measures to increase childcare services and fixed national targets.

In terms of the debate about demographic trends, there is some evidence to point to the fact that improved access and affordability of childcare services is the best way to promote women's activation in the labour market (Hilgeman and Butts 2004; Giullari and Lewis 2005).

Historically, the focus of EU equal rights policies has been on encouraging women to enter the official labour market by creating a level playing field. They have therefore focused on formal equality (Giullari and Lewis 2005: 6; Guerrina 2005). Giullari and Lewis (2005: 6) have put forward a particularly poignant analysis of this policy bias. They argue that "little attention has been paid to the pursuit of gender equality in respect to unpaid work at the household level. It is also significant that the principle of equality is deployed in EU level documents in such a way as to eclipse the equally difficult issue of choice". It is interesting to note that EES reinforces this trend, whereby the focus on women's activation has been at the expense of a more concerted effort for the achievement of substantive equality. Even the renewed focus on the reconciliation between work and family life is less about challenging gender power hierarchies than it is about providing a viable framework for increasing women's employment rates. In this context, these policies may have a positive outcome in terms of demographic trends, but such an achievement will be at the expense of social justice, as the newly established dual breadwinner model will simply crystallize gender power hierarchies in the public and the private sphere.

The latest Commission Green Paper on demographic change highlights quite how entrenched these trends have become. The European Commission published in 2005 a Green Paper, *Confronting demographic change*, outlining the challenges facing EU Member States over the next couple of decades. The basis for the Commission's consultation process is that "Europeans would like to have more children. But they are discouraged from doing so by all kinds of problems that limit their freedom of choice, including in finding housing" (European Commission 2005: 2). The Green Paper recognizes the difficulties faced by many women/families to reconcile their care responsibilities with employment in the official labour market. This conflict of interests, in turn, has led to a downturn in intergenerational solidarity as evidenced in the decline in fertility rates.

The Green Paper focuses on five key issues/areas: (1) Work-life balance; (2) Integration of young people in the official labour market; (3) Working life cycles; (4) (Re-) integration of the elderly in the official labour market; (5) Intergenerational solidarity. The main focus of the paper is the forecasted decline in working age population. Current forecasts estimate a decline of 20.8 million workers between 2005 and 2030 (European Commission 2005). Ultimately, this policy document concentrates on the long term impact of demographic trends on the economic well being of the Single Market. The following quote summarizes the rationale for policy action in this field: "A low birth rate is a challenge for the public authorities. Never in history has there been economic growth without population growth" (European Commission 2005: 5). The assumption that underpins this change in policy focus is that economic stagnation and/or decline will result from demographic decline. Promoting substantive equality and challenging the gender power hierarchies that ultimately have produced these trends are less of an issue for European policy makers.

Clearly this paper is the result of increasing public policy concern over an ageing population and the impact it will have on the long term survival of the European social model. The strategies adopted thus far by the Member States to deal with this challenge have been: (1) Raising compulsory retirement age; (2) Support for non-linear, non-standard career patterns; (3) Life-long learning. Finally, the Green Paper identifies three key factors that will have an impact on Europe's demographic trends: (1) Lack of a demographic motor, (2) Immigration; (3) Enlargement.

The Green Paper implicitly recognizes the impact of gender power hierarchies on Europe's demographic transition; however, there is little in the way of a critique of those socio-economic structures that serve to limit women's choices and have led to a decline in birth rates. Reconciliation between work and family life is introduced as a strategy for encouraging women/families to have more children, and thus becomes instrumental to promoting intergenerational solidarity. The assumption made by the Commission is that Europeans are having fewer children because of economic necessity, as opposed to a change in culture. The key preoccupation for the Green Paper is how to encourage women to enter the labour market whilst continuing to fulfil the social function of reproduction (European Commission 2005). Little or no consideration is given to the issue of substantive equality.

Comparing the demographic situation across a range of countries highlights that there is a positive correlation between the implementation of family friendly policies and the maintenance of sustainable birth-rates (Del Boca et al. 2004). The Green Paper acknowledges the difficulties entrenched in changing socio-cultural norms and attitudes. Citing a 2004 Eurobarometer survey, it points out that the vast majority of European men (84 per cent) have not taken advantage of new rights for working fathers such as paternity and parental leave.

Given the potential bestowed upon work-life balance measures to promote substantive equality, it is interesting to note some of the questions posed by the European Commission during this consultation process:

> How can a more balanced distribution of household and family tasks between men and women be encouraged? Should the award of certain benefits or advantages (leave, etc.) be linked to an equal distribution of tasks between the sexes? How best to ensure an adequate income for both parents on parental leave? (European Commission 2005: 5)

These are pertinent and important questions. However, the issue that remains unanswered is how can these proposals be enforced? Even the discussion of parental leave seems to disregard current trends, whereby women/mothers are the main beneficiaries of the leave entitlements. The next section will explore the ways in which the EES can help to develop a multidimensional approach to the dilemma posed by the conflicting interests of care and employment.

The EES, Demographic Trends and Gender Power Hierarchies – Priorities and Outcomes

At a superficial level the shift in policy focus and rhetoric outlined in the previous section seems to acknowledge feminist critiques of equal opportunities policies. In particular, it appears to be answering calls for greater links between public and private spheres, and to ensure greater recognition of women's double burden. This section looks at how the EES can be a tool for the achievement of the policy objectives outlined in the Commission's Green Paper. In other words, it will assess the ways in which it can be used to establish a multidimensional approach to equality, particularly in view of recent feminist criticisms of the new Lisbon strategy (Rubery et al. 2003; Pfister 2006).

What I am particularly interested in looking at is how reconciliation between work and family life is seen as a way to ease women's choices about mothering and employment, and thus can become a useful tool both in the context of activation policies and in easing the pressure of current demographic trends (see for instance, Del Boca et al. 2004). Giullari and Lewis (2005: 6) have argued that there is a link between the de-familialization of care and women's employment choices. This policy option, however, also serves to mask the problem of women's double burden and the continued reliance on women's unpaid work in the private sphere. As they further explain: "the de- familialization of care work necessarily follows, and there is no further discussion of gender inequalities in unpaid work. Nevertheless, very different ideas about the desirability of 'choice' in regard to the performance of unpaid work exist, both at the level of national governments and among people, and the willingness to undertake informal care work is unlikely to become less important in the future" (Giullari and Lewis 2005: 6).

This analysis leads them to conclude that women's agency is ultimately limited by the social function of care and the persistence of power structures and inequalities in the domestic sphere (Giullari and Lewis 2005: 18). The lack of political will for putting forward a sustained challenge to traditional gender roles further compounds this problem. These issues are not too far removed from current debates about the EES. The Commission's 2002 *Evaluation of the European Employment Strategy* provides an interesting example in this context. By drawing attention to the potential long term effects of establishing a dual breadwinner model on children it implicitly opens the debate about the role and position of working mothers in Europe. As Rubery et al (2003: 483) further outline, "here there is explicit questioning of the goal of the EES to promote dual-earner households where there are children present as a means of meeting the twin targets of equal opportunities and a high employment rate".

This latest statement supports the findings of a number of earlier studies that have pointed towards the emergence of a conservative agenda within European employment policies, particularly as regards the position of working mothers (Caracciolo di

Torrella 2000; Guerrina 2005, 2003; McGlynn 2001a, 2001b, 2000). The findings of these studies draw attention to the enduring conflict between women's participation in the official labour market and traditional assumptions about the social function of mothering. Yet, this discussion takes on a whole new dimension when taking into consideration current demographic trends and the impact that this particular position has had and continues to have on women's choices about mothering.

This analysis supports the findings of Hilgeman and Butts' (2004: 20) study about the relationship between the availability of care services and fertility rates. In particular, they found that childcare is one of the most significant variables in determining fertility rates. In particular, they argue that childcare services, rather than parental leave arrangements, may provide a more suitable avenue for reconciling the conflict of responsibilities faced by working women. This argument is based on extensive evidence that parental leave and general policies for the reconciliation between work and family life have not succeeded in engendering a change in social norms and practices, thus leading to a more equitable distribution of work in the family.

Giullari and Lewis (2005: 10) also warn against the shortcomings of an approach to labour market policy that underestimates the complexities of care in the private sphere. More specifically, they look at the impact the commodification of care will have on gender equality and gender justice. From this position the shift towards the adult worker model shifts the responsibility of care to the public sphere but fails to challenge gender norms that continue to portray women as the primary carers. This is a powerful argument that challenges what has recently become accepted wisdom about the link between declining birth rates and women's employment practices. It is thus not women's participation in the official labour market that leads families to have fewer children, but it is women's double burden that makes motherhood a more difficult choice. This analysis thus shifts the responsibility of declining birth rates from women to social structures/norms that assume gender based divisions of care.

Despite the rhetoric that a shift from the male breadwinner model towards the adult worker model should help to ease the pressure on women's choices, it does not reflect the social reality in Europe. Evidence from states that have made the most significant progress (e.g. the Netherlands; Sweden) towards the establishment of these arrangements is that there remain significant gender differences in employment patterns. In these countries, horizontal segregation of the labour market tends to be common place, and women's participation in paid employment has not engendered a significant change in gender divisions of labour in the family (Kay 2003; Giullari and Lewis 2005; Kugelber 2006: 152-3).

From a policy perspective, the establishment of the adult worker model seems to have positive outcomes for fertility rates, in as far as the introduction of flexible employment patterns and more readily available part-time work allow women to reconcile work and family life. However, it ultimately fails to challenge gender norms and power hierarchies. Ultimately, this model is based on the assumption that women are and will continue to be the primary carers. Moreover, it fails to challenge the presumed link between time spent at the workplace, commitment to work and productivity (Kugelberg 2006: 153). If women's contributions to the household income continue to be secondary, then the adult worker model can only have limited emancipatory power.

Conclusions – Lessons of the European Experience

This chapter has sought to explore the link between the establishment of women's activation policies and demographic trends. More specifically, it sought to assess how women's expectations and perceptions of the impact of mothering on their ability to participate in the official labour market has led to specific choices about the ideal number of children. The evidence presented points to a 'new' social trend whereby women have exercised agency by withdrawing from the social function of reproduction. The chapter has also sought to link this analysis to current debates taking place at the European level about women's activation. In this context, I put forward the following questions: What is the impact of active labour market policies on women's ability to reconcile work and family life? What are the overall objectives of these policies in terms of: (a) The equal opportunities agenda, particularly with reference to substantive equality; (b) The current decline in birth rates; (c) The establishment of the adult worker model? Through the application of gender sensitive lens to the analysis presented here, it is possible to bring to light a number of conflicting discourses, the aim of which is not to challenge traditional gender power hierarchies.

The analysis of the current transition towards the dual breadwinner family in particular highlights some of the interests that are at work in this particular policy area. On the one hand, economic pressures brought about by the impending demographic crisis necessitate a novel approach to social and employment policy. On the other hand, there is recognition that social and cultural changes need to be accommodated by policies. At first glance this appears to be a rather positive picture for the future of gender policies in Europe. However, Lewis and Giullari's (2005) criticism of the adult worker model highlights the dangers of embarking upon this particular policy approach without detailed understanding of the impact of gender power hierarchies on women's choices and women's ability to negotiate their position within the family and the official labour market.

What starts to transpire from current discourses on activation is that women are seen predominantly as a reserve army of labour that can help to ensure long term economic growth of the European Single Market. If this is the case, then these policies will have only limited impact on redressing gender power hierarchies and inequalities in the public and private spheres. The establishment of the adult worker model will simply shift some of those power dynamics from the private to the public and will ultimately increase women's double burden.

Evidence from a number of studies points to the dichotomy between rhetoric and reality in the redistribution of unpaid work in the family. Whereas an increasing number of men would accept the discourse of sharing domestic and care work, evidence shows that there has been only a superficial change in family dynamics and practice. There are three key questions that emerge from the analysis presented here that warrant further exploration: Is low fertility a sign of women's agency? Is social engineering acceptable in order to forestall economic downturn in Europe? Is substantive equality going to be the by-product of this process?

Finally, in terms of the impact of the EES on the establishment of a substantive equality regime, many questions remain to be addressed. There is increasing evidence that, following a short period in which gender became central to the achievement of the EES, it is now being increasingly marginalized (Pfister 2006; Rubery et al 2003). Persistent focus on quantity of work rather than quality of employment is likely to have negative repercussions on women employment in the labour market, as they continue to make up the vast majority of atypical workers. The shift in favour of economic efficiency and growth seem to have been achieved at the expense of social justice (Fagan et al 2005; Busby 2005). As noted in this chapter, this may ultimately have a positive effect on demographic trends, but it will only serve to mask the persistence of gender inequalities.

References

Aliaga, C. (2005), 'Gender Gaps in the Reconciliation between Work and Family Life' *Statistics in Focus*, 4/2005. Eurostat, <http:// www.eds-destatis.de/en/downloads/sif/nk_05_04.pdf>.

Annesley, C. (2006), 'Women's Agency and Welfare Reform: Engendering the 'Adult Worker Model' Welfare State'. Paper presented to the "Policy-making, Gender and Citizenship Seminar", ESRC Research Seminar Series on *Gender, Participation and Citizenship – Political World(s) in Crisis*. 24 March 2006.

Babb, P., Butcher, H., Church, J., and Zealey, L. (2006) *Social Trends, Number 36*. (Basingstoke: Palgrave Macmillan).

Bock, G. and Thane, P. (1994), 'Introduction' in Bock, G. and Thane, P. (eds) *Maternity and Gender Policies: Women and the Rise of the European Welfare States 1880s-1950s* (London and New York: Routledge).

Busby, N. (2005), 'Pulp Fiction or Hard Fact? The Development of a European Employment Policy', *Journal of Contemporary European Research* 1(2): 29-38.

Caracciolo di Torrella, E. (2000), 'A Place for Maternity in the European Union' in McGlynn, C., (ed.) *Legal Feminisms: Theory and Practice*. (Dartmouth: Ashgate).

Cousins, C. (1999), *Society, Work and Welfare in Europe*. (Basingstoke: Palgrave Macmillan).

Craig, L. (2007), 'Is Gender Inequity in Time Allocation Associated with Low Fertility?' Paper presented at the Population Studies Association of America Annual Meeting 2007. <http://paa2007.princeton.edu/>.

Crompton, R. (2001), 'Gender Restructuring, Employment and Caring', *Social Politics* 8(3): 266-91.

Daly, M. (1994), 'Comparing Welfare States: Towards a Gender Friendly Approach' in Sainsbury, D. (ed.) *Gendering Welfare States*. (London: Sage) pp. 101-117.

Del Boca, D., Paqua, S. and Pronzato, C. (2004) 'Why are Fertility and Women's Employment Rates So Low in Italy? Lessons from France and the UK'. Institute for the Study of Labour (IZA, Bonn), Discussion Paper No. 1274, August 2004. <http://www.iza.org/>.

Duncan, S. (1995), 'Theorising European Gender Systems', *Journal of European Social Policy* 5(4): 263-284.

Duncan, S. and Edwards, R. (1999), *Lone Mothers, Paid Work and Gendered Moral Rationalities*. (London: Macmillan).

Duncan, S. (2000), 'What's the Problem with Teenage Parents? And What's the Problem with Policy?' *Critical Social Policy* 27(3): 307.

England, P. (2005), 'Gender Inequality in Labour Markets: The Role of Motherhood and Segregation', *Social Politics* 12(2): 264-88.

Esping-Andersen, G. (1990), *The Three Worlds of Welfare Capitalism*. (Cambridge: Polity).

European Commission (2004), *The Social Situation in the European Union 2004*. <http://ec.europa.eu/employment_social/publications/>.

European Commission (2005), *Green Paper – Confronting Demographic Change: a New Solidarity Between the Generations*. COM(2005)94 final. <http://europa.eu.int/comm/employment_social/news/2005/mar/comm2005-94_en.pdf>.

Eurostat (2005), *Europe in Figures – Eurostat Yearbook 2005*. (Luxembourg: Office for the Official Publications of the European Union).

Eurostat (2006), 'A statistical view of the life of women and men in the EU 25', <http://epp.eurostat.ec.europa.eu/pis/portal/docs/PAGE/PGP_PRD_CAT_PREREL/PGE_CAT_PREREL_YEAR_2006/PGE_CAT_PREREL_YEAR_2006_MONTH_03/3-06032006-EN-BP1.PDF>.

Fagan, C., Rubery, J., Grimshaw, D., Smith, M., Hebson, G.; Figueiredo, H. (2005) 'Gender Mainstreaming in the Enlarged European Union: Recent Developments in the European Employment Strategy and the Social Inclusion Process', *Industrial Relations Journal* 36(6): 568-91.

Giullari, S. and Lewis, J. (2005), 'The Adult Worker Model Family, Gender Equality and Care – The Search for New Policy Principles and the Possibilities and Problems of a Capabilities Approach', *Social Policy and Development Programme Paper*, No. 19. UN Research Institute for Social Development, <http://www.unrisd.org/>.

Guerrina, R. (2002), 'Mothering in Europe: A Feminist Critique of European Policies on Motherhood and Employment', *The European Journal of Women's Studies* 9(1): 49-68.

Guerrina, R. (2003), 'Employment Policy and the Family in the European Union' in Ackers, P. (ed) *Employment Relationship and Family Life*. Cross-National Research Papers, 6(4): 41-49.

Guerrina, R. (2005), *Mothering the Union: Gender Politics in the EU*. (Manchester, Manchester University Press).

Haas, B. (2005), 'The Work-Care Balance: Is It Possible to Identify Typologies for Cross-National Comparisons?', *Current Sociology* 53(3): 487-507.

Hakin, C. (2003), 'A New Approach to Explaining Fertility Patterns: Preference Theory', *Population and Development Review* 29(3): 349-374.

Hilgeman, C. and Butts, C.T. (2004), 'Family Policy, Women's Employment, and Below-Replacement Fertility in Developed Countries: A Hierarchical Bayesian

Approach' *Mathematical Behavioural Sciences at UC Irvine, Technical Reports*, MBS 04-11. <http://www.imbs.uci.edu/tr/abs/2004/mbs04_11.pdf>.

Kay, T. (2003), 'The Work-Life Balance in Social Practice', *Social Policy & Society* 2(3): 231-9.

Kugelberg, C. (2006), 'Constructing the Deviant Other: Mothering and Fathering at the Workplace', *Gender, Work and Organization* 13(2): 152-173.

Lewis, J. and Bennett, F. (2003), 'Themed Issue on Gender and Individualisation' *Social Policy and Society* 3(1): 43-5.

Lewis, J. (1992), 'Gender and the Development of Welfare Regimes', *Journal of European Social Policy* 2(3): 159-73.

Lewis, J. (2001), 'The Decline of the Male Breadwinner Model: Implications for Work and Care', *Social Politics* 8(2): 152-69.

Lewis, J. (2003), 'Economic Citizenship: a Comment', *Social Politics* 10(2): 176-85.

Lewis, J. (2006), 'The Adult Worker Model Family, Care and the Problem of Gender Equality', *Benefits* 14(1): 33-8.

McDonald, P. (2000), 'Gender Equality in Theories of Fertility Transition', *Population and Development Review* 26(3): 427.

McGlynn, C. (2001a), 'Reclaiming a Feminist Vision: The Reconciliation of Paid Work and Family Life in European Union Law and Policy', *Columbia Journal of European Law* 7, 241-72.

McGlynn, C. (2001b), 'European Union Family Values: Ideologies of "Family" and "Motherhood" in European Union Law', *Social Politics* 8(3): 325-50.

Muehlberger, U. (2000), 'Women's Labour Force Attachment in Europe: An Analytical Framework and Empirical Evidence for the Household' *IRISS Working Papers*, No. 2000-07. <http://ideas.repec.org/s/irs/iriswp.html>.

Paraskeva, M.A. (2003), 'Reconciliation Between Work and Family as a Means to Promote Women's Participation in the Labour Market'. <http://www.eurochambers.be/activities/women.shtml>.

Pfister, T. (2006), 'Transformations of Social and Economic Citizenship in the Transnationalising Context of European Integration – Gender Equality as Necessary Requirement and Crucial Test' Paper presented at the ESRC research seminar *Policy making, gender and citizenship*; University of the West of England, 24 March 2006.

Rubery, J.; Smith, M. and Fagan, C. (1999) *Women's Employment in Europe*. (London and New York: Routledge).

Rubery, J.; Smith, M.; Anxo, D.; Flood, L., (2001) 'The Future Labour Market supply: The Critical Role of the Family', *Feminist Economics* 7(3): 33-69.

Rubery, J., Grimshaw, D., Fagan, C., Figueiredo, H. and Smith, M. (2003), 'Gender Equality Still on the European Agenda – but for how long?', *Industrial Relations Journal* 35(5): 477-97.

Sainsbury, D. (1994), *Gendering Welfare States*. (London: Sage).

Stier, H., Lewin-Epstein, N., and Braun, M. (2001) 'Welfare Regimes, Family-supportive Policies, and Women's Employment along the Life-course', *American Journal of Sociology* 106: 1731-60.

Chapter 4

The European Employment Strategy and the Europeanization of Gender Equality in Employment

Ayse Idil Aybars

This chapter locates gender equality in employment in the European Employment Strategy (EES), and explores its implications in four European Union (EU) Member States exemplifying a four-fold welfare regime typology, which consists of the addition of a fourth, Southern welfare model (Castles 1995; Ferrera 1996; Trifiletti 1999), to Esping-Andersen's (1990) now classical three-fold typology. These Member States are Spain (Southern welfare regime), Denmark (social-democratic welfare regime), France (conservative welfare regime), and the UK (liberal welfare regime), each with considerably different starting points and current settings for gender equality in the labour market. The focus on the welfare regime typology aims to highlight how gender equality arrangements differ across Member States with distinct welfare legacies and what the EES implies in different welfare settings.

Although gender equality in employment was predominantly promoted through the components of a 'hard' legislative framework, such as Treaty provisions and Directives, for most of the history of the EU, it is also a core element of the more recent 'soft' approach to employment and social policy in the EU, best illustrated by the EES. Being one of the areas where the Open Method of Coordination (OMC) is applied in one of its most fully-developed forms, the EES has significant implications for gender equality in employment, which was, until 2005, one of its ten 'priority areas'. The EES highlights the differences amongst the Member States in terms of gender equality in employment, which are closely connected to their welfare state structures. This is particularly important as the EU 'hard' legislative approach has, for a long time, emphasized the importance of establishing a common legal framework for gender equality, regardless of the diversity of welfare regimes and gender equality practices prevailing in individual countries. In this context the analysis of the EES offers important insights on what novelty is brought by the 'soft' EU approach to employment and social policy in an area with an advanced 'hard' legal background.

The assessment of the impacts of the Community method on national gender equality frameworks is relatively easier due to its more tangible outcomes in terms of the national transposition of EU regulations and the relative 'oldness' of the process implying an abundance of research in the area. In contrast, the OMC poses significant challenges regarding the identification of outcomes not just because it is more recent but particularly because it is non-binding. With a view to explaining the transformation at the national level, which takes place in response to the European initiatives in employment and social policy, 'Europeanization' provides a significant analytical tool by revealing that the outcome of supranational governance at national level can be continuing diversity, although all Member States are bound by the same supranational discourse and policy vision.

This chapter first locates gender equality in employment in the EES in three phases (1997-2002, 2002-2005, and 2005 onwards), and then focuses on the differences amongst welfare regimes in the area of gender equality in employment that come to the fore as a result of the non-binding, pluralistic and voluntary approach of the OMC. It finally spots the potential strengths and weaknesses of the approach in terms of its implications for 'Europeanization', which is taken here as a process whereby the EU-level 'hard' and 'soft' initiatives in the area of gender equality in employment lead to changes in the existing gender equality legislation, policies and ideas at the national level.[1]

Gender Equality in the EES

The EES is part of an attempt, at the EU level, to increasingly use 'soft' policy instruments in employment and social policy.[2] As gender equality in employment had mainly been regulated through the 'hard' legislative framework of the classical Community method for almost half a century, the launch of the EES at the Luxembourg Summit in 1997[3] represented a very significant step in the direction of a 'soft' co-ordination approach in the field.[4] The EES is one of the European

1 Nevertheless, it is important to note that this study does not focus on Europeanization as a one-way process, whereby policies developed at the supranational level affect national settings in a top-down manner. It rather focuses on Europeanization as a two-way, interactive process, in which Member States, to varying extents, also have considerable influence on shaping the policies adopted by the EU.

2 The main reasons behind this are the increasing pressure dictated by the economic integration process (Hafner-Burton and Pollack 2000; De la Porte 2002; Pochet 2005); as well as the changes in labour market and family structures (Vandenbroucke 2002; Zeitlin 2005a).

3 For the development of the EES and OMC through subsequent European Summits and meetings, see de la Porte 2002; Regent 2003; Sabel and Zeitlin 2003; Trubek and Mosher 2001; Barbier 2004.

4 It is important to note, however, that this chapter does not attempt to trace a chronological dividing line between 'hard' and 'soft' approaches, which rather co-exist and complement each other. The soft approach to gender equality was evident from the 1980s onwards, when equality legislation started to be accompanied by non-binding political instruments, such as recommendations, resolutions, proposals and action programmes on equal opportunities for women and men (Ostner and Lewis 1995; Hoskyns 1996). On the other hand, there are still notable attempts at the EU level towards 'hard' regulation of gender equality, not least the amendment of the Equal Treatment Directive in 2002 (Masselot 2004), and the endeavour to consolidate the existing gender equality legislation in the European Constitution (Shaw 2005).

policies where the OMC is applied in one of its most fully developed forms.[5] The 'soft' disposition of this new procedure stems from, first, its reliance on soft policy instruments for its realization (Mazey 2002; Trubek and Mosher 2001), involving agreement on common targets, exchange of best practices, the use of benchmarking, periodic reporting, experimental policy learning, multi-lateral surveillance and monitoring. Second, the OMC is considered 'soft' due to its non-binding character: the method does not involve any sanctions for the Member States which do not comply with the objectives (De la Porte 2002; Trubek and Trubek 2005). However, it entails 'peer pressure' for the Member States to address the common guidelines and objectives and to adapt their policies accordingly (O'Connor 2005; Pochet 2005). Third, as employment and social policy are politically sensitive areas (Chalmers and Lodge 2003; Sabel and Zeitlin 2003), traditionally left to Member State authority, it was difficult for the Commission to 'coerce' the Member States into further supranationalization in this policy sector (Mazey 2002). Hence the new 'soft' European approach is 'nation-state friendly', facilitating the achievement of coordinated decisions among the Member States, and entailing intergovernmental cooperation, with a proliferation of actors contributing to the processes of policy-making and implementation (de la Porte 2002; Regent 2003).

With these features, it has been argued, the OMC institutionalized a flexible, participatory method of governance, rather than one based on top-down, uniform rules strengthened by sanctions (Trubek and Mosher 2001; Regent 2003), and 'one-size-fits-all lawmaking' (Sabel and Zeitlin 2003). As a crucial new mode of European governance (Hemerijck 2002; Mazey 2002; Radaelli 2003b), it has been seen as a move away from 'hard law' to 'soft law' (Trubek and Mosher 2001; De la Porte 2002; O'Connor 2005), symbolising a shift in emphasis from harmonization to convergence of results, permitting a diversity of national policies (Palier 2003; Radaelli 2003b), with 'a capacity for reconciling European action with national diversity' (Zeitlin 2005a: 7).

How, then, is gender equality in employment incorporated into this new framework? The EES, from the Luxembourg Summit of 1997 until the Barcelona European Council of 2002, was based on a pillar structure, composed of the four pillars of employability, entrepreneurship, adaptability, and equal opportunities. Gender equality was thus considered as one of the four building blocks of the new approach as 'Pillar IV' on equal opportunities. As devised in the 1999 Employment Guidelines, this Pillar included four specific guidelines: integrating gender equality across all the four Pillars; tackling gender gaps in employment; reconciling work and family life; and facilitating the reintegration of women in employment (CEC 1999). Starting from the 2001 Employment Guidelines (CEC 2001), the number of specific guidelines were reduced to three, combining the last two elements. During this first stage, the female employment target of 60 per cent to be attained by 2010 was put

5 The OMC in employment, as illustrated by the EES, has a strong institutional foundation as opposed to most other areas where it is used, such as social exclusion, pensions, etc. This is due to the fact that it has a Treaty basis. The Treaty of Amsterdam incorporated the Title VIII on Employment into the Treaty (for a more detailed discussion, see Pollack and Hafner-Burton 2000; Hemerijck 2002; Regent 2003; Sabel and Zeitlin 2003; Pochet 2005).

forward by the Lisbon European Council of 2000, and the mid-term rate of 57 per cent to be attained by 2005 was set by the Stockholm European Council of 2001. Table 4.1 outlines the three phases of the EES in terms of its implications for gender equality, while Table 4.2 locates gender equality in the transformation of the EES.

Table 4.1 Three phases of the EES in terms of gender equality

PHASE I	PHASE II	PHASE III
1997 Luxembourg Summit **2002 Barcelona European Council**	**2002 Barcelona European Council** **2005 Mid-term Review**	**2005 EES Mid-term Review**
• One of Four Pillars • Lisbon Strategy (2000) established 60 per cent female employment target to be attained by 2010 • Stockholm European Council (2001) established 57 per cent mid-term target for female employment rate	• One of 10 Priorities for Action • Targets for 2010 Reconciliation of work and family life • Childcare for 90 per cent of 3-6 year olds • Childcare for 33 per cent of 0-3 year olds • Substantial reduction in gender gaps in employment, unemployment and pay with a view to eliminating gender pay gap	• EES streamlined with BEPGs • No specific gender guideline, but a number of references to women's labour market situation, particularly in GL 18

The EES was revised and entered into a second stage after the Barcelona European Council of March 2002, which replaced the Pillar structure with three 'overarching objectives' of full employment, job quality and productivity, and social cohesion and inclusion, to be achieved through ten 'priorities for action' (CEC 2003). Gender equality, within this framework, became one of the latter as priority number six, losing some of its visibility under the previous structure. Nevertheless, in addition to the existing targets relating to gender, European targets concerning reconciling employment and family life have been established for the first time: to provide childcare to at least 90 per cent of children between three years old and the mandatory school age and at least 33 per cent of children under three years of age by 2010, as well as targets on achieving substantial reductions in gender gaps in employment, unemployment and pay, with a view to eliminating the gender pay gap by 2010, which showed the importance attached to increasing female employment rates and childcare at the EU level (Rubery et al. 2003, 2004; O'Connor 2005).

Table 4.2 Gender equality in the different stages of the EES

1999 Employment Guidelines	2001 Employment Guidelines	2003 Employment Guidelines	2005 Employment Guidelines
Four Pillars: 1. EMPLOYABILITY 2. ENTREPRENEURSHIP 3. ADAPTABILITY 4. EQUAL OPPORTUNITIES: GL 19. Gender mainstreaming GL 20. Tackling gender gaps GL 21. Reconciling work and family life GL 22. Facilitating reintegration into the labour market	Four Pillars: 1. EMPLOYABILITY 2. ENTREPRENEURSHIP 3. ADAPTABILITY 4. EQUAL OPPORTUNITIES: GL 16. Gender mainstreaming GL 17. Tackling gender gaps GL 18. Reconciling work and family life	Three Objectives: 1. FULL EMPLOYMENT 2. IMPROVING QUALITY AND PRODUCTIVITY AT WORK 3. STRENGTHENING SOCIAL COHESION AND INCLUSION Ten priorities for action: 1.Active and preventive measures for unemployed/ inactive 2. Job creation and entrepreneurship 3. Adaptability and mobility in the labour market 4. Development of human capital and lifelong learning 5. Increase labour supply and promote active ageing 6. Gender Equality 7. Integration of disadvantaged people in labour market 8. Make work pay 9. Transform undeclared work into regular employment 10. Address regional employment disparities	Objectives and Priorities for Action: 1. FULL EMPLOYMENT 2. IMPROVING QUALITY AND PRODUCTIVITY AT WORK 3. STRENGTHENING SOCIAL AND TERRITORIAL COHESION Integrated Guidelines (GL 17 to 24): 17. Implement employment policies aiming at achieving full employment, improving quality and productivity at work, and strengthening social and territorial cohesion 18. Promote a lifecycle approach to work 19. Ensure inclusive labour markets, enhance work attractiveness, and make work pay for job-seekers 20. Improve matching of labour market needs 21. Promote flexibility combined with employment security and reduce labour market segmentation 22. Ensure employment-friendly labour cost developments and wage-setting mechanisms 23. Expand and improve investment in human capital 24. Adapt education and training systems in response to new competence requirements

The year 2005 witnessed another significant turning point for the EES, with the mid-term review of the Lisbon strategy. Under the new title of the Community Lisbon Programme, the EES has been streamlined with the Broad Economic Policy Guidelines (BEPGs), setting up the Integrated Guidelines for Growth and Jobs. This new framework covers actions in the 'three main areas' of knowledge and innovation for growth, making Europe a more attractive place to invest and work, and creating more and better jobs. While there was no specific reference to gender in the Integrated Guidelines for Growth and Jobs (EC 2005), the Employment Guidelines 2005-2008 (CEC 2005) (numbers 17 to 24 of the new Integrated Guidelines), incorporated explicit references to the importance of increasing female participation and reducing gender gaps in employment, unemployment and pay; and of promoting better reconciliation of work and private life and the provision of accessible and affordable childcare facilities (particularly GL 18: Promote a lifecycle approach to work). Still, the lack of a specific guideline on gender equality brings a concern with a further loss of visibility of the gender equality policy objective (Fagan et al 2006).

Still, it is worth noting that, in March 2006, the Commission adopted a Roadmap for equality between women and men (EC 2006), outlining six priority areas for EU action on gender equality, including equal economic independence for women and men, and reconciliation of private and professional life,[6] whereby it made significant references to Lisbon and Barcelona objectives. On the basis of the roadmap, moreover, a European Pact for Gender Equality was annexed to the Presidency Conclusions of the European Council meeting on 23-24 March 2006,[7] encouraging action at the Member State as well as the EU levels in the following fields: measures to close gender gaps and combat gender stereotypes in the labour market; measures to promote a better work-life balance for all; and measures to reinforce governance through gender mainstreaming and better monitoring. The Pact aimed to 'contribute to fulfilling EU ambitions on gender equality as mentioned in the Treaty',[8] thereby underlining the complementarity between the 'hard' and 'soft' frameworks. What is important to underline is that the Pact was envisaged to be integrated into the follow-up mechanisms of the Partnership for Growth and Employment, and to promote the implementation of gender mainstreaming within the streamlined Lisbon Strategy. Within this framework, Member States were encouraged to include a gender equality perspective in their National Reform Programmes (NRP), and the European Commission and Council were invited to do so in their Annual Progress Reports.

Gender Equality in Different Welfare Models

A very important novelty introduced by the OMC is its recognition of the diversity amongst the Member States in terms of their welfare and labour market policies (see

6 Other priority areas include equal representation in decision-making; eradication of all forms of gender-based violence; elimination of gender stereotypes; and promotion of gender equality in external and development policies.

7 Brussels European Council, 23-24 March 2006, Presidency Conclusions, 7775/1/06, Brussels, 18 May 2006 (Annex II).

8 Ibid., p.27.

among others Pochet 2005; Zeitlin 2005a). It has been argued that the new method has, indeed, been developed as 'soft policy coordination' because, across the EU, the European Social Model 'is implemented in many different ways through legal and institutional structures that vary tremendously yet are deeply embedded in national life and costly to change' (Trubek and Mosher, 2001: 6). Its decentralized approach, as opposed to the Community method, is based on the acceptance of divergence among, and even within, the Member States, which are free to define the most appropriate measures for implementing their employment and social policies (De la Porte 2002; Regent 2003).

In terms of the structure of governance implied by the OMC, therefore, one of the most significant questions regarding gender equality, which has been mainly regulated through legal harmonization, is raised by the new method's celebrated encouragement of diversity and the absence of legal sanctions. Within the EES, although the key discourse emerging from the European context and adopted by national actors is similar, the steps to be taken by the Member States to achieve the transformation that would bring them in line with the European discourse depend on their welfare regime structures (De la Porte 2002; Chalmers and Lodge 2003; O'Connor 2005). This section focuses on the four countries identified above, exemplifying a four-fold welfare regime typology, in order to highlight the differences in the gender components of their welfare regimes.

As an exemplar of the Southern European welfare regime, the most distinctive characteristic of Spain in terms of gender equality is the 'familialistic' orientation of the welfare state, implying a crucial role played by the family as an institution of welfare production and distribution of income and services (Salido 2002). The importance of the family in Spain can be seen in the predominance of intergenerational dependency and solidarity, low fertility and low female labour market participation rates, which are closely related to the influence of the Catholic religion and a dictatorial regime until 1975 (Salido 2002; Moreno Minguez 2004). The central position of the family, however, is constantly undermined by a lack of state support and services for families (Flaquer 2000; Moreno 2004) in particular for working mothers (Moreno Minguez 2004). The state takes no responsibility for the reconciliation of women's two roles, leading to the 'reproduction of a system based on a very limited amount of family-friendly public measures', which creates 'a situation of mutual dependency of men and women in which the former provide income and the latter care services' (Flaquer 2000: 29). This certainly had a negative impact on the labour force participation of women with familial tasks, and constituted an important obstacle for the integration of women with caring tasks in the labour market (Moreno Minguez 2004).

As an exemplar of the social-democratic welfare regime, Denmark is characterized by a welfare system based on egalitarianism, solidarity, universalism, generous benefit levels, and a comprehensive social citizenship (Esping-Andersen 1990; Nielsen and Kesting 2004). It is marked by high de-familialization effects (Esping-Andersen 1990), implying a heavily service-oriented welfare state that takes direct responsibility for the care of children, the elderly, and the helpless, together with providing generous income support for working women (Kjeldstad 2001; Roseberry 2002). Considering the high degree of individualization in social and taxation policies, as well as the recent activation efforts tying benefits to labour market participation, it is not surprising to find the highest rates of female labour market participation in countries exemplifying this welfare regime (Nielsen and Kesting 2004). Along with other exemplars of this regime, Denmark is a pioneer in the promotion of equal opportunities for women and men, and is generally described as a 'woman-friendly' welfare state (Kjeldstad 2001; Siim and Borchorst 2005).

France is an exemplar of the conservative welfare regime, characterized by a mix of statist, corporatist, and familialist traditions. The corporatist legacy in the conservative regime, which includes most of the continental European countries, implies a strict linkage of entitlements to work performance, a system particularly privileging civil servants, and a strong influence of the Catholic Church in social reform (Esping-Andersen 1990; Hemerijck 2002). Although France largely illustrates the conservative model with its income maintenance system and de-commodifying effects, its inclusion in this category becomes problematic when it comes to gender equality in employment. Three main factors can be identified to account for this: (1) the influence of the Catholic Church in the development of the continental welfare regime, (2) the extensive family-friendly public policy approach of the French welfare state, and (3) the high female labour force participation. These three points are closely intertwined and stem from the fact that Esping-Andersen's typical example to the continental welfare regime, at least in his earlier work (1990), was Germany. France rather stands as an exception to the conservative regime with its highly developed women-friendly policies, which have led to it being categorized close to the Scandinavian model in various gender-oriented typologies. France was one of the first nations to embark on a significant expansion of family services in the 1970s, following Denmark and Sweden which initiated the process a decade earlier (Esping-Andersen 1999; Hemerijck 2002). Nevertheless, the justification behind French family-friendly policies fundamentally differs from that in Scandinavian countries: French policies reflect a preoccupation with maintaining high birth rates, which has traditionally manifested itself in an emphasis on the protection of the family and working mothers (Fagnani and Letablier 2005). Still, although the influence of the Catholic Church was felt in the protectionist and pronatalist approach of the welfare state, social policies in France have rather been marked by a 'republican' understanding of secularism, equality, citizenship and solidarity, inscribed by the French Revolution of 1789. This implied a different path for the French welfare state, and entailed, above all, higher support for female participation in employment in the form of family-friendly policies.[9] The relatively high levels of female labour market participation are mainly explained by the progressive nature of French family-friendly policies in content and coverage compared to those of its counterparts in the continental welfare model (Le Feuvre and Andriocci 2001).

The UK is an exemplar of the liberal welfare regime in Esping-Andersen's (1990) 'three worlds of welfare capitalism'. This model is characterized mainly by individualism, heavy predominance of the market, means-tested assistance, low de-

9 This is acknowledged by Esping-Andersen in his later work (1999, 2002), which distinguishes between continental welfare regime members like Germany, on the one hand, and France, on the other, in terms of the commitment to the male breadwinner model and the influence of familialism.

familialization effects, and 'residualism' in transfers (Esping-Andersen 1990, 1999). A very crucial feature of this model is that it is the market which is the main welfare provider, rather than the state as in the case of Denmark or France, or family in the case of Spain. The model traditionally favours individualism and free reign of the market, 'with the welfare state cast as a minimal and residual player' (Esping-Andersen 2002: 2). The implication of these characteristics for gender equality is that childcare and domestic division of labour between men and women have been traditionally conceived by the British welfare state as private issues (O'Connor et al. 1999; Daguerre and Taylor-Gooby 2004). Therefore, as in the conservative and Southern European models, family services are underdeveloped in the liberal model, although the justification behind this differs: while the conservative model leaves this task to families themselves, the liberal model sees it as 'a natural market activity' and 'an individual responsibility' (Esping-Andersen 1999, 76). The Liberal model is thus characterized by low de-familialization effects, as it does not provide wide-ranging services to families (Hemerijck 2002). Despite all these, the UK has remarkably high levels of overall and female employment. Still, female employment is heavily concentrated in part-time jobs, displaying the insufficiencies of British policies for reconciling work and family life (Silvera 2002; Kilpatrick and Freedland 2004).

In the context of the EES, it is argued that, depending on the welfare structures, some countries can easily adapt to it, while others have to make a great effort to comply with it. In terms of gender equality in employment, the countries exemplifying the social-democratic welfare regime, with remarkably high service provision, a central role for the state and the social partners, as well as progressive gender arrangements, are those belonging to the former group (De la Porte 2002; Sabel and Zeitlin 2003). Sweden and Denmark have already attained high levels of female employment, and exceeded the Lisbon target of 60 per cent female employment to be attained by 2010 (De la Porte 2002; O'Connor 2005). Denmark and Sweden, together with Belgium, have also been the only three countries that attained the childcare target of 33 per cent for children under three. On the other hand, the UK, as an example of the liberal welfare regime, has also reached the general and female employment targets (De la Porte 2002; O'Connor 2005), but remains remarkably weak at reducing gender pay gaps, as well as the provision of accessible and affordable childcare, which are well established in its welfare system based on the dominance of the market as against the state or the family. The EES implies the most comprehensive and structural transformations and the biggest pressure for change for the Member States with conservative and Southern European social policy traditions. These welfare states rely on a 'strong' male-breadwinner/female carer model, where women's situation in the labour market and the overall employment rate are still well behind the EU average (De la Porte 2002). The exception is France, which has already reached the mid-term target rate for female employment (O'Connor 2005). In the countries belonging to the Southern model, the services provided by the state are marginal, and the role of the family is central in welfare provision. On the other hand, the countries with a conservative welfare legacy have considerably improved their care services (De la Porte 2002).

In the next section, the impact of the EES on the four countries exemplifying the four-fold welfare regime typology will be put under the spotlight through two separate but closely connected lenses: (1) their employment levels, and (2) the recommendations they received from the European Council up until 2004 in the area of gender equality.

Evolution of Employment Trends

Generally speaking, although women's labour market participation is lower than that of men across the EU, there is a process of convergence in women's and men's rates of participation in all Member States, although to varying degrees (O'Connor et al. 1999; Daguerre and Taylor-Gooby 2004). At EU level, female activity rates have doubled since the 1960s, from less than 30 per cent of the active population to almost 60 per cent (Silvera 2002). Table 4.3 displays the male, female and overall employment trends during the period between 1990 and 2004 in the four countries. The year 1997 has been taken as a key date as it represents the launch of the EES with the Luxembourg Jobs Summit. It is therefore a significant year in terms of assessing the main changes in employment trends occurring in the four countries in association with the EES, although no causal relationship is claimed here. The Table below allows us to trace the employment trends in two seven-year periods, namely, between 1990-1997, and 1997-2004.

Table 4.3 Employment rates (share of persons of working age – 15-64 – in employment, per cent) in 1990, 1997, 2004

	1990			1997			2004		
	Men	Women	Total	Men	Women	Total	Men	Women	Total
Denmark	80.1	70.6	75.4	81.3	69.4	75.4	79.9	72.0	76.0
Spain	71.9	31.8	51.8	66.1	35.2	50.7	74.9	49.0	62.0
France	69.7	50.3	59.9	66.3	51.7	58.9	68.1	56.7	62.4
UK	82.1	62.8	72.5	77.4	64.0	70.6	78.9	66.6	72.7
EU-15	74.3	48.7	61.5	70.8	50.9	60.8	72.4	56.7	64.6

Source: OECD (2006)

There are two points to be made regarding these figures. The first relates to locating the four countries in a continuum of employment rates, and identifying the best and the worst performers. In this respect, Denmark offers the most progressive picture in terms of gender equality in the labour market, in line with the view of Scandinavia as 'sex equality's Promised Land' (Roseberry 2002: 217). Indeed, one of the most important characteristics of the Danish labour market is the near-maximum activity rate for both men and women (Kjeldstad 2001; Esping-Andersen 2002a; Hemerijck 2002). From 1990 to 2004 Denmark had the highest rates of both overall and female employment, and the highest rates of male employment since at least 1997. Compared to other EU countries, moreover, the gap between the male and female employment rates in Scandinavian countries in general, and Denmark in particular, is relatively low and is in the course of disappearing (Silvera 2002).

The UK also has above EU-15 average rates of overall, male and female employment, being second after Denmark. It is one of the few countries which have already attained the female employment targets of the Lisbon Strategy for 2010, although it must be underlined that the precarious part-time character of female employment in the UK raises questions concerning the pursuit of gender equality. The major growth in female employment has been occurring since the beginning of the 1990s, mainly due to private sector expansion, particularly private service sector expansion (OECD 2005). This contrasts with the other countries where the growth has been in the pubic services sector (Kjeldstad 2001).

Next in terms of employment rates is France, which occupies a middle ground in terms of overall, male and female employment levels, with its figures remaining close to the EU-15 average over the period. Despite its increasing female employment rate, its overall employment rate was almost identical to the Spanish rate in 2004. France emerges as another country offering a relatively positive picture for female employment, where the activity models for men and women converge (Fouquet et al. 2000). The female employment rate was 58 per cent in 2004, implying that France has succeeded in attaining the 2005 mid-term Lisbon target of 57 per cent, and is rapidly approaching the target of 60 per cent by 2010.

Spain is at the lowest end of the spectrum of female and overall employment rates, although its male employment rates have been very close to or higher than France throughout the whole period. In comparison with the EU, the Spanish employment rates remained low for both sexes for a long period of time (Salido 2002, Valiente 2003), although Spain has been rapidly catching up as is evident in Table 4.3. Despite the significant increase in the rates of female employment since 1990, there has been a relatively low participation rate for women in employment (Moreno 2004). Moreover, the difference between men's and women's employment rate remains much more marked in Spain than the remaining three countries (Moreno Minguez 2004; Fouquet et al. 2000).

The second point relates to the assessment of the EES in terms of its association with the changes in overall female and male employment trends in the four countries. For this purpose, it is necessary to focus on the two periods of 1990-1997 and 1997-2004 respectively. The comparison of the first two columns of Table 4.3 shows that the growth in male, female and overall employment rates was much less significant throughout the first period. Between 1990 and 1997, Spain, France and the UK witnessed a remarkable decline in male employment rates, ranging from three per cent in France to six in Spain. Female employment growth was also not very significant in this first period, when Spain saw the greatest increase with about three per cent. Finally, overall employment declined slightly in Spain, France and the UK.

The second seven-year period, which followed the launch of the EES, witnessed more noteworthy changes. Almost all male, female and overall employment levels rose sharply. The highest increases were in Spain where female employment increased by 14 per cent, male employment rates by nine per cent, and the overall employment rate by 11 per cent. On the other hand, the smallest increases and even decreases took place in Denmark, which saw a drop of one per cent in male employment rates, and an increase of less than three per cent in female. This can be explained by the fact that Denmark already had a very favourable labour market situation for both sexes. Moreover, it was indeed the source of inspiration behind the EES, which implies that the Danish labour market has not been significantly affected by the Strategy. On the other hand, the association of the EES with the change in the Spanish labour market may have been much stronger because Spain had a remarkably low starting point compared to the rest of the countries. Finally, the UK and France have only been slightly affected by the EES as these two countries were close to or above the EU average.

In summary, these figures clearly establish that Denmark, as an exemplar of the social-democratic welfare regime, and the UK, as an exemplar of the liberal welfare regime, are remarkably close to each other in terms of employment performance. On the other hand, France and Spain, exemplars of the conservative and Southern regimes respectively, tend to group together, displaying a remarkable gap with the first group, although France rather occupies a middle ground between the first group and Spain. The two ends of the continuum are therefore occupied by Denmark and Spain, with the UK and France in the middle, the former closer to Denmark and the latter to Spain. Another clear picture emerging from Table 4.3 is the significant pace gained after 1997, which coincides with the EES, although no causation is argued here. Nevertheless, it is worthwhile noting a possible EES association with the improving employment situation in each country, albeit to varying extents. Still, it is important not to overestimate the increasing levels of female employment since the start of the EES, as the character of this employment also needs to be taken into consideration: for instance, while women form the majority of low-paid, low-skill, unstable part-time workers in the UK, they overwhelmingly occupy temporary jobs in Spain.

Council Recommendations on Gender Equality

Council Recommendations constitute a second important axis in identifying the outcomes of the EES in the national settings marked by distinct welfare regimes. These documents form a significant part of the EES, and were issued annually until the streamlining of the EES with the BEPGs in 2005 as a response to the National Action Plans (NAP) for Employment and the Joint Employment Reports (JER) by the Commission and the Council. The streamlining of the EES with BEPGs meant that the NAPs became National Reform Programmes to be issued every three years, and thus the structure of the EES has changed. This section examines the Recommendations issued between the years 2000-2004. These documents assess the situation of the Member States in terms of the European objectives and targets, identifying the areas where each Member State needs to improve its performance, and drawing attention to the most pressing problems in the national labour markets.

The Recommendations therefore give significant clues as to the welfare structure and gender arrangements of each Member State, as well as their position with regard to the European guidelines and benchmarks. This section puts these pressing issues emerging in relation to each of the four countries under the spotlight, with a view to pointing to the differences in their gender equality arrangements, which are closely connected to their welfare regime structures. Table 4.4 outlines the Recommendations on gender equality in the labour market directed to each of the four countries throughout the period between 2000 and 2004.

Table 4.4 Council recommendations on gender (2000-2004)

Spain	Denmark	France	UK
• Raise female employment rates to EU average • Intensify efforts to mainstream gender • Close gender gaps in employment and unemployment; • Improve provision of care facilities • Reduce fixed-term contracts, increase part-time contracts	• Promote training and job opportunities for unemployed women • Find ways to reduce occupational and sectoral segregation • Develop a substantial gender mainstreaming approach • (From 2002 onwards, no recommendation on gender)	• (Until 2004 no recommendation on gender) • Facilitate transition of people under fixed-term contracts to avoid labour market segmentation • Build effective pathways to work and training for unemployed young people and immigrants, notably women	• Expand and improve quality of childcare to enable women's employment • Give special attention to lone parents' needs • Strengthen efforts to reduce gender pay gaps and segregation by involving social partners and establishing targets and indicators • Implement ALMP (in full) to tackle inactivity and long-term unemployment traps, particularly for lone parents and deprived communities

The Recommendations directed to Spain between 2000 and 2004 emphasized the remarkably low employment and high unemployment levels, high long-term unemployment trends, and the existence of very large employment and unemployment gender gaps in the country, which placed it amongst the worst performers in the EU-15. Throughout the period, gender equality was constantly on the agenda: several recommendations on gender were directed to Spain each year, and were often repeated in subsequent years, showing the urgency of the need to tackle the problem. The areas of particular concern were the low female employment rates, insufficient efforts to establish gender mainstreaming, wide gender gaps in the labour market, absence of affordable childcare facilities, high share of fixed-term contracts which mainly concern women, and lack of incentives to increase female labour force participation.

The evaluation of Recommendations shows that Denmark stands in stark contrast to Spain in terms of almost all the labour market indicators in general and the gender equality dimension in particular. Denmark emerges as the country with the highest male and female employment rate in the EU, and one of the lowest unemployment rates, which has already succeeded in attaining the Lisbon employment targets for 2010. Thus, as opposed to Spain, which received numerous recommendations signalling the urgent need to prioritize gender equality in the labour market, in the case of Denmark, gender equality did not constitute the key focus of the Recommendations, apart from a concern with high gender segregation in different sectors and occupations. The latter emerges as Denmark's main problem and stands out as an area requiring immediate action, although it too ceased to be pointed out in the Recommendations over the years, which focused, instead, on more alarming issues such as the ageing population, labour shortages, and integration of immigrant groups in the labour market.

Having achieved the mid-term target for female employment, France is another country which received a limited number of recommendations on gender equality. Nevertheless, the Recommendations identified numerous other areas in need of improvement, particularly the relatively low employment and high unemployment levels, low participation of the older workers, the youth and immigrants, and insufficient social dialogue. Although France did not receive any recommendation on gender issues until 2004, the final Council Recommendations underlined the need for facilitating the transition of people under fixed-term contracts – who are mostly women – into permanent contracts to avoid labour market segmentation, and for increasing work and training opportunities for unemployed young people and for immigrants, notably women.

Finally, the UK was evaluated in the Council Recommendations as a country with a favourable labour market performance, and above-average employment rates which exceeded the Lisbon targets for both men and women. Nevertheless, important structural problems were identified, mainly in relation to inactivity and long-term unemployment (particularly for lone parents), above-average gender pay gaps, lack of affordable childcare facilities, low skills levels, and job quality problems. The UK therefore emerges as another country which continuously received recommendations concerning gender equality. It was consistently warned about the need to improve the access to and affordability of care services, to tackle problems relating to the gender pay gap and the quality of childcare provisions, to encourage female full-time work, to focus on the needs of lone parents, and to take measures against gender segregation in the labour market.

What is important to note here is that the Recommendations, particularly to those countries identified as having structural problems such as Spain and the UK, were consistently repeated, which raises questions as to the effectiveness of the 'soft' approach adopted by the EES in bringing about the desired levels of change. They, moreover, point to the fact that the 'tailor-made' approach of the EES leads different problems to come to the fore in each individual Member State, and therefore strongly underlines the specific social policy legacies of the Member States under consideration.

Implications for Gender Equality in the EU

What, then, can be said about the implications of this tailor-made approach, which allows Member States discretion in devising their own national policies while providing the terms of progress towards gender equality in employment? While it is still early to assess the actual implementation at the national level, significant measures have been taken by the Member States in accordance with the recommendations they have been receiving. Indeed, it has been argued that the new method has modified national systems in line with the common discourse that has emerged (Barbier 2004; Pochet 2005; Trubek and Trubek 2005), and that it has been particularly effective in expanding the terms of national policy debates on gender equality in employment and gender mainstreaming (Zeitlin 2005a, 2005b). However, this common discourse, providing 'cognitive coordination', has not yet changed the basic structures of national social and employment policies, 'which remain indeed very diversified in terms of their outcomes' (Barbier 2004: 22).

In the case of gender equality, progress through the 'hard' legal framework has often been criticized for putting forward no more than minimum standards and lowest-common denominator solutions for the implementation of common goals (Ostner and Lewis 1995; Hoskyns 1996). Although the Directives are legally binding upon the Member States, they provide no indication of the form and methods required to transpose the aspired goals at national level (Cichowski 2004). Nevertheless, Article 119 EC and the subsequent gender equality Directives, along with the activism of the European Court of Justice (ECJ), pushed the Member States to adapt their legislation on certain important employment-related issues (Ostner and Lewis 1995). In addition, the constitutionalization of gender equality at Amsterdam and the status of a 'Community social norm' assigned to it (Wobbe 2003) contributed to the establishment of 'an advanced legal framework' for gender equality in employment at EU level (Hoskyns 1996, 113).

Against this background provided by the 'hard' legal approach, the most important question mark relating to the 'soft' framework of the EES concerns its non-binding character, which entails the danger that EU social policy in general and gender equality policy in particular would not be effectively implemented at the level of Member States. Secondly, its recognition and encouragement of diversity may complicate the governance of social policy in the EU even further. Yet the appearance of a common discourse of social policy in the EU, a new 'common policy vision' (Palier 2003; Pochet 2005), should not be underestimated. Here, however, it seems necessary to keep in mind the distinction between convergence of dynamics and procedures on the one hand, and the convergence of substantive policy outcomes on the other (Barbier 2005; Palier 2003).

While the 'common language and categorical framework to discuss and evaluate different solutions to similar problems' (Zeitlin 2005b, 11) seems to entail a deeper integration process concerning the social systems of the Member States, it must be kept in mind, first, that this common language does not preclude the existence of diverging, even conflicting views about the same concepts in different national contexts (Barbier 2005). The actual processes of policy design and implementation remain largely national, reflecting national social, institutional and political contexts, which remain different (Barbier and Sylla 2002; Palier 2003; Zeitlin 2005b). Second, the lack of formal sanctions paves the way for the whole process to be voluntary in nature: the procedure based on an annual benchmarking exercise itself encourages 'window dressing', whereby countries make every effort to be seen as having attained the target in a very limited time, 'at times overestimating domestic results to get a better 'score', rather than engaging in serious long term reforms' (Collignon et al. 2004, 9). Finally, it is very difficult to trace whether the change that has actually occurred since 1997 in the national contexts can be attributed to the EES or other factors (Trubek and Trubek 2005). As Barbier shows with the concept of 'activation', it might well be the case that most of the concepts were already gaining significance in different national settings due to global economic developments and the action taken by other international organizations, significantly the OECD with its 'Jobs Study' of 1994 (Barbier 2005; Barbier and Sylla 2002).

Nevertheless, one of the most significant outcomes of the EES is that it provides national actors with a new orientation and European resources as a tool to promote their own domestic political agenda (Palier 2003; Barbier 2005; Zeitlin 2005b). Furthermore, the strategy certainly serves 'to increase the salience and urgency of particular issues and policy approaches' (Zeitlin 2005b: 11). The process thus entails important elements of social interaction between various levels and actors of policy-making (Palier 2003; Pochet 2005), as well as of socialization, as implied by the learning exercise.

Although it is much more difficult to trace a substantive policy change at this stage, it is nevertheless possible to discern a considerable change in administrative structures and policy-making bodies, or a procedural change, as a result of the EES since 1997 (Pochet 2005; Zeitlin 2005b). This is illustrated, for example, by the increasing number of experts with detailed knowledge about the European orientation (Pochet 2005), and the increasing legitimacy of the *Service des droits des femmes et de l'égalité* in the French stage of policy-making, which significantly gained from the consolidation of a 'Brussels arena' (Barbier and Sylla 2002; Barbier 2005). Moreover, it would not be wrong to argue that gender equality is one of the areas which have been most influenced by EU-level action and most open to learning within the framework of the EES. However, it seems that for the moment at least, the EES remains 'a source for procedural rather than for substantive convergence' (Barbier 2005: 440), as illustrated by the still very different ways to accommodate gender in the labour market in different welfare structures.

Conclusion: Does 'Europeanization' Provide the Answer?

From the perspective of gender equality in employment, the EES does not seem to be leading to a 'European welfare state', in which the outcomes are equal across the board. The question to be asked, however, concerns whether the formation of a

European welfare state, in which the boundaries amongst the social systems of the Member States are increasingly blurred, is indeed the goal of European initiatives? This is where 'Europeanization' comes into play as a significant analytical tool to explore the different impacts of European policies on domestic settings. In one of the most encompassing definitions of 'Europeanization', Radaelli (2003a, 30) refers to this process as one of:

> (a) construction (b) diffusion and (c) institutionalization of formal and informal rules, procedures, policy paradigms, styles, 'ways of doing things', and shared beliefs and norms which are first defined and consolidated in the EU policy process and then incorporated in the logic of domestic (national and sub-national) discourse, political structures, and public policies.

What is important in this process is that it is contingent upon institutional factors, and that the issue of the diversity of national (policy, political, welfare) systems is left open, with the consequence that 'Europeanization' will produce diversity rather than convergence, because domestic institutions differ widely (Radaelli 2003a). It is thus an asymmetrical process (Featherstone and Radaelli 2003), implying 'clustered convergence' (Börzel and Risse 2003), 'domestic adaptation with national colours' (Risse et al. 2001), and, thus, a 'differential Europe' (Héritier 2001).

Going back to the four national settings which have been the focus of this chapter, it is obvious that gender inequality and gender differentiation are still prevalent in all of them, albeit to varying degrees. Each of the four countries, exemplifying a four-fold welfare regime typology, has significant gender imbalances in the labour market, although the specific problems that come to the fore, as well as the extent of the problems, vary across distinct welfare regimes. Denmark and the UK, as exemplars of the social-democratic and liberal welfare regimes respectively, have relatively high employment and low unemployment in terms of both overall and female rates, and they seem to form a cluster with remarkable distance from France and Spain. On the other side of the coin, the two labour markets have very high gender segregation and wage gaps, which come to the fore as urgent issues to be tackled. Still, there are crucial differences between the two, particularly in terms of part-time employment and gender pay gaps, which are much more pronounced in the UK.

France and Spain, as exemplars respectively of the conservative and Southern European welfare regimes, form another cluster, particularly in terms of overall employment and unemployment rates that are close to the EU average in both cases; gender pay gaps, which are relatively modest compared to the first two countries; and part-time work, which was not the facilitator of female employment growth in either case, but has started to increase more recently. Nevertheless, Spain is clearly the 'laggard' in terms of female employment levels, which are one of the lowest in EU-15, and female unemployment rates, which are one of the highest, although the gap in both between Spain and the rest of the EU-15 countries has been declining significantly. Moreover, the rapid economic growth and transformation of the welfare state as well as of the labour market in Spain has led to a massive increase in temporary and precarious employment, which mainly affects women.

There are clear differences amongst the four countries in terms of gender equality in the labour market, which are closely related to their welfare regime structures. The analysis in this chapter shows that each country continues to preserve its specific context, and that there is almost no convergence of outcomes among the four, although there are clearly parallel developments which are driven by the common targets established at European level through the Lisbon Strategy, and by common policy goals. It thus seems appropriate to place the four countries on a continuum of gender (in)equality in the labour market, where Denmark, exemplifying the social-democratic welfare regime, fares relatively better in terms of almost all indicators, followed by the liberal model of the UK, the conservative tradition of France, and the Southern European welfare legacy of Spain.

In this context, it can be argued, particularly in the light of the 'soft' policy mechanism promoted by the EES, that Europeanization provides an appropriate tool for looking at the development of gender equality in employment in the EU and its Member States, since neither 'hard' nor 'soft' approaches have been able to bring about 'convergence' of outcomes in different national settings. It is nevertheless crucial to underline that, despite the apparent diversity of outcomes, the existence of a 'common policy vision', a 'cognitive framework' for gender equality, with its emphasis on female employment rates, gender mainstreaming, and work-life balance among others, should not be underestimated, particularly in terms of its implications for a 'European social model' distinct from its counterparts in the globalizing world.

References

Barbier, J.C and Sylla, N.S. (2002), *La Stratégie européenne pour l'emploi: les representations des acteurs en France*. Rapport de Recheche, Centre d'Etudes de l'Emploi.

Barbier, J.C. (2004), 'Research on "Open Methods of Coordination" and National Social Policies: What Sociological Theories and Methods?', Paper presented at the RC19 International Conference, Paris, 2-4 September 2004.

Barbier, J.C. (2005), 'The European Employment Strategy, A Channel for Activating Social Protection?' in Zeitlin J. and Pochet, P. with Magnusson, L. (eds.) *The Open Method of Coordination in Action: The European Employment and Social Inclusion Strategies*. (Brussels: P.I.E-Peter Lang).

Börzel, T. A. and Risse, T. (2003), 'Conceptualizing the Domestic Impact of Europe', in Featherstone, K. and Radaelli, C.M. (eds.) *The Politics of Europeanization*. (Oxford: Oxford University Press).

Castles, F.G. (1995), 'Welfare State development in Southern Europe', *West European Politics* 18(2): 291-313.

Chalmers, D. and Lodge, M. (2003), 'The Open Method of Co-ordination and the European Welfare State', ESRC Centre for Analysis of Risk and Regulation, Discussion Paper No. 11, June 2003, The London School of Economics and Political Science, <http://www.lse.ac.uk/collections/CARR/pdf/Disspaper11.pdf>.

Cichowski, R.A. (2004), 'Women's Rights, the European Court, and Supranational Constitutionalism', *Law & Society Review* 38(3): 489-511.

Collignon, S., Dehousse, R., Gabolde, J., Jouen, M., Pochet, P., Salais, R., Sprenger, R.U., de Sousa, H.Z. (2004), 'The Lisbon Strategy and the Open Method of Co-ordination: 12 Recommendations for an Effective Multi-level Strategy', *Notre Europe* Policy Paper No. 12, < http://www.notre-europe.eu/en/axes/>.

Council of the European Union (1999), Council Resolution of 22 February 1999 on the 1999 Employment Guidelines (1999/C 69/02). *Official Journal of the European Communities*, C 69, 12/03/1999, pp. 2-8.

Council of the European Union (2001), Council Decision of 19 January 2001 on Guidelines for Member States' employment policies for the year 2001 (2001/63/EC). *Official Journal of the European Communities*, L 22, 24/01/2001, pp. 18-26.

Council of the European Union (2003), Council Decision 2003/578/EC of 22 July 2003 on Guidelines for the Employment Policies of the Member States. *Official Journal of the European Union*, L 197, 05/08/2003.

Council of the European Union (2005), Council Decision of 12 July 2005 on Guidelines for the Employment Policies of the Member States (2005/600/EC). *Official Journal of the European Union*, L205, 6.8.2005.

Daguerre, A. and Taylor-Gooby, P. (2004), 'Adaptation to Labour Market Change in France and the UK: Convergent or Parallel Tracks?' in Taylor-Gooby, P. (ed.) *Making a European Welfare State? Convergences and Conflicts over European Social Policy*. (Oxford: Blackwell Publishing).

De la Porte, C. (2002), 'Is the Open Method of Coordination Appropriate for Organising Activities at European Level in Sensitive Policy Areas?', *European Law Journal* 8(1): 38-58.

Esping-Andersen, G. (1990), *The Three Worlds of Welfare Capitalism*. (Cambridge: Polity Press).

Esping-Andersen, G. (1999), *Social Foundations of Post-industrial Economies*. (Oxford: Oxford University Press).

Esping-Andersen, G. (2002), 'Towards the Good Society, Once Again?', in Esping-Andersen, G., Gallie, D., Hemerijck, A. and Myles, J. (eds.) *Why We Need a New Welfare State*. (Oxford: Oxford University Press).

European Commission (2005), Communication from the Commission to the Council and the European Parliament, 'Common Actions for Growth and Employment: The Community Lisbon Programme', COM (2005) 330 final. Brussels, 20.7.2005.

European Commission (2006), Communication from the Commission to the Council, the European Parliament, the European Economic and Social Committee and the Committee of the Regions, 'A Roadmap for equality between women and men 2006-2010' COM (2006) 92 final. Brussels, 01.3.2006.

Fagan, C., Grimshaw, D. and Rubery, J. (2006), 'The Subordination of the Gender Equality Objective: The National Reform Programmes and 'Making Work Pay' Policies', *Industrial Relations Journal*, 37(6): 571-592.

Fagnani, J. and Letablier, M.T. (2005), 'La politique familiale Française', in M. Maruani (ed.) *Femmes, genre et sociétés: L'état des savoirs*. (Paris: La Découverte).

Featherstone, K. and Radaelli, C.M. (2003), 'A Conversant Research Agenda', in Featherstone K. and Radaelli, C.M. (eds.) *The Politics of Europeanization*. (Oxford: Oxford University Press).

Ferrera, M. (1996), 'The "Southern Model" of Welfare in Social Europe', *Journal of European Social Policy* 6(1): 17-37.

Flaquer, L. (2000), 'Is there a Southern European Model of Family Policy?' in Pfenning, A. and Bahle, T. (eds.), *Families and Family Policies in Europe: Comparative Perspectives*. (Frankfurt am Main: Peter Lang).

Fouquet, A., Gauvin, A. and Letablier, M.T. (2000), 'Des contrats sociaux entre les sexes différents selon les pays de l'Union européenne', in Majnoni d'Intignano, B. (ed.) '*Egalité entre femmes et hommes: aspects économiques*. (Conseil D'Analyse Economique, Paris: La Documentation Française).

Hafner-Burton, E. and Pollack, M. (2000), 'Mainstreaming Gender in the European Union' *Journal of European Public Policy* 7(3): 432-56.

Hemerijck, A. (2002), 'The Self-Transformation of the European Social Model(s)', in Esping-Andersen, G., Gallie, D., Hemerijck A. and Myles J. (eds.) *Why We Need a New Welfare State*. (Oxford: Oxford University Press).

Héritier, A. (2001), 'Differential Europe: National Administrative Responses to Community Policy', in Cowles M.G. et al. (eds.) *Transforming Europe: Europeanization and Domestic Change*. (Ithaca: Cornell University Press).

Hoskyns, C. (1996), *Integrating Gender: Women, Law and Politics in the European Union*. (London: Verso).

Kilpatrick, C. and Freedland, M. (2004), 'The United Kingdom: How is EU Governance Transformative?' in Sciarra, S., Davies, P. and Freedland, M. (eds.) *Employment Policy and the Regulation of Part-time Work in the European Union*. (Cambridge: Cambridge University Press).

Kjeldstad, R. (2001), 'Gender Policies and Gender Equality', in Kautto, M. et al. (eds), *Nordic Welfare States in the European Context*. (London: Routledge).

Le Feuvre, N. and Andriocci, M. (2001), *Background Data Report: France*. A report of the EU-funded project 'Employment and Women's Studies: The Impact of Women's Studies Training on Women's Employment in Europe', <http://www.hull.ac.uk/ewsi>.

Masselot, A. (2004), 'The New Equal Treatment Directive: Plus Ça Change...', *Feminist Legal Studies* 12(1): 93-104.

Mazey, S. (2002), 'Gender Mainstreaming Strategies in the EU: Delivering on an Agenda?' *Feminist Legal Studies* 10(3): 227-240.

Moreno, L. (2004), 'Spain's Transition to New Risks: A Farewell to "Superwomen"', in Taylor-Gooby, P. (ed.), *New Risks, New Welfare: The Transformation of the European Welfare State*. (Oxford: Oxford University Press).

Moreno Minguez, A. (2004), 'El familiarismo cultural en los Estados de Bienestar de sur de Europa: transformaciones de las relaciones entre lo público y lo privado', *Sistema* 182, 47-74.

Nielsen, K. and Kesting, S. (2004), 'Demise Mystery or Miracle – Globalization's Impact on the Danish Model', in Greve, B. and Jespersen, J. (eds.), *Globalization and Welfare*. (Roskilde: Roskilde University Press).

OECD (2006), *Factbook 2006: Economic, Environmental and Social Statistics*. Paris: OECD.

OECD (2005), *Babies and Bosses: Reconciling Work and Family Life, Vol.4, Canada, Finland, Sweden and the United Kingdom*. (Paris: OECD Publications).

O'Connor, J.S., Orloff, A.S. and Shaver, S. (1999), *States, Markets, Families: Gender, Liberalism and Social Policy in Australia, Canada, Great Britain and the United States*. (Cambridge: Cambridge University Press).

O'Connor, J.S. (2005), 'Employment-anchored Social Policy, Gender Equality and the Open Method of Policy Coordination in the European Union', *European Societies* 7(1): 27-52.

Ostner, I. and Lewis, J. (1995), 'Gender and the Evolution of European Social Policies', in Leibfried, S. and Pierson, P. (eds.) *European Social Policy: Between Fragmentation and Integration*. (Washington, DC: The Brookings Institution).

Palier, B. (2003), 'The Europeanization of Welfare Reforms', paper presented at the RC19 Conference, Toronto, 21-24 August 2003.

Pochet, P. (2005), 'The Open Method of Co-ordination and the Construction of Social Europe: A Historical Perspective', in Zeitlin, J. et al. (eds.) *The Open Method of Coordination in Action: The European Employment and Social Inclusion Strategies*. (Brussels: P.I.E-Peter Lang).

Radaelli, C.M. (2003a), 'The Europeanization of Public Policy', in Featherstone, K. and Radaelli, C. M. (eds.) *The Politics of Europeanization*. (Oxford: Oxford University Press).

Radaelli, M.C. (2003b), 'The Open Method of Coordination: A New Governance Architecture for the European Union?', Report No. 1/2003, SIEPS, <http://www.sieps.se/publ/rapporter/rapporter_2003_en.html>.

Regent, S. (2003), 'The Open Method of Coordination: A New Supranational Form of Governance?', *European Law Journal* 9(2): 190-214.

Risse, T., Cowles, M.G. and Caporaso, J. (2001), 'Europeanization and Domestic Change: Introduction', in Cowles, M. G. et al. (eds.) *Transforming Europe: Europeanization and Domestic Change*. (Ithaca: Cornell University Press).

Roseberry, L. (2002), 'Equal Rights and Discrimination Law in Scandinavia,' in P. Wahlgren (ed.) *Stability and Change in Nordic Labour Law*, Scandinavian Studies in Law, 43, pp. 215-256.

Rubery, J., Grimshaw, D., Fagan, C., Figueiredo H. and Smith, M. (2003), 'Gender Equality Still on the European Agenda – But For How Long?', *Industrial Relations Journal* 34(5): 477-497.

Rubery, J., Figueiredo, H. Smith, M. Grimshaw, D. and Fagan, C. (2004), 'The Ups and Downs of European Gender Equality Policy', *Industrial Relations Journal*, 35(6): 603-628.

Sabel, C.F. and Zeitlin, J. (2003), 'Active Welfare, Experimental Governance, Pragmatic Constitutionalism: The New Transformation of Europe', International Conference of the Hellenic Presidency of the EU, 'The Modernisation of the European Social Model & EU Policies and Instruments', Ioannina, Greece, 21-22 May 2003.

Salido, O. (2002), 'Women's Labour Force Participation in Spain', *Working Paper 02-15*, Unidad de Politicas Comparadas (CSIC), Madrid.

Shaw, J. (2005), 'The Social Implications and Possibilities of the Constitutional Treaty', Report for the *Platform of European Social NGOs*, 18 February 2005, <http://www.socialplatform.org>.

Siim, B. and Borchorst, A. (2005), 'The Women-friendly Welfare States Revisited', in Kildal, N. and Kuhnle, S. (eds.) *Normative Foundations of the Welfare State: The Nordic Experience*. (London: Routledge).

Silvera, R. (2002), *Articuler Vie Familiale et Vie Professionnelle en Europe: Un Enjeu pour l'Egalité*. (Paris: La Documentation Française).

Trifiletti, R. (1999), 'Southern European Welfare Regimes and the Worsening Position of Women', *Journal of European Social Policy* 9(1): 49-64.

Trubek, D.M. and Mosher, J.S. (2001), 'New Governance, EU Employment Policy, and the European Social Model', *Jean Monnet Working Paper* No. 6/01.

Trubek, D.M. and Trubek, L.G. (2005), 'The Open Method of Coordination and the Debate over 'Hard' and 'Soft' Law', in Zeitlin, J. and Pochet, P. with Magnusson, L. (eds.) *The Open Method of Coordination in Action: The European Employment and Social Inclusion Strategies*. Brussels: P.I.E-Peter Lang.

Valiente, C. (2000), 'Reconciliation Policies in Spain', in L. Hantrais (ed.) *Gendered Policies in Europe: Reconciling Employment and Family Life*. (London: Macmillan).

Valiente, C. (2003), 'Pushing for Equality Reforms: The European Union and Gender Discourse in Post-Authoritarian Spain', in U. Liebert (ed.) *Gendering Europeanisation*. (Brussels: Peter Lang).

Vandenbrouke, F. (2002), 'The EU and Social Protection: What Should the European Convention Propose?' Paper presented at Max Plankt Institute for the Study of Societies MRIfG Working Paper 02/06, available at: <http://www.mpi-fg-koeln.mpg.de/pu/workpap/wp02-6/wp02-6.html>.

Wobbe, T. (2003), 'From Protecting to Promoting: Evolving EU Sex Equality Norms in an Organisational Field', *European Law Journal* 9(1): 88-108.

Zeitlin, J. (2005a), 'Social Europe and Experimentalist Governance: Towards a New Constitutional Compromise?', *European Governance Papers (EUROGOV)*, No. C-05-04.

Zeitlin, J. (2005b), 'Conclusion: The Open Method of Coordination in Action: Theoretical Promise, Empirical Realities, Reform Strategy', in Zeitlin, J. and Pochet, P. with Magnusson, L. (eds.) *The Open Method of Coordination in Action: The European Employment and Social Inclusion Strategies*. (Brussels: P.I.E-Peter Lang).

Chapter 5

The OMC and the EES: Broadening the Possibilities for Gender Equality?

Julia S. O'Connor

Gender equality, in the sense of equal treatment of men and women *in the labour market*, has been identified as a principle of the European Union since the Treaty of Rome. Although not prominent in the early years it has been the subject of several Directives since 1976 and has gained greater salience with the recognition, particularly since the early 1990s, that the employment growth central to EU economic progress is heavily dependent on increased female labour market participation. This has placed gender equality in the European Employment Strategy (EES) frame and as a result it is a relevant area of interest for examination of the open method of coordination (OMC).

The OMC is the process through which the employment anchored social policy framework of the European Union, in particular the reforms stemming from the Lisbon Strategy, are formulated. It has been the subject of considerable analysis and commentary ranging from the highly positive, at least in terms of its potential (e.g. Trubeck and Trubeck 2005 and Zeitlin 2005), to the relatively negative which points to inherent limitations particularly when compared to hard law alternatives (e.g. Chalmers and Lodge 2003). This chapter focuses on the potential and limitations of the OMC for enhancing social policy objectives in the EU, in particular the potential for broadening the possibilities for gender equality beyond the labour market participation objectives of the European Employment Strategy. This is discussed with reference to the development of EU gender equality initiatives since the mid-1990s.

These issues are analyzed in three sections followed by conclusions. The immediately following section outlines the OMC as it relates to gender equality in the changing Employment Guidelines put into practice in Member States by the National Action Plans from 1998 to 2004 and by the National Reform Programmes since 2005. It also outlines the parallel development of broader gender equality initiatives with particular reference to their commitment to a gender mainstreaming strategy, taking as its point of reference the European Commission definition of gender mainstreaming as:

> The systematic integration of the respective situations, priorities and needs of women and men in all policies and with a view to promoting equality between women and men

> and mobilizing all general policies and measures specifically for the purpose of achieving equality by actively and openly taking into account, at the planning stage, their effects on the respective situation of women and men in implementation, monitoring and evaluation. (European Commission 1996: 2)

The second section examines the progress in gender equality measures as reflected in the Joint Employment Reports and the reports on equality between men and women with reference to the labour market gender equality objectives outlined in the EES. It draws on the work of the European Commission's Expert Group on Gender and Employment (EGGSE), in particular their evaluation of the National Action Plans and their commentary on the changes in the Employment Guidelines over time.[1]

The third section points to the possibilities and limitations of the OMC for broadening the potential for labour market related gender equality. It identifies limitations in terms of gender equality and links these, first, to the two-way supranational-member state interface, in particular the trade-off between two principles that underlie the OMC, subsidiarity and the implementation of agreed common objectives; second, it links them to the failure to realize the potential of the OMC in this area through the involvement of stakeholders at the national level not only in formulating national employment plans/national reform programmes but also in monitoring their implementation. In addition it points to the constraints of the context within which the EES and the associated employment guidelines have been modified. The post-Lisbon EU context demonstrates clear tensions at the EU institutional level centered on the balance between the elements of the Lisbon Strategy: on the one hand, giving primacy to making the EU, 'the most competitive and dynamic knowledge-based economy in the world capable of sustainable economic growth' with more jobs *and the associated byproduct of fulfillment of social objectives* and, on the other hand, *giving equal primacy to 'more and better jobs and greater social cohesion*' (my emphasis). This mirrors the tensions evident to varying degrees across Member States and is particularly reflected in the social, economic and political constraints and possibilities associated with the achievement of objectives in employment-related policy areas that have structural and redefinition elements. Redefinition is considered in terms of the redefinition of the division of responsibility between the family, the state and the market for service provision as in childcare, and the conceptual redefinition of gender equality from equality of treatment to the promotion of equality between men and women in gender mainstreaming as outlined in the Commission definition above, both redefinitions occurring in the context of structural constraints, in particular labour market developments that include the creation of a significant proportion of poor quality employment. While the unrealized possibilities of the OMC are identified in the early part of this section, it concludes with a discussion of the potential of the OMC

1 See DG Employment, Social Affairs and Equal Opportunities website for access to a wide range of reports by the Expert Group. These include synthesis reports for 2004, 2005 and 2006 on the EES and annual reports on employment related themes. These are all based on 30 country reports by national experts – the EU27, Norway, Iceland and Lichtenstein, <http://ec.europa.eu/employment_social/gender_equality/gender_mainstreaming/gender/exp_group_en.html>.

process for gender equality objectives in the context of the 2008 synchronization of the already integrated economic and employment OMC with the social OMC. The paper concludes with an overview of key trends and conclusions.

EU Commitments to Gender Equality in the Open Method of Coordination Era

In March 2000 the Lisbon Council set a ten year strategic goal for the European Union: 'to become the most competitive and dynamic knowledge-based economy in the world capable of sustainable economic growth with more and better jobs and greater social cohesion'. The modernization of the European Social Model was identified as central to the achievement of this goal. The open method of coordination (OMC) was the governance mechanism by which this was to be achieved; this was identified as 'a means of spreading best practice and achieving greater convergence towards the main EU goals'. The OMC is a means of political coordination to achieve agreed common objectives in employment, social protection and social inclusion but without legal constraints on the member states. A system of social indicators as a means of comparing good practice and measuring progress is central to this process. The common objectives are translated into national policies through national action plans from 1998 to 2004 and national reform programmes since 2005.[2] These strategies are evaluated by the European Commission and in consultation with the European Council a Joint Employment Report is issued annually. This report contains country-specific information and recommendations as well as a comparison and synthesis of developments from a European point of view. The OMC process was identified as such in the Lisbon Strategy but had already been established in economic policy in the Broad Economic Policy Guidelines and more directly related to gender equality in the European Employment Strategy/Luxembourg Process launched at the Luxembourg Jobs Summit in November 1997.

The Gender Dimension of the EES

The EES is a widely analyzed process (e.g. Zeitlin and Pochet 2005). My concern in this chapter is with its role in relation to gender equality and the broadening of possibilities for its achievement in the labour market. The EES was the culmination of considerable concern about low employment growth and high unemployment, reflected for example in the 1993 White Paper on Growth, Competitiveness and

2 The annual National Action Plans on employment from 1998 to 2004 were replaced by National Reform Programmes in 2005. A parallel change was made in the OMC on social inclusion from National Action Plans on Social Inclusion which were prepared for 2001-2003 and 2003-2005 to National Reports on Strategies for Social Protection and Social Inclusion prepared for 2006-2008; these strategy reports incorporate thematic sections on social inclusion, pensions and health and long-term care. From 2008 onwards the social OMC will be synchronized with the already synchronized economic and employment OMC. This is discussed in the last section of this chapter.

Employment, the 1994 Essen Strategy[3] and most immediately in the new Title on Employment in the Amsterdam Treaty agreed in 1997. That Treaty has several elements that strengthen the Community's approach to employment, including a commitment to achieve a high level of employment as one of the EU's key objectives, its recognition as a 'common concern' of Member States, the need to develop a coordinated strategy and the 'mainstreaming' of employment policy in the sense that the employment impact of all community policies must be recognized. The recognition of the centrality of employment for EU policy is reflected in its inclusion in the Treaty as a Title in its own right like the monetary and economic articles and not just as a chapter. The Luxembourg Jobs summit created the procedure, now known as the OMC, whereby Member States prepare National Action Plans for Employment[4] in accordance with the Employment Guidelines prepared by the Commission and adopted by the Council. Member State's policies are examined yearly through a Joint Employment Report developed by the Commission and the Council; associated with this, the Commission may propose and the Council adopt recommendations to individual Member States.

The EES and the Employment Guidelines have gone through considerable changes since 1997 and this is evident in the treatment of gender equality within the guidelines. Equal opportunities was one of the four pillars of the Employment Guidelines on which the National Action Plans were based between 1998 and 2002 and there were specific guidelines on gender mainstreaming, tackling gender gaps and reconciling employment and family life. In 1999 gender mainstreaming was introduced across all four pillars. Following the revision of the EES by the Barcelona European Council in 2002 the Guidelines for 2003 and 2004 were based on three objectives – full employment, improving quality and productivity at work and strengthening social cohesion – and ten priorities for action, one of which was gender equality.[5] This mandated Member States to encourage female labour market participation and a reduction in gender gaps in employment and unemployment through an integrated approach combining gender mainstreaming and specific policy actions.

The EES went through its most significant change in 2005 as a result of the midterm review of the Lisbon Strategy. This review was strongly informed by the slow performance of the EU in terms of the economic growth and employment objectives identified at Lisbon in 2000 (European Commission 2004). The review led to the adoption by the European Council of 'Integrated Guidelines for Growth and Jobs (2005-08)' in 2005 (European Commission 2005). These comprise of sixteen

3 The Essen European Council in December 1994 agreed on five key objectives to be pursued by Member States: (i) the development of human resources through vocational training; (ii) the promotion of productive investment through moderate wage policy; (iii) improvement of the efficiency of labour market institutions; (iv) the identification of new sources of jobs through local initiatives; (v) the promotion of labour market access for specific target groups including young people, long-term unemployed people and women.

4 Since 2005 this is part of the National Reform Programme.

5 The Barcelona Council is significant in terms of the identification of targets relating to the reconciliation of employment and family life, specifically targets relating to childcare provision.

Broad Economic Policy Guidelines – six macro- and ten micro-economic guidelines – presented in the first two parts and eight Employment Guidelines presented in the third part of the document. Based on the Integrated Guidelines Member States are required to draw up National Reform Programmes focusing on economic and employment policy for a three year period with annual implementation reports in the years when National Reform Programmes are not being produced. *An annual Joint Employment Report is still prepared.*

None of the 'Integrated Guidelines for Growth and Jobs (2005-08)', in particular, none of the Employment Guidelines – Guidelines 17 to 24 – identifies a gender dimension in its title but the importance of action on gender inequality as an element of employment policy is evident in the preamble and Guideline 18. The preamble identifies the overarching objectives and priorities for Member States' employment policies as the implementation of policies aimed at achieving full employment, improving quality and productivity at work, and strengthening social and territorial cohesion. Equal opportunities and combating discrimination are deemed essential for progress and gender mainstreaming and the promotion of gender equality are to be ensured in all action taken (Council of the European Union 2005a). The 2010 employment objectives are re-affirmed: these are to achieve an employment rate of 70 per cent overall, at least 60 per cent for women and of 50 per cent for workers aged 55-64 by 2010 and to reduce unemployment and inactivity. The 2002 Barcelona Council childcare objectives are identified as targets and benchmarks – these are the provision of childcare by 2010 to at least 90 per cent of children between 3 years and the mandatory school age and at least 33 per cent of children under 3 years of age. Measures to promote a lifecycle approach to work (Guideline 18) include 'resolute action to increase female participation and reduce gender gaps in employment, unemployment and pay' and 'better reconciliation of work and private life and the provision of accessible and affordable childcare facilities and care of other dependants'.

This brief overview points to the lessening prominence of gender over time in the Employment Guidelines paralleled by increased iteration of the importance of gender mainstreaming although not of indicators that would facilitate examination of its success or failure. Before considering the progress or not in the gender equality objectives from 1997-2006, it is essential to recognize that the EES does not operate in isolation; it must be situated in parallel to other EU gender equality policies. With this in mind we consider the parallel process of gender equality action taking place under the headings of the *Framework Strategy for Gender Equality (2001-2005)*, the *Roadmap for equality between men and women 2006-2010*, the *European pact for gender equality (2006)* and the commitment to gender mainstreaming in the Structural Funds. We have already made reference to the gender mainstreaming definition outlined in the European Commission 1996 document: 'Incorporating equal opportunities for women and men into all Community policies and activities'. Clearly here we are talking about a policy strategy or practice but gender mainstreaming is also used in the *interrelated* sense of 'incorporating gender into mainstream analysis' (Mazey 2000: 333) or as a form of theory, 'a process of revision of key concepts to grasp more adequately a world that is gendered, rather than the establishment of a separatist gender theory' (Walby 2005: 321). We come back to these issues in the third section where we discuss the imprecise nature of mainstreaming as a strategy whether this be in the area of gender or other dimensions of social exclusion. It is important to stress here that despite the EU Commission definition, gender mainstreaming as used in the EES is confined to labour market related gender equality.

Gender Equality Framework, Roadmap and Pact

The goal of eliminating inequalities and promoting equality between men and women in the European Union can be traced back to Article 119 of the Treaty of Rome – now Article 141 of the EC Treaty – which requires Member States to ensure that the principle of equal pay for men and women for equal work or work of equal value is enforced. While this was primarily a measure to prevent market distortion, it along with other articles made it possible for the Commission to prepare five gender equality directives between 1975 and 1986, three others in 1992, 1996 and 1998 and the amendment of the Directive on Equal Opportunities in 2002.[6]

In 1996 the European Commission adopted a formal commitment to gender mainstreaming and the Amsterdam Treaty recognized mainstreaming equality between men and women as a key objective. Specifically, Article 3(2) of the EC Treaty, as amended by the Amsterdam Treaty 1997, provides that the EU should aim to eliminate inequalities, and to promote equality between men and women in all its activities.[7] Gender mainstreaming as a strategy implies a commitment to incorporate gender into all areas and all levels of public policy, rather than considering gender as a discrete policy issue. It shifts the focus from equality of treatment to equality of gender impact: policy makers are obliged to ask whether or not policy has a negative impact on men or women.[8] Efforts to promote equality are not restricted to the implementation of specific measures to help women or men. Gender mainstreaming

6 Directive on Equal Pay (75/117); Directive on Equal Treatment (76/207); Directive on Equal Treatment in Matters of Social Security (79/7); Directive on Equal Treatment in Occupational Security Schemes (86/378); Directive on Equal Treatment between men and women engaged in an activity including agriculture, in a self-employed capacity, and on the protection of self-employed women during pregnancy and motherhood (86/613); Directive on Pregnant Workers (92/85/EEC) – originally negotiated by the social partners under the provision of the 1992 Maastricht reforms; Directive on Parental Leave (96/34/EC) – originally negotiated by the social partners under the provision of the 1992 Maastricht reforms; Directive on Burden of Proof (98/52/EC) re indirect discrimination and burden of proof; Directive on Equal Treatment (2002/73/EC); this amendment of the 1976 directive states that the principle of equal treatment means that there shall be no direct or indirect discrimination on the grounds of sex in the public or private sectors, including public bodies in relation to conditions for access to employment, vocational training, employment and working conditions including dismissal and membership or organizations or workers or employers. It also proscribes harassment related to sex and harassment of a sexual nature.

7 While this does not create legally enforceable rights it does represent a Treaty-based political commitment to gender mainstreaming.

8 In considering gender one cannot assume homogeneity amongst either men or women. There is consistent evidence of differences in labour market experience and ability to exercise citizenship rights depending on level of education, occupation and location within the labour market and this is as true for women as for men (O'Connor, 1996: 78-100).

involves mobilizing all general policies and measures for the purpose of achieving equality by actively and openly taking into account at the planning stage their possible effects on the respective situation of men and women (gender perspective). This means systematically examining measures and policies and taking into account possible differential effects on men and women when defining and implementing them (European Commission 1996). Movement from aspiration to practice depends on whether, or not, gender mainstreaming commitments are a formality to meet reporting criteria or have policy import and equally importantly whether or not they are accompanied by measurable implementation criteria. This brings into focus the issue of social indicators and the measuring of progress which were envisaged as central to the OMC process. While significant progress has been made in the development of a framework of indicators at the EU level their systematic use at member state level is uneven and generally at a very early stage.

The *Community Framework Strategy on Gender Equality (2001-2005)* was agreed in 2000. Its purpose was to establish a framework for action within which all Community activities could 'contribute to attain the goal of eliminating inequalities and promoting equality between women and men, as set out in Article 3(2) of the Treaty'. The Strategy committed to tackle structural gender inequalities by operationalizing and consolidating gender mainstreaming and to continue to require the implementation of specific actions in favour of women (European Commission 2000).[9]

Building on the 2001-2005 Framework Strategy, a *Roadmap for equality between women and men 2006-2010* was issued in March 2006 by the European Commission (2006a) and reaffirmed the dual strategy of gender mainstreaming and specific measures. It identified six priority areas: equal economic independence for women and men; reconciliation of private and professional life; equal representation in decision-making; eradication of all forms of gender-based violence; elimination of gender stereotypes; and promotion of gender equality in external and development policies. It outlined priority objectives and actions for each area and pointed out that in many of the areas 'the centre of gravity' for action rests with Member States. To achieve equal economic independence for women and men the priority objectives include reaching the Lisbon employment targets and elimination of gender pay gaps. Flexible working arrangements for men and women, increasing care services and better reconciliation policies such as parental and paternity leave are identified as essential to enhancing the reconciliation of private and professional life. The Commission commits to monitor and strengthen gender mainstreaming in the Integrated Guidelines for Growth and Jobs and in the streamlined OMC process in pensions, social inclusion, health and social care; and to present a communication on

9 The Employment and Social Affairs gender mainstreaming website identifies several dimensions of the 'Commission method' including this dual approach, gender impact assessment and gender proofing, mobilizing all Commission services, anchoring responsibility, training for an awareness raising among key personnel, monitoring, benchmarking and break down of data and statistics by sex and establishing structures including a group of Commissioner on Equal Opportunities, <http://ec.europa.eu/employment_social/gender_equality_gender_mainstreaming/general_overview_en.html>.

the gender pay gap in 2007 (see below). It also commits to presenting a Communication on Demography addressing the issue of reconciliation and supporting the Barcelona childcare targets.

The *European pact for gender equality* was issued as an Annex to the Presidency Conclusions of the Brussels European Council in March 2006. Taking into account the gender equality roadmap and the need to contribute to fulfilling the EU gender equality objectives, close the gender gaps in employment and social protection and contribute to meeting the demographic challenges by promoting work-life balance for men and women, the pact is aimed at encouraging EU and Member State level action to (i) close gender gaps and combat gender stereotypes in the labour market; (ii) promote a better work-life balance for all and (iii) reinforce governance through gender mainstreaming and better monitoring. It concludes that it, and the annual report on equality between women and men, should be integrated into the established follow-up mechanisms of the partnership for growth and employment and aim to promote the implementation of gender mainstreaming in action taken within the strategy. When reporting on the implementation of their National Reform Programmes for jobs and growth, Member States are encouraged to include a perspective on gender equality, especially in relation to Guideline 18 on promoting a life cycle approach to work. The Commission and the Council are encouraged to do likewise in the annual progress report on the partnership for growth and employment (European Commission 2006b).

This outline of the key objectives of the gender dimensions of the EES and the other EU gender equality strategies indicates that at least in terms of commitments there is considerable overlap between the two. We now turn to an examination of whether or not this commitment is reflected in policy commitment at member state level. The more significant issue of policy outcome is also considered.

Gender Equality Practice in the Open Method of Coordination Era

The *2007 Report on equality between men and women in the EU* points out that: Since the launch of the Lisbon Strategy in 2000, six of the eight million jobs created in the EU have been taken by women. In 2005, the rate of female employment rose for the twelfth consecutive year, to stand at 56.3 per cent, i.e. 2.7 points above its 2000 level, compared with a 0.1 point rise in the rate of male employment. If this favourable trend continues, the Lisbon objective of 60 per cent female employment by 2010 will be attained (European Commission 2007: 5). But the report also identifies major gaps that are 'always to women's disadvantage.' These include a significant and stable gender pay gap. In 1998 gender pay gaps averaged 16 per cent in the EU15 – these ranged from 7 to 24 per cent (European Commission 2002). In 2005 they still averaged 14 per cent in the EU15 ranging from 5 to 22 per cent (European Commission 2007a).

The *Joint Employment Report for 2006/2007 (JER)* also acknowledges the increase in the employment rate for women but concludes that 'the potential contribution of women to increasing the aggregate employment rate is still not fully exploited' (Council of the European Union 2007: 10). It points to the need for further policies to promote child and elder care and the reconciliation of work and family life. Despite the EU average female employment rate of 57 per cent in 2006, the rate was still below 50 per cent not only in Poland and Malta – EU members since 2004 – but also in Greece and Italy who had had the experience of the EES since 1998.[10] The majority of Member States made no reference to specific measures aimed at promoting female employment and reducing gender pay gaps in the 2006 Implementation Reports on their National Reform Programmes. Ten Member States set childcare place targets in their Reform Programmes but few report on progress towards the EU target and overall progress towards this remains slow.[11] Furthermore, reference to strengthening the role of men in reconciling work and family life is absent (Council of the European Union 2007: 10).

These patterns were already evident in 2002 when the European Commission (2002) carried out a five year review of the EES. While overall that report was positive and identified 'significant changes in national employment policies, with a clear convergence towards the common EU objectives set out in the EES policy guidelines' (2) and concluded that gender equality received an important impetus through the EES, it acknowledged considerable gender gaps. Furthermore, the impact evaluation associated with this report points out that the national evaluation reports provide hardly any impact assessment of their policies on gender gaps and where it does exist, as in Denmark and the UK, it is lacking in precision. Member States tended to see effects as indirect and long-term or impossible to measure. Furthermore, in most Member States the reduction in the gender gap in employment was seen to be due to the increase in female labour force participation associated with economic growth rather than to the implementation of the Employment Guidelines. Yet, the persistence of gaps was associated with the factors identified in the Employment Guidelines, for example, childcare non-availability and limited availability of family friendly policies in some countries and labour market segregation in others (European Commission, Employment and Social Affairs 2002).

An increasingly pessimistic perspective on the potential for gender equality through the EES is evident from a series of reports and articles by the coordinators of the European Commission's Expert Group on Gender and Employment (EGGSE) in their evaluation of the National Action Plans and their commentary on the changes in the Employment Guidelines over time and particularly on their format since 2005 (Rubery et al. 2003; Rubery et al. 2004 and 2006; Rubery 2005; Rubery, Grimshaw and Figueiredo 2005; Fagan, Grimshaw and Rubery 2006).[12]

The 2004 synthesis report on the country evaluations by national experts noted that most countries reported their gender equality activity only under the gender equality guideline (Guideline 6) and Sweden was the only member state to have a national action plan that made gender mainstreaming fully visible. Improvement in

10 Overall the employment gender gap was 15 per cent in 2005 and the full-time equivalent was 21.4 per cent and the latter is decreasing more slowly than the former (European Commission 2006c).

11 Austria, Belgium, Denmark, Germany, Spain, Ireland, Italy, Luxembourg, Portugal and the UK.

12 See footnote 1 re the Expert Group.

the position relating to gender mainstreaming was evident in only two of the EU25 Member States: in Portugal and the UK improvement in gender related information and greater recognition of gender gaps were noted. Only limited evidence was noted 'of any linkage between the setting of national employment targets for women and the development of a policy programme to support the objective' (2004: 227). The situation was even more dismal in relation to the gender pay gap. The report concludes that failures were evident not only on the part of Member States but also in relation to the Council Recommendations which promote a labour market model that includes high levels of part-time work 'that may be inappropriate or counterproductive for gender equality in some Member States'. While the Council was found to be more likely to address the gender pay gap than were Member States it failed to identify the gendered nature of particular policies such as mobilizing the inactive, or to identify failures by Member States to adopt an inclusive strategy to implement such an approach. In general there was an inadequate response to the challenges of gender equality in Member States. Gender mainstreaming outside of Guideline 6 was weak and patchy. While there was a lack of political commitment, especially in new Member States, institutional arrangements for promoting gender mainstreaming and gender equality were being put in place. Even in the EU15 Member States, where some improvements were evident, the negative gender impacts of new policies tended not to be identified, for example the gender implications of active ageing and associated pension reforms. Rubery et al (2004: 233) conclude with a call for Council recommendations that explicitly link 'the general thrust of employment policies and the objective of gender equality. Such a link would highlight the need to focus more strongly on *the enhancement of job quality* within the employment strategy' (emphasis added).[13] This brings into sharp relief the balance between the growth and competitiveness objective, on the one hand, and the 'more and better jobs and greater social cohesion' objective of the Lisbon Strategy on the other hand (see discussion below).

The 2006 synthesis report of the Expert Group, which focuses on the first implementation reports on the National Reform Programme/s prepared for the 2005-2008 period, identifies a continuing decline in the visibility of gender and the attention to gender equality policies and gender mainstreaming in Member State documents and links this to the disappearance of the specific gender guidelines following the earlier removal of the equal opportunities pillar (Rubery et al. 2006). Furthermore, concern with employment in relation to the other guidelines varies across Member State National Reform Programme/s and within the employment guidelines concern with gender varies and there is 'a general failure to gender mainstream the NRP reports. Almost all Member States are regarded as providing either very limited or no gender

13 The report includes a critique of the employment review chaired by Wim Kok (European Commission 2004) arguing that the EU must focus not just on jobs but on better jobs especially for those disadvantaged in the labour market such as women (Rubery et al 2004: 62-5).

mainstreaming in the chapters not related to employment' (ibid: 47).[14] The only country experts to report some improvement were those for Greece, Spain and Italy and in the latter it was from a zero base; those for France, Ireland, Latvia and Luxembourg report less visibility in 2006 than in 2005 (ibid: Table 4.3 (Ch.4) pp. 47-49).

Positive actions in some Member States were noted – for example, Sweden's new National gender equality objective – but this was outweighed by regression in other countries, even countries sharing the same social democratic welfare regime classification, specifically Denmark and Finland. The former's action plan is criticized for not including any specific equality legislation and for placing the responsibility for achieving equality on the individual. Meanwhile gender has been almost absent in the Finnish National Reform Programme/s since the gender guideline was removed. It is noted that some positive gender equality initiatives were not included in the NRPs but some countries have included these in their National Action Plans on social inclusion; for example both France and Luxembourg identify the barriers to employment associated with childcare and commit to initiatives in this regard in their social inclusion plans (France 2006: 25; Le Grand-Duché de Luxembourg 2006: 16-17 and 24-25) (the proposed synchronization of the two processes is discussed below).

An important factor identified in the 2006 synthesis report is the tendency for the focus on gender in National Reform Programme/s to be employment-linked rather than gender-linked. This is reflected in the relatively greater and sometimes exclusive emphasis on increasing female labour market participation to achieve employment rate targets without attention to whether or not this policy has a negative impact on men or women. In the context of variation in the quality of employment and the disproportionate creation of poor quality jobs, a gender-linked focus would necessitate addressing the question of whether or not the employment opportunities available to formerly under-represented groups in the labour market, such as women, are likely to be disproportionately of poor quality.

This review of labour market gender equality issues in the OMC era, that is, from 1998 to 2007, presents a rather negative picture. First, with the exception of labour market participation and some improvement in childcare provision there has been no marked positive movement in any of the indicators, in particular there is 'nothing to indicate that the [gender pay] gap is narrowing in any significant way' (European Commission 2007b, 2). The Commission's Communication on tackling the pay gap between women and men recognizes that women continue to be affected by direct and indirect discrimination. It points to the complexity of the phenomenon, the need to improve the capacity to analyze it and the need to engage Member States and the social partners. The 2007 *Report on equality between men and women in the EU* concludes that Member States need to take action to:

- eliminate the gender pay gap;
- strengthen gender mainstreaming in the implementation of employment policies;

14 Further evidence of this is provided in the Expert Groups report on gender mainstreaming (Rubery et al 2006: 76) which concludes that the focus on gender mainstreaming is 'rather narrow and patchy'.

- continue efforts to allow for the reconciliation of employment and family life.

It is noteworthy that these are the gender equality objectives of the EES Employment Guidelines although as illustrated in the previous section their relative prominence has been lessened over time. This brings us to the second important conclusion of this review, that is, that the reduced prominence of gender in the employment guidelines over time is associated with a lessening of commitment to gender equality by Member States as reflected in their Employment Action Plans and particularly in the implementation of their National Reform Programmes 2005-08.

In parallel to this negative pattern two new gender equality initiatives must be recognized, specifically, the *Roadmap on gender equality* and the *Gender equality pact.* These are important in situating the EES in a broader context but they can be seen, at least in part, as a reflection of the failure of the EES and the associated OMC to make significant progress in gender equality beyond the lessening of gender differences in labour market participation. As pointed out above the five year review of the EES found that Member States tended to link this to employment growth rather than directly to OMC linked gender equality commitments (European Commission 2002). Since women were underrepresented in the labour market, their increased participation, even with a constant or slightly declining male level of participation, inevitably led to a more gender-balanced labour market – in this context quality as well as quantity of employment must be factored in if we are to get meaningful answers about gender equality. In addition to the gender-equality-specific initiatives – the Roadmap and the Gender equality pact – it is noteworthy that the Commission has issued a Communication on tackling the pay gap between women and men (European Commission 2007b) and that the Commissioner for Employment Social Affairs and Equal Opportunities made a commitment in March 2007 to present a Communication on childcare in 2008. This follows a statement in the 2006 *Report on equality between men and women in the EU* that Member States should step up efforts to meet the Barcelona childcare targets and other care service targets (European Commission 2006c).

Examination of the evidence on gender equality measures in the OMC era, particularly the failure to achieve progress in some measures, raises the issue of a gulf between Member State policy commitment and implementation of at least some of the guidelines which they have participated in formulating. The OMC is built on the assumptions of policy exchange and mutual learning through establishing policy guidelines, setting benchmarks, targets and a monitoring system to identify good practice and evaluate progress through peer group review. In view of the success of some indicators of gender equality, such as labour market participation, it must be asked if there are particular difficulties concerning the OMC process in areas of gender equality broadly conceived, specifically those which involve structural and redefinition elements, such as childcare and the qualitative dimensions of employment in the context of worldwide structural changes in labour markets.

The Limitations and Possibilities of the OMC for Enhancing Gender Equality in a Changing Context

Gender equality is an objective of the EU and as such is reflected in considerable output of frameworks, strategies and pacts for gender equality broadly conceived, that is, in the sense of promoting equality between men and women. Gender equality is also a means to the end of achieving high levels of employment, which was recognized as a 'common concern' of Member States in the Amsterdam Treaty. In the latter sense gender equality is often rather narrowly conceived as equality in labour market participation. The evidence relating to labour market gender equality in the OMC era reflects these differences and illustrates the limitations of the OMC. This does not mean that the radical potential, including the potential for gender equality broadly conceived, inherent in the OMC cannot be realized. We now consider these possibilities and reasons why they have not been realized.

Radical Potential of the OMC Process

A review of gender equality outcomes over the first decade of the OMC era illustrates the disjuncture between commitments at the supranational level, implementation and, especially, outcomes at the Member State level. This is not to suggest that a causal argument linking an iterative process such as the OMC and particular *outcomes* could be easily made. It is recognized that the methodological challenges to such an exercise would be substantial. What is apparent at this stage is that we have very little evidence to suggest that examining such an argument would be warranted in terms of several of the key indicators of gender equality. Furthermore, the evidence relating to the prior stage of *policy outputs* as reflected in commitments in these areas is almost as weak.[15] Yet, reviews of the operation of the EES demonstrate positive influences in several countries and policy areas including putting equal opportunities higher on the political agenda (see Zeitlin and Pochet (eds) 2005). What is at issue is the kind of commitments on which progress can be identified and the limitations of the process particularly from the point of view of gender equality objectives in the context of the trade-off between subsidiarity and adherence to agreed common objectives trade. Both are principles underlying the OMC and the former means that objectives agreed at the EU level and committed to in National Action Plans / National Reform Programmes may be variously interpreted at Member State level. For example, Rubery (2005) points out that the absence of specification of what a gender equal society means 'allows Member States extreme freedom in presenting their policies as promoting gender equality' (Rubery 2005, 404).

The OMC assumes mobilization of national stakeholders around the formulation and implementation of the National Action Plans / National Reform Programmes. Effective involvement of stakeholders would necessitate wide dissemination of comparable data on key social outcome indicators. The radical potential of the OMC lies in these elements. Active national debate on recommendations agreed

15 Martinsen (2007) also recognizes this difficulty in her analysis of the Europeanization of gender equality and concentrates on policy outputs.

between Member States and the EU is dependent on the involvement of all relevant national actors. Otherwise the process is merely an exercise for a minority of officials (Scharpf 2002: 654). Atkinson has made a similar argument relating to the social outcome indicators. He argues that the involvement of social partners, non-governmental and grass-roots organizations and the academic community is essential to disseminate knowledge and to modify indicators as appropriate (Atkinson 2002: 630). The evidence on involvement of national stakeholders in formulation and implementation of National Actions Plans is not encouraging (O'Connor 2005). There is considerable ongoing activity in relation to portfolios of social indicators and the associated data by the European Commission and Eurostat (European Commission Employment Social Affairs and Equal Opportunities DG 2006a, 2007). This bodes well for commitment to increased concern with implementation in the revised EES; however these portfolios and the data compendium do not address employment quality, although the latter provides information on gender pay gaps and occupational segregation. Yet there is potential for addressing the quality issue in the proposed contextual indicators that would be relevant for the framing of national policy contexts.

Hierarchy of Objectives?

Apart from the limitations of the present operation of the OMC, we identify two other reasons for the relatively poor performance on gender equality outcomes, specifically: the tensions within EU institutions relating to policy priorities for meeting objectives; and the tensions at Member State level relating to objectives that have structural and redefinition elements. While the non-binding nature of the OMC process must be borne in mind, the economic and political context within which the EES and the associated employment guidelines have been modified is also relevant to considering progress or its absence in indicators of labour market gender equality through this process. In 2003 the European Commission (2003) proposed a streamlined framework for the open coordination of social protection and inclusion OMC processes, that is, social inclusion, pensions and health and long-term care and eventually a process relating to making work pay. The longer term objective was to synchronize these streamlined processes with the already streamlined employment and economic strategies from 2008 onwards when both systems would be on a three year reporting cycle. It was envisaged that this synchronization would enhance the mutual reinforcement of the social, economic and employment processes. The streamlining took account not only of experience of Member States and other stakeholders of the OMC process (European Commission 2006) but also of the revision of the Lisbon Strategy that followed the report of the High Level Group chaired by Wim Kok (European Commission 2004) and the integrated guidelines for economic and employment policies 2005-2008 (European Commission 2005a).

The revision process demonstrates clear tensions at the EU institutional level centered on the balance between those who give primacy to making the EU 'the most competitive and dynamic knowledge-based economy in the world capable of sustainable economic growth' with more jobs and those who argued that 'more and better jobs and greater social cohesion' be given equal primacy. The Kok report pointed to the failures of the Lisbon process in terms of the key competitiveness, employment and transition to knowledge economy objectives; it called for the refocusing of objectives and targets on growth and employment and argued for more explicit benchmarking and peer pressure on Member States and public affirmation of success and failure in implementation of programmes. The report argued that fulfillment of the social objectives would result from economic and employment growth. The alternative emphasis by the 'socially-oriented' stakeholders stressed the equal importance and mutual reinforcement of social, employment and economic policies and drew on the extensive EU documentation on social policy as a productive factor. This was supported not only by non-governmental organizations, for example the European Anti-Poverty Network (EAPN), the European Federation of National Organizations Working with the Homeless (Feantsa) and the European Social Platform, but also by some elements of the European Commission and the European Parliament.[16] It is noteworthy that the Communication to the 2005 Spring European Council by the President and Vice-President of the Commission (European Commission 2005b) and the Council conclusions reflected the change in approach advocated by the Kok report. The Council conclusions called for a refocusing of priorities on growth and employment arguing that Europe must renew the basis of its competitiveness, increase its growth potential and its productivity and strengthen social cohesion, placing the main emphasis on knowledge, innovation and the optimization of human capital (Council of the European Union 2005b: paragraph 5). This tension or at least contradiction is evident in the increasing assertion of a commitment to gender mainstreaming at the EU level and its active promotion by DG Employment and Social Affairs while DG Economic and Financial Affairs emphasizes competitiveness and flexibility although advocating a context of flexicurity, that is the successful combination of flexibility for employers and security for workers.[17]

This mirrors the tensions evident to varying degrees across Member States and is reflected particularly in the social, economic and political constraints and possibilities associated with the achievement of objectives in employment related policy areas that have structural and redefinition elements. Redefinition arises in two senses in relation to gender equality: one concerns the redefinition of the division of responsibility between the family, the state and the market for service provision as in childcare. The other is the conceptual redefinition of gender equality from equality of treatment and/or positive action with its objective of equality of outcome to the promotion of equality between men and women in gender mainstreaming (see European Commission definition in the introduction to this chapter). The policy

16 A division between 'socially-oriented' and 'economically oriented' actors within the European Commission has been noted by several analysts (Guillén and Palier 2004; Pochet 2005). Pochet includes trade unions, centre-left governments and Members of the European Parliament in the former group and centre-right governments in the latter (above, p. 38).

17 Initially used to describe the successful combination of flexibility and security in the Danish and Dutch labour markets in the 1990s, flexicurity now has a more general connotation. In Employment in Europe 2006 the European Commission identifies flexicurity regimes based on one dimension of flexibility – external flexiblity.

implications of this redefinition are highly demanding and have implications at each stage in the policy process from planning to outcome. Redefinitions in both senses, that is in relation to division of responsibility and conceptually, are occurring in the context of changing labour market structures nationally and globally, reflected in the changing composition and distribution of manufacturing employment and most sharply in increasing service sector employment. Underlying these changes is the fundamental issue of the balance in the quality of employment being created and the disproportionate dependence of some people, especially members of groups previously under-represented in the labour market, on poor quality employment (O'Connor 2005a).

Childcare is recognized in the EU as essential to the reconciliation of employment and family life (O'Connor 2005b). This is strongly stressed in most National Reform Programmes, and formerly in National Action Plans, and associated Commission documents where such reconciliation is seen as pivotal to increased labour market participation. This is paralleled by the several OECD reports in the *Babies and Bosses* series (OECD 2005). In these, and more explicitly in an earlier OECD report, childcare was framed as an important contributor to the prevention of educational difficulties (OECD 2001). In an article on childcare in the EU published in 2000, Randall (2000) pointed out that those countries that were relatively advanced in childcare provisions in the 1970s were still the leaders in the late 1990s and that convergence remained weak. Furthermore, she concluded that EU childcare policy was 'better able to influence the terms in which childcare is discussed than substantive policy' (Randall 2000: 367). While she was addressing the result of policy largely in the pre-OMC period her conclusion still applies. Progress is dependent on national historical policy legacies and reflects the division of responsibility for services between state, market, family and the voluntary sector, current social policy and labour market priorities and the advocacy of national social forces. Much of the success of this advocacy in relation to gender equality measures was due to the use of the courts to enforce compliance by Member States with directives (O'Connor 2005b). This possibility was always missing in relation to childcare and is not relevant under the OMC process. Despite the slow progress in childcare and the apparent lessening of salience in the Implementation Report (2006) on the NRP 2005-08, it is identified in the Integrated Economic and Employment Guidelines as a key element in the reconciliation of employment and family life. In its identification as a policy commitment in several Member State NRPs we can at least speak of some level of 'cognitive Europeanization', understood as 'the shaping and reshaping of the perceptions of, and attitudes towards, social problems and the way to tackle them' (Radaelli 2000). Perhaps of more significance in terms of childcare outcomes is activity under the Structural Funds, in particular the European Social Fund. In relation to OMC activity the social inclusion process may be of particular importance in the childcare area. We return to this below in discussing the 2008 synchronization of the OMC processes.

Gender mainstreaming is the area of least progress identified in the previous section. Despite widespread affirmation at the EU and Member State level, this is not surprising in view of the fact that like childcare it has a redefinition element. If the European Commission definition outlined in the introduction to this chapter is adhered to, gender mainstreaming demands redefinition of policy goals to incorporate the promotion of equality between women and men as a policy objective in all policy areas and the adoption of gender impact assessment at all stages of the policy process. However, as pointed out earlier the scope of gender mainstreaming as it applies in EU documents, and the EES in particular, is centred on economic and labour market related policies and activities and does not focus on the issue of the relationship between gender representation and policy-making (re the latter see Beveridge et al 2000) and this is an inherent limitation. Gender mainstreaming is easily asserted at a rhetorical level but its implementation, even when confined to economic and labour market policies and activities, would necessitate significant questioning of taken for granted policy practice. In particular, in the absence of clearly measurable outcome indicators, promoting gender equality through the strategy of gender mainstreaming is merely an abstract aspiration. These characteristics are not confined to gender mainstreaming. They arise even more cogently in some other dimensions of social exclusion where mainstreaming is discussed, for example in the area of poverty, another dimension of social exclusion on which action is a high priority at the EU level and which is not systematically incorporated into the policy process in all its stages. Furthermore, there is an interaction across areas of exclusion which complicates impact assessment. While the Commission definition of gender mainstreaming is a highly demanding one, it remains aspirational if not accompanied by prescriptions for gender impact assessment based on measurable criteria.

But the problems with gender mainstreaming are more fundamental than this. Despite its salience in policy terms over the past decade and a half, mainstreaming is a contested concept and imprecise strategy irrespective of the area in which it is applied. It has been the focus of much academic and policy debate over the past decade – the former is reflected in numerous articles and special issues of journals (see Mazey 2000 for special issue of *Journal of European Public Policy*; Beveridge and Shaw, 2002 for Special Issue of *Feminist Legal Studies*; Walby 2005a for special issue of *International Feminist Journal of Politics*; and Walby 2005b for special issue of *Social Politics*). Some of the key EU documents have been referred to above but it is a strategy advocated by several other cross-national or supranational organizations, for example, the UN Commission on the Status of Women and various other UN units, the ILO, the World Bank and the Council of Europe (UN 1997; 2008; Council of Europe 1999). Yet, reports on its implementation point to its contested nature and associated limitations including a gulf between its formal implementation and addressing gender inequality in a transformative or agenda setting way (Booth and Bennett 2002; Daly 2005; Rees 2005) the complexity of impact assessment (Roggeband and Verloo 2006); the limitations associated with resource and data availability (Veitch 2005) and the constraints imposed by the wider economic context (Perrons 2005).[18]

Underlying the barriers to the achievement of labour market gender equality in all areas, and most prominently in relation to pay, are the more fundamental issues

18 The assessment of gender mainstreaming at the EU level is considerably more optimistic than are assessments of its implementation at member state level – re the former see Haffner-Burton and Pollack who analyze its implementation in five issue areas.

of the structure of the labour market, the balance in the quality of employment being created and the disproportionate dependence of some groups on poor quality employment. While the majority of jobs being created in the EU are of reasonable or good quality, the European Commission 2001 Employment in Europe report indicated that 25 per cent of jobs created in the EU15 were of low quality including 8 per cent in the 'dead-end' category, that is offering neither job security nor employer provided training, and over half of these have low pay and productivity (European Commission 2001). Women and young people were more likely to be in low pay/low productivity jobs and the gender earning gap was greatest in these jobs. There is no evidence to indicate that this pattern has changed in recent years. Furthermore, the intensification of globalization of production is increasing competitiveness pressures and makes the synchronization of the economic and employment OMC with the social OMC essential if their mutual reinforcement is to be achieved.

The 2008 Synchronization: The Possibilities

The Lisbon Strategy aimed 'to bring together economic, employment and social policies by focussing them on the commonly defined [and mutually reinforcing] objectives of improving competitiveness, moving towards full employment and promoting social inclusion' (Council of the European Union 2000). It is envisaged that the synchronization of the social OMC with the OMC processes for employment and economic strategies from 2008 onwards will enhance the mutual reinforcement of the social, economic and employment processes. Such mutual reinforcement has been a consistent theme in EU policy statements since the 1990s. The Integrated Guidelines for Growth and Jobs reflect integration of the employment guidelines with the broad economic policy coordination process. On the one hand one might argue that this potentially balances the relative weights of the economic, employment and social policy streams; on the other hand, it is noteworthy that the flexibility emphasis of the macro and micro economic guidelines are not formulated using a gender mainstreaming lens and neither are the employment guidelines. While the evidence presented in this paper on what has transpired in terms of gender equality under the integrated guidelines is not encouraging it is possible, but certainly not guaranteed, that a broader synchronized process as is envisaged from 2008 may facilitate greater recognition of the mutual incompatibility of some of the objectives and approaches pursued at present and allow for the positive interaction of social, economic and employment factors. It is noteworthy that Rubery et al (2003) point out that the 2003 Joint Report on Social Inclusion raises issues relating to gender equality in employment that are almost entirely absent in the Joint Employment Report. Furthermore, the Danish National Reform Programme Implementation Report (2006) notes that it only includes those aspects of social policy that are relevant to the Lisbon Strategy. Significantly, it asserts that 'An *active social policy* must be utilized in order to handle the social problems that lie beyond unemployment' (the Danish Government 2006: 49). In theory this is what was envisaged by the Lisbon Council which identified the building of a more socially and economically inclusive EU as an essential element in the achievement of the Lisbon Strategy.

Conclusion

This analysis of gender equality in the context of the OMC as it operates in the EES points to some achievements, unrealized potential and some possibilities. First, there is a major difference in the policy implications of gender equality in the sense of eliminating inequalities in labour market participation and gender equality more broadly conceived; that is in the sense of promoting equality between men and women as is the objective of gender mainstreaming strategy outlined by the European Commission. This difference tends not to be identified in EU policy documents or Member State policy documents. Commitments to gender mainstreaming are consistently made not only in EU level documents over the past decade but in National Action Plans and the more recent National Reform Programmes prepared by Member States but the evidence for recognition of the demanding implications of such a strategy as outlined in the EU Commission definition is sparse. Furthermore, evidence for the implementation of the more easily specified gender equality commitments is variable not only across Member States, some of whom have already met the Lisbon labour participation targets and a few of whom have reached the Barcelona childcare targets, it is also variable across commitments. Taking the EU as a whole, with the exception of considerably increased gender equality in labour market participation and some improvement in childcare provision, there has been no marked positive movement in other indicators of labour market gender equality; in particular the European Commission concluded in 2007 that there is 'nothing to indicate that the [gender pay] gap is narrowing in any significant way' (European Commission 2007b: 2).

While the EES has been successful in putting gender equality on the policy agenda there are clear limitations in the implementation of commitments at Member State level in relation to gender equality broadly conceived. Promoting equality between men and women requires changes in labour market structure if the quality of employment open to new labour market entrants, who are disproportionately women, is to be improved. It also requires redefinition of the state-market-family relationship in service provision if employment and caring demands are to be reconciled in ways that allow for participation in the labour market on equal terms for men and women. While the latter is widely acknowledged in EES documents, and particularly in the parallel gender equality stream of documents, the Gender Equality Roadmap, Framework and Pact, the structural barriers to labour market gender equality receive little or no attention. This is at least in part linked to what is identified above as the 'hierarchy of objectives' – economic, employment and social in that order – evident in the revision of the Lisbon Strategy. It is also linked to the scope of gender mainstreaming as it applies in EU documents and the EES in particular, which is centred on gender mainstreaming of labour market related policies and does not focus on the issue of the relationship between gender representation and policy-making.

In considering the OMC and Member State policy commitments in the EES it is important to bear in mind that subsidiarity is a fundamental principle underlying the OMC and that policy commitments in the EES are not the result of a top-down process. Büchs (2008) usefully draws on the 'two-level game' terminology, used by

Putnam (1988) in relation to diplomacy and domestic politics, to characterize the OMC: On the one hand, Member States try to have an influence on OMC objectives and, on the other, 'selectively use the OMC in national policy-making processes' (2008: 22). The EES is a negotiated process and the OMC involves a trade-off between subsidiarity and implementation of commonly agreed objectives. This allows Member States to prioritize employment creation policies without according equal weight to the gender impact of policies. This cannot be divorced from the wide-ranging but imprecise nature of the strategy of gender mainstreaming.

The potential of the OMC as envisaged by the Lisbon Council is considerable – it is built on the assumptions of policy exchange and mutual learning through establishing policy guidelines, setting benchmarks, targets and a monitoring system to identify good practice and evaluate progress through peer group review. While it broadens the possibilities for gender equality, its potential is not realized. In particular, there is a failure to broaden the discussion of policy formulation, implementation and monitoring through the involvement of stakeholders at Member State level and a failure to disseminate comparable data on key social indicators beyond a narrow policy elite. The ongoing development of a range of social indicators and associated data is a potential resource for national stakeholders to monitor commitments and their implementation. It is noteworthy that there is an increased emphasis on implementation of commitments in the revised EES.

Finally, the reduced salience of gender equality commitments at each successive reform of the employment guidelines has tended to be replaced by general commitments to gender mainstreaming but the contested nature of this concept and the imprecise nature of the gender mainstreaming strategy gives considerable leeway to Member States in terms of meeting commitments in this area. However, the EES does not operate in isolation, it must be situated in parallel to other EU gender equality activity including the *Roadmap for equality between men and women 2006-2010* and the *European pact for gender equality (2006)* both issued by the Commission, and the commitment to gender mainstreaming in the Structural Funds. While strong on gender equality commitments, the two Commission documents are largely dependent on Member States for action on the priorities outlined. A second parallel process that may offer more tangible potential for labour market gender equality objectives is the synchronization of the present integrated economic and employment OMC process and the social OMC in 2008. This could create the conditions for realizing the potential of the OMC process for broadening policy possibilities by facilitating the recognition of the contradictions and mutual incompatibilities of the objectives and approaches pursued in economic, employment and social processes. This is essential for the attainment of key labour market gender equality objectives. But this will be realized only if it is based on a more balanced interaction of social, employment and economic policies than is evident at present at the EU and Member State levels. This is unlikely to occur unless it becomes a policy objective and focus of political discourse involving a wide range of stakeholders at the level of Member States and unless this is reflected in the policy commitments agreed between Member States and the Commission.

References

Atkinson, T. (2002), 'Social Inclusion and the European Union' *Journal of Common Market Studies* 40(4): 625-43.

Beveridge, F., Nott, S. and Stephen, K. (2000), 'Mainstreaming and the Engendering of Policy-making: A Means to an End?' *Journal of European Public Policy* 7(3), 385-405.

Beveridge, F. and Shaw, J. (eds.) (2002), 10(2) *Feminist Legal Studies*, Special Issue on *Mainstreaming Gender in European Public Policy.*

Booth, C. and Bennett, C. (2002), 'Gender Mainstreaming in the European Union: Towards a New Conception and Practice of Equal Opportunities?' *European Journal of Women's Studies* 9(4): 430-446.

Breitenbach, E. and Galligan, Y. (2006), 'Measuring Gender Equality: Reflecting on Experiences and Challenges in the UK and Ireland' *Policy and Politics* 34(4): 597-614.

Büchs, M. (2008), 'The Open Method of Coordination as a 'two-level game' *Policy and Politics* 36(1): 21-37.

Chalmers, D. and Lodge, M. (2003), *The Open Method of Co-ordination and the European Welfare State* ESRC Centre for Analysis of Risk and Regulation, LSE, Discussion Paper No:11.

Council of Europe (1999), *Gender Mainstreaming: Conceptual Framework, Methodology and Presentation of Good Practices*. Council of Europe. EG (1999) 3.

Council of the European Union (2005a), 'Council Decision of 12 July 2005 on Guidelines for the Employment Policies of the Member States' (2005/600/EC) *Official Journal of the European Union* L205/21-27.

Council of the European Union (2005b), *Presidency Conclusions, Brussels, 22-23 March, 2005.*

Council of the European Union (2007a), *Joint Employment Report 2006/2007*, EPSCO, 6706/07.

Council of the European Union (2007b), *Presidency Conclusions, Brussels. European Council 8-9 March 2007.*

Daly, M. (2005), 'Gender Mainstreaming in Theory and Practice' *Social Politics: International Studies in Gender, State and Society* 12(3): 433-450.

European Commission (1996), 'Incorporating Equal Opportunities for Women and Men into all Community Policies and Activities', COM (96)67 final.

European Commission (2000), Community *Framework Strategy on Gender Equality (2001-2005)*, COM (2000)335.

European Commission (2002), *Communication to the Spring European Council, Taking Stock of Five Years of the European Employment Strategy* Brussels: European Communities, COM (2002) 416 final.

European Commission (2003), *Strengthening the Social Dimension of the Lisbon Strategy: Streamlining Open Coordination in the Field of Social Protection.* Brussels: Communication from the Commission, COM (2003) 261 final.

European Commission (2004), *Facing the Challenge. The Lisbon strategy for Growth and Employment, Report from the High Level Group chaired by Wim*

Kok, November 2004, Luxembourg: Official Publications of the European Communities.

European Commission (2005a), *Communication to the Spring European Council Working Together for Growth and Jobs Integrated Guidelines for Growth and Jobs (2005-08)*, Luxembourg: Office of Official Publications of the European Communities.

European Commission (2005b), *Communication to the Spring European Council, Working Together for Growth and Jobs. A New Start For The Lisbon Strategy Communication From President Barroso In Agreement With Vice-president Verheugenl*, SEC (2005) 192-193.

European Commission (2006a), Communication from the Commission to the Council, the European Parliament, the European Economic and Social Committee and the Committee of the Regions *A Roadmap for Equality Between Women and Men – 2006-2010*, COM (2006) 92 final.

European Commission (2006b), 'European Pact for Gender Equality' Annex II to the Presidency Conclusions (2/15) *Bulletin of the European Union* 3-2006.

European Commission (2006c), *Report from the Commission to the Council, the European Parliament, the European Economic and Social Committee and the Committee of the Regions on Equality Between Women and Men – 2006*. Brussels, COM (2006) 71 final.

European Commission (2006), *Portfolio of Overarching Indicators and Streamlined Social Inclusion, Pensions and Health Portfolios*. Brussels. <http://ec.europa.eu/employment_social/spsi/common_indicators_en.htm>.

European Commission (2007), *Indicators for Monitoring the Employment Guidelines Including Indicators for Additional Employment Analysis*. Brussels. Latest update 23/10/2007. http://ec.europa.eu/employment_social/employment_strategy/pdf/2007compendium_en.pdf.pdf.

European Commission (2007a), *Report from the Commission to the Council, the European Parliament, the European Economic and Social Committee and the Committee of the Regions on Equality Between Women and Men – 2007*, COM (2007) 49 final.

European Commission (2007b), *Communication from the Commission to the Council, the European Parliament, the European Economic and Social Committee and the Committee of the Regions Tackling the Pay Gap Between Women and Men*, COM (2007) 424 final.

European Commission (2002), *Impact Evaluation of the European Employment Strategy Technical Analysis Supporting*, COM (2002) 416 final of 17.7.2002 *Taking Stock of Five Years of the European Employment Strategy.*

European Economic and Social Committee (2007), *Opinion on the Proposal for a Council Decision on Guidelines for Employment Policies of the Member States*, COM (2006) 815 final – 2006/0271 (CNS).

Fagan, C., Grimshaw, D. and Rubery, J. (2006), 'The Subordination of the Gender Equality Objective: The National Reform Programmes and 'Making Work Pay' Policies', *Industrial Relations Journal* 37(6): 571-592.

France (2006), Rapport sur les stratégies pour la protection sociale et l'inclusion social 2006-2008. <http://ec.europa.eu/employment_social/spsi/docs/social_inclusion/2006/nap/france_fr.pdf>.

Guillén, A.M. and Palier, B. (2004), 'Introduction: Does Europe Matter? Accession to EU and Social Policy Developments in Recent and New Member States' *Journal of European Social Policy* 14(3): 203-10.

Hafner-Burton, E. and Pollack, M. (2000), 'Mainstreaming Gender in the European Union' *Journal of European Public Policy* 7(3): 432-56.

Le Grand-Duché de Luxembourg (2006), *National Strategy Report on Social Protection and Social Inclusion.*<http://ec.europa.eu/employment_social/spsi/docs/social_inclusion/2006/nap/luxembourg_en.pdf.

Martinsen, D.S. (2007), 'The Europeanization of Gender Equality – Who Controls The Scope of Non-discrimination?' *Journal of European Public Policy* 14(4): 544-562.

Mazey, S. (2000), 'Introduction: Integrating Gender – Intellectual and 'Real World' Mainstreaming' *Journal of European Public Policy* 7(3): 333-45.

O'Connor, J.S. (1996), 'Trend Report: From Women in the Welfare State to Gendering Welfare State Regimes', *Current Sociology*, 44(2): 1-124.

O'Connor, J.S. (2005a), 'Employment-Anchored Social Policy, Gender Equality and the Open Method of Coordination in the European Union' *European* Societies 7(1): 27-52.

O'Connor, J.S. (2005b), 'Policy Coordination, Social Indicators and the Social-policy Agenda in the European Union' *Journal of European Social Policy* 15(4): 345-361.

O'Connor, J.S. (2007), 'Convergence in European Welfare State Analysis: Convergence of What?' in Clasen, J. and Siegel, N.A. (eds) *Exploring the Dynamics of Reform: The Dependent Variable Problem in Comparative Welfare State Analysis*. (Cheltenham: Edward Elgar), pp. 217-243.

OECD (2001), *Starting Strong. Early Childhood Education and Care.* Paris: OECD.

OECD (2005), *Babies and Bosses: Reconciling Work and Family Life* (series covering Australia, Austria, Canada, Denmark, Finland, Ireland, Japan, New Zealand, the Netherlands, Portugal, Switzerland, Sweden and the UK). Paris: OECD.

Perrons, D. (2005), 'Gender Mainstreaming and Gender Equality in the New (Market) Economy: An Analysis of Contradictions' *Social Politics: International Studies in Gender, State and Society* 12(3): 389-411.

Pochet, P. (2005), 'The Open Method of Co-ordination and the Construction of Social Europe. A Historical Perspective' in Zeitlin J., Pochet, P. (eds.), with Magnusson, L. *The Open Method of Coordination in Action The European Employment and Social Inclusion Strategies*. (Brussels: P.I.E.-Peter Lang), pp. 37-82.

Putnam, R.D. (1998), 'Diplomacy and Domestic Politics: The Logic of Two-level Games' *International Organization*, 42(3): 427-60.

Radaelli, C. (2000), 'Whither Europeanization? Concept Stretching and Substantive Change' EIoP, European Integration on line Papers, 4: 8, <http://eiop.or.at/eiop/texte/2000-008a.htm>.

Randall, V. (2000), 'Childcare Policy in the European States: Limits to Convergence' *Journal of European Public Policy* 7(3): 346-68.

Rees, T. (2005), 'Reflections on the Uneven Development of Gender Mainstreaming in Europe' *International Feminist Journal of Politics*, 7(4): 555-574.

Roggeband, C. and Verloo, M. (2006) 'Evaluating Gender Impact Assessment in the Netherlands (1994-2004): A Political Process Approach' *Policy and Politics* 34(4): 615-32.

Rubery, J. (2005), 'Gender Mainstreaming and the OMC. Is the Open Method Too Open for Gender Equality Policy' in Zeitlin, J. and Pochet, P. (eds.), with Magnusson, L. *The Open Method of Co-ordination in Action The European Employment Strategy and Social Inclusion Strategies*. (Brussels: P.I.E.-Peter Lang), pp. 391-416.

Rubery, J., Grimshaw, D., Fagan, C., Figueiredo, H. and Smith, M. (2003), 'Gender Equality still on the European Agenda' *Industrial Relations Journal* 34(5): 477-497.

Rubery, J., Grimshaw, D., Smith, M. and Figueiredo, H. (2004), *Gender Mainstreaming and the European Employment Strategy*, prepared as part of the work by the co-ordinating team of the Expert Group on Gender Inclusion and Employment commissioned by the Equal Opportunities Unit in the European Commission.

Rubery, J., Grimshaw, D. and Figueiredo, H. (2005), 'How to Close the Gender Pay Gap in Europe: Towards the Gender Mainstreaming of Pay Policy' *Industrial Relations Journal* 36(3): 184-213.

Rubery, J., Grimshaw, D., Smith, M. and Donnelly, R. (2006), *The National Reform Programme 2006 and the Gender Aspects of the European Employment Strategy. The Co-ordinators' Synthesis Report* prepared as part of the work by the co-ordinating team of the Expert Group on Gender Inclusion and Employment commissioned by the Equal Opportunities Unit in the European Commission.

Scharpf, F.W. (2002), 'The European Social Model: Coping with the Challenges of Diversity' *Journal of Common Market Studies* 40(4): 645-70.

The Danish Government (2005), *Denmark's National Reform Programme*, <http://www.um.dk/NR/rdonlyres/15E3C091-7A14-493C-82C9-2204B3A9964A/0/TheDanishNationalReformProgramme.pdf>.

The Danish Government (2006), *Denmark's National Reform Programme First Progress Report*, <http://ec.europa.eu/growthandjobs/pdf/nrp/DA_nrp_en.pdf>.

Trubeck, D.M. and Trubeck, L.G. (2005), 'The Open Method of Co-ordination and the Debate over "Hard" and "Soft" Law' in Zeitlin, J. and Pochet, P. (eds.), with Magnusson, L. *The Open Method of Co-ordination in Action The European Employment Strategy and Social Inclusion Strategies*. (Brussels: P.I.E.-Peter Lang), pp. 83-103.

UN (1997), 'Gender Mainstreaming' Extract from *Report of the Economic and Social Council for 1997*, <http://www.un.org/womenwatch/daw/csw/GMS.PDF>.

UN (2008), OSAGI (Office of the Special Adviser on Gender Issues and Advancement of Women) Department of Economic and Social Affairs <http://www.un.org/womenwatch/osagi/statementsandpapers.htm>.

Veitch, J. (2005), 'Looking at Gender Mainstreaming in the UK Government' *International Feminist Journal of Politics*, 7 (4): 600-606.

Walby, S. (2005a), 'Introduction: Comparative Gender Mainstreaming in a Global Era' *International Feminist Journal of Politics*, 7 (4): 453-70.

Walby, S. (2005b), 'Gender Mainstreaming: Productive Tensions in Theory and Practice' *Social Politics: International Studies in Gender, State and Society* 12(3): 321-343.

Zeitlin, J. (2005), 'The Open Method of Co-ordination in Action. Theoretical Promise, Empirical Realities, Reform Strategies' in Zeitlin, J. and Pochet, P. (eds.), with Magnusson, L. *The Open Method of Co-ordination in Action. The European Employment Strategy and Social Inclusion Strategies*. (Brussels: P.I.E.-Peter Lang), pp. 447-503.

Zeitlin, J. and Pochet, P. with Magnusson, L. (eds.) (2005), *The Open Method of Coordination in Action: The European Employment and Social Inclusion Strategies*. (Brussels: P.I.E-Peter Lang).

Chapter 6

The OMC, Gender Policy and the Experience of Poland as a New Member State

Małgorzata Fuszara

The Open Method of Coordination (OMC) raises both hopes and fears. Gender equality policy is not mentioned directly among the areas to which it is applied. Two issues appear important in this context. First, does the policy of gender equality in the European Union (EU) contain elements which render it suitable for the methods employed in the OMC? Second, in the areas where the OMC is employed, is attention paid to the principle of gender equality and to women's interests? It is worth noting that the OMC is applied in areas such as employment policy, poverty eradication, social exclusion and adequate and sustainable pensions, that is, areas in which the issue of gender equality is particularly important.

The OMC seems to be appropriate in situations where, in certain areas, no further unification of legal regulations and social policy solutions in the EU by means of hard law is possible or desirable, and yet the EU perceives a need for convergent solutions to be adopted in the Member States. This is where the soft law methods of the OMC may be of use. Instead of implementing another directive, the focus is on setting common objectives for all Member States, on establishing common indicators as a means of measuring progress, and on monitoring the results. Mutual learning and progressing on the basis of one another's experience are the basic methods which are expected to lead to establishing best practice for a given area and a given country. The mechanism employed in this method is likened to a radar, by means of which the best solutions are sought (Raedelli 2003). The method is usually applied in the areas where almost every country has already designed certain social and legal solutions based on its own traditions. Therefore, it is concerned not with the regulation of areas previously unregulated, but rather with modifying, reforming, and amending already functional solutions. It is often emphasized in literature that the inclusion of the new Member States from Central and Eastern Europe could not have left the OMC unaffected (Pochet 2005).

The new countries contributed their own experience and their own systems of regulations, sometimes different than those prevailing in the 'old' Member States. As is often the case, this can be treated as an advantage, because in this way a greater number of options and experiences became available for use. On the other hand, it can be perceived as a disadvantage, in that new, previously unknown experiences appeared, which meant in turn that the choice had to be made among a greater variety of deeply different solutions, some of which had never been implemented in many countries and the influence of which on the systems already in existence in the 'old' Member States was difficult to predict.

While in the case of hard law there is a model which must be implemented in all countries, the OMC allows for the establishment of solutions in a bottom-up manner and for making a selection from a variety of possible solutions. When this method is applied, only a framework is established as a result of a joint discussion: basic objectives to which the countries aspire, conditions to be met, and indicators for measurement of progress. Exchange of experiences and learning together from the results of experiences in other countries is expected to produce the best solution for each country.

The OMC has basic indisputable advantages. In accordance with the subsidiarity principle, it makes it possible to approximate the policies of Member States in areas which are not regulated by hard law. Even just a discussion focused on setting common objectives and indicators for their measurement forces the participants to reflect upon and to critically analyze their current social policy and legal solutions. It also demands that the participants become more open to new solutions which do not directly follow from the given country's experience. Most often this results in attaching greater importance to the areas under discussion as well as in progress in the search for solutions. Also, the Member States' policies may become more convergent in areas where there is no strict EU-wide regulation.

The OMC requires political will to strive to achieve the objectives, since it is (like any 'soft' method) mostly voluntary and not supported by force or sanctions. This on the one hand appears as its great asset, but on the other hand as a kind of in-built fault. Mandatory rules, such as regulations and directives, are imposed on Member States and must be followed. As exemplified by Poland before accession, this gives stronger arguments to non-governmental organizations in pressurizing the government to meet standards and to introduce new regulations. The existence of the *acquis communautaire* was often the only truly effective method for NGOs to force the government to introduce certain solutions in the pre-accession period. In particular, the experiences of Polish women's organizations are instructive in this respect. The organizations employed a broad strategy of citing EU regulations when lobbying for the introduction of solutions to prevent discrimination and promote equal opportunities for men and women before the accession (Fuszara 2006). The OMC may equip NGOs with arguments as well, since it refers to the examples of other countries and solutions implemented there. However, it is a much weaker type of argument, because no state can be forced to implement 'soft law', and therefore the arguments will only succeed if the objectives are deemed worthy of pursuit by the government in power.

The method also requires self-discipline and political stability which are necessary conditions for long-term policy-making. This is often not easily achievable, particularly with respect to areas such as gender equality. Therefore, when contemplating the application of the OMC, one must not overlook the difficulties that might result from its application. In the light of these observations, despite the OMC's many advantages, this chapter will focus on the difficulties which may appear with regard to its application. It will refer to the recent experiences of

Poland, which a short time ago was still a candidate for accession to the EU. The process of accession was in many ways the pre-cursor to the process of application of the OMC and shared many similar features. For example, during the pre-accession period Poland participated in a number of so called 'twinning projects', some of which touched upon the subject matter of gender equality. Pre-accession experiences such as these may be important in discussing the usefulness of the OMC as a tool for shaping gender equality policy in the Member States.

This chapter looks first at the basic problems inherent in this method, which often give rise to controversies: which practice can be described as best practice, and how to establish the indicators? It then considers Poland's pre-accession experience with twinning projects and mutual learning. The chapter then examines Poland's experience since accession with gender equality programmes using the OMC and, finally, draws some conclusions.

'Best Practices', Indicators and Benchmarking

The countries of Central and Eastern Europe recently went through the process of harmonizing their law with the law of the EU. It was a very interesting process. Its assumption was simple: it required mostly (although not exclusively) that the EU directives be implemented. In the area of gender equality this process turned out to be not as simple and not as easy to evaluate as one might expect. All countries of Central and Eastern Europe had previously maintained a wide-ranging system of legal protection of women's labour and of motherhood. They often also declared gender equality in their constitutions, which was quite rare in the 'old' Member States.

Technically, the implementation process required only an evaluation of whether the candidate state had sufficiently well harmonized its law with EU law. In other words, that meant an evaluation of the old and newly introduced regulations against the directives. However, analyses conducted in the candidate states often compared the old regulations with the new ones. This in turn resulted in attempts to evaluate whether the old or the new regulation is better from the point of view of the interests of women and gender equality. Such evaluations were rendered even more difficult by the fact that simultaneously not only the legal regulations but also the social and political situation in the country was changing. Under new circumstances, in a market economy and with very high unemployment, the old regulations have a different impact on the situation of women than they used to have in a system where unemployment did not exist, pay differences were inconsequential, and careers depended on political loyalty. Rights connected with, for example, protection of mothers or childcare absences were not only greater but also more often used in practice, since there was no unemployment, no danger of job loss and no risk to career development. Contemporary research shows that in the opinion of both employers and employees, women often do not take advantage of their rights – once commonly taken advantage of – because it is important for them to keep their jobs. Moreover, it appears that there are significant differences between women employed in the public sector, where women take advantage of their full rights, and those employed in private businesses who, according to the respondents, 'guard their desks.' For them, it is not any kind of ban that makes them forego the rights; it is sufficient for them to be aware that 'the employer would not be happy' if the women fully exercised their rights (Fuszara 2007a). For such reasons it is very difficult to establish objectively what constitutes best practice from the perspective of women's employment. The old regulations may produce a very different effect under new circumstances.

Similar problems are encountered when comparing the situation of women in different EU Member States. In countries and at times when unemployment is low, long maternity leave and childcare leave may be perceived as favourable to women. In other countries and at times when unemployment is high and there is a risk of women being pushed out of the labour market, the same solutions are often seen as unfavourable to women, because employers may avoid employing women who might want to exercise their rights. Such controversies are complex in character. They have not only an economic aspect but also a legal, political and worldview aspect, and disputes centered around such subject matters may have a decisive impact on what is deemed to be best practice, and therefore may influence the definition of the objectives to be achieved.

A further difficulty may consist in a lack of political stability and frequent changes of governments in power, if each of the successive governments has a different stance as to what constitutes best practice in the area of gender equality. In many countries, including Poland, policy with regard to women and gender equality changes radically depending on which political party is in power. Lack of political stability may therefore be an added difficulty in establishing objectives and indicators.

An analysis of parliamentary debates, electoral programs and gender policy shows that particularly in the area of women's rights and gender equality the old division into 'leftist' and 'rightist' political options is resurrected, even though it has largely lost its significance in other areas. With reference to issues other than gender it is often difficult to decide whether a party has a left-wing or a right-wing program, in the traditional sense of these terms. Economic programs as well as social policy often differ very little between parties, even if their justifications are different. However, in debates centered around the situation of women, including legal regulations with regard to women and gender equality, the right-left division reappears. The representatives of these two options have radically different visions of roles, aspirations and ambitions of women. Each political wing is convinced that it is their suggestions which are 'pro-women' and in line with the expectations and interests of women in Poland. Not long ago in parliamentary debates the division was even clearer. Representatives of the left spoke of the necessity to introduce regulations ensuring equality, while representatives of the right claimed that gender equality was a fact already, and gender discrimination was a figment of leftist and feminist imagination. The process of harmonization with EU law, in addition to other consequences, influenced the tone of the debate about the situation of women and gender equality. To a large extent it managed to eliminate the old view that Poland had already achieved gender equality, and in particular the view that gender equality was not an issue worth debating. At present, at least on the official level, lack of gender equality is no longer questioned. However, there still are deep differences in terms of both objectives to achieve (is it better for women to be able to stay with the children at home for longer, or is it better if they return to the labour market as swiftly as possible?) and the ways and means of achieving them (Fuszara 2006).

Currently the problem is not that one of the political options (that is, the left) has a programme for women while the other option (that is, the right) has no such programme. The problem is that their visions of 'interests of women' are entirely different. This causes great difficulties in establishing indicators which would make it possible to decide which of the policies is more and which is less women-friendly. A good example is the regulation with regard to the length of maternity leave. So far in Poland, since 1991, power has swung between left and right with every election: the party who was in opposition during the previous term of office came to power with the next election. Right-wing governments, every time they came to power, attempted to make maternity leave and childcare leave longer, including in the legal regulation a provision which guaranteed the woman her job once the leave was used. This was presented as a women-friendly solution which accommodates the women's wish to reconcile professional and family life. However, research shows that only women who are employed in the public sector take advantage of the maternity-related rights (Fuszara 2007b). Generally women aim to return to work as soon as possible after childbirth, for fear of losing their jobs despite the legal guarantees. The employers use a range of 'tricks' (including a generally unwilling attitude to employing women as such or making the post redundant as soon as a woman returns to work, etc.) to remove from their companies the employees who take advantage of their rights, despite the existing right to work. There is also another important aspect of this state of affairs. If a mother uses her rights – for example, a breastfeeding mother exercises her right to leave work earlier, which in practice makes her workday shorter – may result in a larger workload for her colleagues. As a consequence, women often feel the pressure from many sides, both from the employers and from co-workers, not to take full advantage of their rights (Fuszara 2007b).

Research also shows that the majority of women do not welcome the introduction of longer maternity leave and other similar solutions, fearing that this may result in a worse situation of women in general on the labour market. Such fears are well justified in countries such as Poland where unemployment is high, and the fear of losing one's job is widespread. This is why longer maternity leave periods and the legal right to return to work are considered in different ways. On the one hand, they may constitute an instrument for combining professional work with family life. On the other hand, they may be perceived as a means of excluding women from the labour market. The actual effects of such rights on the Polish labour market may only be evaluated *ex post*. However, due to the above-mentioned instability of the Polish political system, it has not been possible to make such evaluations because the party in power changes often and so does the way gender policy is implemented. *Ex ante* considerations of the impact of such rights are subjective and based on ideological views.

It might be expected that under such circumstances the OMC would be particularly useful, because it includes a comparison of solutions employed in different countries, mutual learning and a search for best practice. However, the methods of comparison appear unreliable in this case: both in countries where women's labour participation is high (Denmark) and in those where it is low (Italy) maternity leave is longer than in Poland. Immediately the question arises of which practice, of which country, should be considered as best practice. In such areas it is particularly difficult to find common indicators which would provide an answer to the question which of the policies is better for women in a particular state or at that particular time.

This brings us to the next important issue which, as far as the OMC is concerned, is the establishment of indicators. On a certain basic level this seems simple and rather uncontroversial. Indicators such as the proportion of working age women who are employed, the proportion of women among the unemployed, the closing of the pay gap between men and women are easy to establish and unlikely to raise a controversy, and it is certainly important to use them. If it was not for the EU's pressure to include such indicators, to make them available and treat them as important measuring tools of gender equality, in many countries such data would still not be included in statistics today. There can also be no doubt that lack of such indicators makes it difficult (if not impossible) to evaluate the situation and policy implemented in a given country by its government. For example, the evaluation of Poland's report on the implementation of the provisions of the United Nations' Convention on the Elimination of Discrimination Against Women (CEDAW) by the Committee on the Elimination of Discrimination against Women, compiled in 2007, shows how difficult it is to evaluate a policy which is conducted without first establishing clear indicators. The evaluation demonstrated how the lack of clear indicators makes not only an internal evaluation difficult, but also makes it difficult for the Committee to evaluate the situation of women in many areas of social life in Poland. The Committee issued the following recommendation for Poland:

> The Committee regrets limited availability of statistical data disaggregated by sex and age and by urban and rural areas, which makes it more difficult for the Committee to assess progress and trends over time in the actual situation of women and their enjoyment of their human rights in all areas covered by the Convention. The Committee calls upon the State party to enhance its data collection and analysis of such data in all areas covered by the Convention so as be able to assess more accurately the actual situation of women and their enjoyment of their human rights, disaggregated by sex and age and by urban and rural areas, as applicable, and to track trends over time, and to design and implement better targeted policies and programs for the promotion of gender equality. It also calls upon the State party to monitor, through measurable indicators, the impact of laws, policies and action plans and evaluate progress achieved towards the realization of women's de facto equality. The Committee requests the State party to include such statistical data and analysis in its next report.[1]

This is only one example of the difficulties which are often faced by persons and institutions whose job it is to monitor the realization of plans when no appropriate indicators are available. Another example can be found in a Polish document entitled 'Evaluation of the system of monitoring of the realization of activities, created for the National Action Plan for Social Integration 2004-2006'. It reads: "Some

1 Concluding Comments of the Committee on the Elimination of Discrimination against Women: Poland, CEDAW, 2 February 2007.

of the indicators cannot constitute the basis for evaluation of whether the action brought the intended results. This is mostly a consequence of using mainly input indicators which are presented as simple numerical values, with no relative points of reference."[2] The example used in the clarification is the number of benefits paid out for educational purposes. According to the persons in charge of monitoring, the number of benefits, without reference to the number of children in need of such benefits, without information on the amount of money paid out as such benefits, and without relating this amount to the actual need, as well as without information on whether those in greatest need received the benefits (eligibility criteria) makes it impossible to evaluate whether this constitutes an indicator of true improvement of educational chances of children whose educational chances were originally low.

Such problems with establishing internal indicators suggest that exchange of experiences with other countries, possibly within the OMC, may lead to improvements and the creation of better indicators. It is undoubtedly a great achievement of the EU that at least some indicators which are necessary in employing the OMC were jointly established. However, difficulties arise not only in their establishment but also – as often mentioned in the literature – in benchmarking: "[...] where benchmarking is cooperative, reaching agreement on the most appropriate bases can be difficult especially if it involves significant changes to existing reporting arrangements" (Arrowsmith, Sisson and Marginson 2004: 320). It has also been pointed out that focusing too hard on established numerical indicators may lead to efforts that are sometimes unnecessary, all in the name of reaching objectives which seemed important some time ago, and also to a tendency to overlook the costs which are to be borne in order to achieve the established numbers (De la Porte 2002: 43).

The ostensibly easy matter of measuring women's and men's labour market participation is a good example of how difficult it can be to evaluate the usefulness of indicators in the area of gender equality. In the literature concerned with the OMC one indicator is commonly referred to: that by 2010, in the entire EU the level of labour market participation is to equal 70 per cent for men and 60 per cent for women (De la Porte 2002). Data on various countries show that labour market participation of men and women varies widely in the European Union. Some countries have already exceeded the rate of women's labour market participation which is the target for 2010, while other still have a long way to go. However, countries differ not only in the overall levels of women's employment, but also in the rates of full-time versus part-time employment. Eurostat data for 2006 suggest that, for example, in the Netherlands as many as 67.5 per cent of women are active on the labour market, but as many as 74.7 per cent of them work part-time. On the other hand, in Bulgaria only 55 per cent of women are employed, but almost all of them work full-time (only 2.7 per cent of women work part-time). A glance at the countries of the EU where the labour market participation rate is the highest

2 'Zabezpieczenie społeczne i integracja społeczna na lata 2006-2008' National Report on Strategies for Social Protection and Social Inclusion.Dokument przyjęty przez Radę Ministrów w dniu 9 października 2006 roku. Aneks 2.4. Ocena systemu monitorowania realizacji działań stworzonego dla Krajowego Planu Działania na rzecz Integracji Społecznej na lata 2004-2006.

reveals that the same countries have a very high rate of part-time employment of women. Over 40 per cent of working women in Austria, Belgium, the Netherlands, Germany, Switzerland and Great Britain work part-time. In Denmark, France and Luxembourg the number is over 30 per cent. On the other hand, in all countries of Central and Eastern Europe women who work part-time constitute less than 15 per cent of all employed women – and in many of these countries less than 10 per cent. If we were to agree that it is important for women to work full-time, since it brings closer the status of men and women, and if we constructed the indicators not on the basis of 'women's employment' but 'women's full-time employment', the comparison would yield very different results. Even this simple example illustrates how important for the entire process is the selection of the indicators. It also draws attention to the fact that the matter is not obvious and settled, particularly if we consider that part-time work may have very different consequences for women in one country than it does in another one. This leads to difficulties in establishing what constitutes best practice, in choosing the indicators and in transplanting a practice from one country to another. A question also appears as to what happens if the indicators established via the OMC are not achieved. The method does not include any means of coercion and uses negative 'naming and shaming' as well as positive 'faming' as sanctions for implementation or non-implementation of certain practices or to praise a drive to achieve certain objectives. However, if the indicators are not well constructed, and countries compete to have their own solutions deemed to be best practice, there is a justified fear that political influence will become decisive in establishing best practice. 'Soft' measures such as naming, shaming and faming are used in the EU rather frequently in practice, including in cases where the Member States are free, for example, to choose a method of implementation of a directive. This occurred, for example in Poland during the discussion on implementation of directives forbidding discrimination in employment for reasons other than gender. The EU officers who were in charge of the pre-implementation conferences visibly preferred, praised, cited and recommended the solutions employed in the countries which had established a single anti-discrimination agency dealing with all types of discrimination. They offered no praise to those who had established separate agencies and mechanisms alongside those already existing for the purpose of combating gender-based discrimination. Although in the opinions of many people such joint agencies might represent a step backwards in the area of gender equality, the officers must have used other criteria of evaluation, because they preferred other solutions and expressed their preference by means of such unofficial but very easy to read instances of 'faming.' In the practical working of the EU such mechanisms are not only used within the OMC but are deployed much more widely and regularly, in a wide range of areas and often in very subtle ways.

Twinning Projects and Mutual Learning

During the EU accession period the countries of Central and Eastern Europe participated in a number of twinning projects. Some of those projects were being realized in the area of gender policy. Twinning projects always consisted of a comparison between the solutions adopted in the various countries participating in the project. This is what makes those experiences worth mentioning in the context of the OMC: comparison between the solutions adopted in the different countries and mutual learning is one of the underlying assumptions of the OMC. For some authors: "The innovative part introduced by the 1997 reform of the enlargement policy in fact originates in the adaptation of a recent method of EU-governance, the open method of coordination (OMC)" (Tulmets 2005: 56), with reference particularly to 'institutional twinnings.' In the years 1998-2002 around 700 twinning projects were approved (Tulmets 2005: 57).

The twinning projects were not based on the assumption of mutual learning. Rather, they were based on the idea of making available to a candidate country a model solution to a problem already functioning in an 'old' member state. In their design, the twinning projects were formed around the idea of the 'old member state teaching the candidate state about the ways and methods employed in the EU. However, many authors find this description to be oversimplified. In fact, the process was much less hierarchical, and it required the candidate countries to express their acceptance of the presented solutions. Moreover, candidate countries themselves chose the areas in which they participated in twinning projects (Tulmets 2005: 57). It is worth noting that the entire project design relied on the hidden assumption that any candidate country can copy and implement a model from any of the 'old' Member States, even though the candidate countries were rooted in different traditions and had differently formed institutions, while the 'old' Member States also had a variety of traditions and solutions to offer.

Two questions arise in this context: the practices of which countries were replicated? Which institutions were though to be best practice? An analysis of the projects (Tulmets 2005) demonstrates that a great majority of the twinning projects were assigned to Germany and France,[3] that is, countries who are the largest financial contributors to the EU. Many of the difficulties that were inherent in the twinning projects are also encountered in the OMC. This is because replicating best practice is one of the most important assumptions in both cases, and in both cases there is the problem of a lack or weakness of indicators which permit a sound evaluation of what constitutes best practice. As the analysis of the twinning projects shows, the candidate countries used various, not necessarily merit-based, criteria when selecting a twinning partner. Estonia, for example, often selected at least one Scandinavian country 'because of growing Scandinavian identity' (Tulmets 2005: 75). Consequently, the process increased the competition among the 'old' Member States, many of whom wanted to make their institutions and their solutions more widely adopted: "in fact, it contributed to increased competition between different national models, without creating harmonization between older Member States' experiences" (Tulmets 2005: 83).

Observations based on participation as an expert in some of the Polish twinning projects in the area of gender equality confirm many comments made by Tulmets (2005) in her article. The candidate countries to which the experts came in order to

3 At the first call for proposals in 1998, Germany won about one third of projects (57 projects from 103), France 40 projects and United Kingdom 23 (Tulmets 2005: 65).

conduct the transfer of best practice had their own institutions, traditions and legal regulations. It was impossible for them to simply copy another country's practice. The projects were often quite a liability for the receiving country, since the imported experts usually had no knowledge on the institutions, traditions and regulations of the target country. In the first stage of the project the foreign experts therefore had to learn about the situation of the target country with the result, in Poland for example, that the Polish expert was essentially a lecturer who informed the foreign visitors of the situation in Poland. During this phase of the project no solutions were being offered which might lead to the improvement of the situation in Poland. Instead, the Polish expert became the 'teacher' with respect to Polish solutions adopted in a given area. Clearly, it was a mutual learning process. The foreign experts not only brought their proposals, but also learned about the methods employed in the candidate countries.

However, due to the inequality between partners embedded in the project, there was no expectation that the models from the candidate countries would be copied, even if they were considered to be in fact better. This situation was not always found acceptable by the receiving candidate countries which had a feeling that it was the foreign experts and not their countries who mostly benefited from the projects. It was, after all, the foreign experts who collected remuneration, travelled and learned, while the benefit to the receiving country was not always immediately clear.

Partially these problems are also to be expected in the application of the OMC. It refers back to the issue of the difficulties with finding indicators well fitted to establishing best practice: different countries use different indicators and different criteria of measuring progress in the area of gender equality. It is often pointed out in the literature that without defining what is understood by gender equality and best practice in the area of gender equality, with no discussion on the issue and no convergence between countries in this area, it is very difficult to employ the OMC (Rubery 2005). Even if common EU objectives have been established, countries differ very much in deciding what leads to equal opportunities or to greater gender equality. Again, this is illustrated by the example of differences between the Netherlands (where women work mostly part-time, which assumes their greater participation in domestic duties) and countries which believe that gender equality is achieved when men and women are involved to the same extent in the work both outside and inside the household. Under these circumstances it was very difficult in the twinning projects to use a model from the 'old' member state in a candidate country undergoing a transformation and facing many problems never encountered in the 'old' EU. Similarly, it will be very difficult to find the best model in the OMC. In the twinning projects, it was the 'old' Member State who decided which solution would be presented as the model. It might be unfitting in the candidate country's situation. It might also differ very much from other models adopted across the EU.

As mentioned earlier, another problem in using the models stems from the lack of stability and continuity in some programmes. This results mostly from political changes, but also from personnel changes. This problem is felt particularly in the new Member States, where the officers who had participated in the twinning projects often left for positions in private companies. The knowledge which they had accumulated brought no benefit to the state institutions but rather helped the officers to achieve higher professional status and benefited the private institutions which they joined. This problem was noticeable not only in the new Member States. Analyses of the twinning projects demonstrated that also the 'old' Member States had to rely on specialists from the private sector, which made many of the projects complicated and expensive (Tulmets 2005).

These experiences from the realization of the twinning projects may be useful in using the OMC, because they draw attention to the shared difficulties of the two frameworks. The traditions, the political and legal system, and the system of institutions already in existence all make it very difficult to transplant a practice from one country to another. It also makes it difficult to predict the consequences of such a transplantation. The new Member States have been party to a lot of such comparisons between solutions of different countries and many evaluations of consequences of replacing old solutions with new, 'imported' ones.

Using other countries' examples and model solutions is of course a well-known and widely used strategy of promoting new solutions. In Poland, experts and NGOs often used the example of legal regulations and practices from other countries when promoting drafts of various legal acts, including the act on the equal status of men and women (Fuszara and Zielińska 1994). Politicians were not always convinced by these examples. Harmonization of law required the country to bring its laws in line with EU legislation, but using examples from particular other countries was not found to be convincing. This is worth remembering since the OMC, just like any soft law solution, requires the political will to do things. It also requires an agreement that certain solutions are worth copying and can be implemented in the practice of other countries. Such agreement is often lacking among politicians whose opinions are often dependent on the political option they represent.

Gender Equality in Programs Using the OMC

This chapter turns now to a slightly different issue: in programmes which are not focused solely on gender policy, but which employ the OMC, is the dimension of gender and gender equality taken into account? It is pointed out in the literature that the OMC may be useful in policy-making, especially in socially sensitive areas such as employment, poverty and social exclusion (De la Porte 2002). In each of these areas the dimension of gender and women's position is essential. This issue is addressed most clearly with reference to employment policy, one of whose four original pillars was the equal opportunity pillar:

The equal opportunity pillar had three guidelines:

- the gender mainstreaming approach. This calls for integrating gender issues transversally into the EEG;
- tackling gender gaps in unemployment rates, ensuring a balanced representation of men and women in all sectors and occupations, taking measures to achieve gender pay equality in both the public and private sectors;

- reconciling work and family life through the design and implementation of family-friendly policies, including affordable, and high-quality care services for children and other dependants, as well as parental and other leave schemes (European Employment Guidelines 2001 for 2002, quoted from C. De la Porte 2002: 48).

Placing gender equality as a necessary dimension in designing solutions in the area of employment has had at least some influence on government documents created in Poland: the situation of women is included in some of the reports produced by the government agencies. For example, the National Report on Strategies for Social Protection and Social Inclusion 2006-2008 (Zabezpieczenie społeczne i integracja społeczna na lata 2006-2008; 2006) includes a section on the situation of women on the labour market. The section describes basic aspects of gender inequality, such as the 12 per cent difference in the level of employment to the advantage of men, higher unemployment among women despite their relatively higher education, and the 17 per cent average pay gap. According to the report:

> The differentiation of the situation of women results mainly from historical and cultural reasons, from a traditional perception of their role in the family and the society at large. For example, in spite of the fact that both of the parents can claim time off in order to care for a newborn, usually it is the women who do so. This is why women can be generally perceived as less interesting candidates for employees. Moreover, certain legal instruments which theoretically have been created in order to protect women on the labour market further lower their attractiveness as employees. Feminist organizations also point to legal aspects which distinguish between the genders, as well as to stereotypes which are still present in school textbooks where they serve to reinforce from the youngest age the traditional perspective, harmful to women. Thus it is not only a labour market problem but rather it is connected with ways of thinking dominant in the society which cannot be expected to change rapidly.

It can be seen as an achievement that government reports of this type include information on the situation of women. This makes it impossible to support the thesis that women are not discriminated against on the labour market, which previously was illustrated with gender-blind statistics and reports.

The question remains whether this in turn leads to introducing changes and methods of achieving equality. It is difficult to give an unambiguous answer. On the one hand, many of the EU programmes, in particular EQUAL, assist in the realization of projects where equality is the aim. Under the influence of the EU Poland has created not only the national mechanism for gender equality but also interdepartamental commissions for gender mainstreaming and other institutions important in the gender equality perspective. However, many programs still do not take this perspective into account. The newest National Development Programme 2007-2013 may serve as an example here. The plan was evaluated in 2006 by experts under the auspices of the Government Plenipotentiary for Equal Status of Men and Women in the perspective of gender equality and the situation of women. The conclusion of the analyses of particular parts of the plan is that the plan only takes into account the gender and women's perspective to a very small extent. However, the critical evaluation of the plan had practically no influence on its final content. It was a critical analysis which resulted in no corrections and was therefore ineffective. In practice, consultations about the plan were held in a very brief period of time, and the minister in charge rushed from one conference to the next where the plan was being evaluated from different perspectives. The minister was present only at the beginning of the conference where the plan was being evaluated in the gender equality perspective. It is difficult to evaluate the influence of the recommendations made there, because an election followed a few months later, resulting in a change of government, including the change of the officer responsible for gender equality and a change in the rank of the appropriate agency. It is worth noting that in the analysis of the plan it was pointed out that it had nothing to say, in legal terms, about gender equality, even though it was produced by a left-wing administration. The plan was not merely analyzed from the gender equality perspective; a number of recommendations were also made, some of which were very detailed. The general recommendations included the following:

- The principle of equal treatment of men and women, according to the EU principle of gender mainstreaming, should be included in the National Development Plan 2007-2013 in a horizontal manner, first of all at the level of values listed in the part devoted to axiology and strategic priorities.
- The diagnosis of the socio-economic situation should be supplemented with an analysis of systemic socio-economic inequalities between men and women.
- Statistical data presented in the National Development Plan 2007-2013 should be supplemented with a division by gender, in order to demonstrate the contribution of women (who constitute more than half of the society) to the process of social, economic and cultural development, and to present their situation in the household, on the labour market and in other areas of public life. This manner of presenting data in official government documents is a requirement of the European Union. Moreover, it is desirable to create budgets which reflect the unpaid labour of women and men in the household.
- The definition of family should be changed so as to be as inclusive as possible and to include various forms of the family, such as single parent families and families in cohabiting relationships.
- Indicators should be established which would make it possible to monitor and evaluate the realization of the National Development Plan 2007-2013 taking into account the social and cultural gender aspects (the so called gender impact assessment method).
- When planning expenditures and allocating means for different purposes, gender budgeting should be employed.
- Representatives of the Polish administration should join the High Level Group for Gender Mainstreaming in the Structural Funds established in May 2004 by the European Commission.
- As far as monitoring and evaluation of the National Development Plan is concerned, indicators should be used which reflect the division into genders. A number of such indicators were suggested.

The experts did not evaluate the Plan highly from a gender perspective. The political change that followed soon after makes it impossible to tell whether the experts' opinion would have otherwise made an impact in the final text. It also makes it impossible to determine whether it was the political change or the fact that a majority of politicians ignores the gender equality issue that lies at the root of the fact that this issue does not constitute an essential element of the Plan.

The search for international programmes in which Poland participates where the OMC is used and where the gender perspective is taken into account brought no optimistic results. It was difficult to find a programme which would satisfy both criteria, that is, both employ the OMC and include the gender perspective. One of the longest-running programmes using the OMC in which Poland participates is the programme on pensions and disability benefits systems, which includes reforms in this area in the countries of Central and Eastern Europe. The programme employs the OMC. Progress reports include comments on indicators and inter-country comparisons. It is pointed out that some countries used other countries' best practices and followed in their footsteps in terms of the systems introduced. However, the reports make no mention of the impact of the solutions that were adopted on the situation of men and women (despite the fact that it is well-known that in the new pension systems gender will be a heavily influential criterion and that for example in Poland under the new system women will in the future receive much lower pensions than men). Were potential solutions compared in this respect? Were some of them more and others less beneficial to women? Unfortunately it seems that the gender impact was not a subject of comparisons and was not included in the criteria used to identify a practice as 'best practice.'

In spite of all these doubts, the OMC may be very promising. It assumes voluntary participation, a willingness to find the best solutions, a desire to harmonize. No one can be forced to participate. Thus, upon the decision to do so, the participating country is aware that it embarks on a joint search for solutions, rather than on a solitary effort to find them. Moreover, the method may be promising also for those who have not joined the process. The group which finds good solutions may serve as a model for those who decided not to participate at first: instead of making efforts to travel the same route, they may simply reach for what appears to be good in the solutions found by others.

References

Arrowsmith, J., Sisson, K. and Marginson, P. (2004), 'What Can "Benchmarking" offer the OMC?', *Journal of European Public Policy* 11(2): 311-328.

Committee on the Elimination of Discrimination against Women Poland (2007), CEDAW, Concluding Comments, Advanced united version.

De la Porte, C. (2002), 'Is the OMC Appropriate for Organizing Activities at European Level in Sensitive Policy Areas?', *European Law Journal* 8(1): 38-58.

Fuszara, M. and Zielińska, E. (1994), 'Progi i bariery czyli o potrzebie ustawy o równym statusie kobiet i mężczyzn' in *Kobiety: Dawne i nowe role. Biuletyn* nr

1/94, (Centrum Europejskie Uniwersytetu Warszawskiego, Ośrodek Informacji i Dokumentacji Rady Europy), pp. 14-24.

Fuszara, M. (2006), Kobiety w polityce, Warszawa, TRIO.

Fuszara, M. (2007a), 'Analiza wyników badań focusowych' w: E. Lisowska (ed.) *Gender Index - narzędzie monitorowania równości kobiet i mężczyzn w miejscu pracy* (Pod UNDP, Warszawa).

Fuszara, M. (2007b), 'Równe traktowanie w procesie rekrutacji' w: E. Lisowska (ed.) *Gender Index - narzędzie monitorowania równości kobiet i mężczyzn w miejscu pracy* (Pod UNDP, Warszawa).

Pochet, P. (2005): 'The Open Method of Co-ordination and the Construction of Social Europe. A Historical Perspective' in: Zeitlin, J. and Pochet, P. (eds) *The Open Method of Coordination in Action* (Brussels: Peter Lang), pp. 1-52.

Radaelli, C. (2003), 'The Open Method of Co-ordination. A New Governance Architecture for the European Union?' Stockholm: SIEPS/Swedish Institute for European Policy Studies.

Rubery, J. (2005), 'Gender Mainstreaming and the OMC. Is the Open Method Too Open for Gender Equality Policy?', in Zeitlin, J. and Pochet, P. (eds) *The Open Method of Coordination in Action* (Brussels: Peter Lang), pp. 391-416.

Tulmets, E. (2005), 'The Introduction of the OMC in the European Enlargement Policy: Analysing the Impact of the New PHARE/Twinning Instrument', *European Political Economy Review* 3(1): 54-90.

"Zabezpieczenie społeczne i integracja społeczna na lata 2006-2008" National Report on Strategies for Social Protection and Social Inclusion. Dokument przyjęty przez Radę Ministrów w dniu 9 października 2006 roku. Aneks 2.4. Ocena systemu monitorowania realizacji działań stworzonego dla Krajowego Planu Działania na rzecz Integracji Społecznej na lata 2004-2006 Ministerstwo Pracy i Polityki Społecznej, Warszawa 2006.

Chapter 7

OMC in the Context of EU Gender Policy from the Point of View of New EU Member States

Kristina Koldinská

When ten new countries joined the European Union (EU) on 1 May 2004, it marked the biggest and also the most significant enlargement in the history of the EU. It was also spoken of as a genuine full stop after the communist era in the countries of Central and Eastern Europe.

Moreover, through its last enlargements (in 2004 and 2007), the EU confirmed its characteristics as an open community of countries that share the same values and all more or less satisfy certain criteria, economic and non-economic. Eight of the ten 2004 entrants have a history of communist rule and membership of the "Soviet bloc" and the same applies to the two latest acceding countries, Romania and Bulgaria. Therefore, when we talk about the new member countries, we particularly have in mind the post-communist countries that currently make up the vast majority of new Member States. What is more, these countries are linked by their present situation as well as their past – they have all had to reform their political and economic systems; and to join the EU they had to adapt their legal order to the requirements of Community law. These new Member States thus represent something of a new phenomenon in the EU and have brought to it many new aspects, in almost all areas, which mainly flow from the legacy that these post-communist countries have to bear.

Social Policy 'Trademarks' of Post-Communist Countries

In social policy, which can be taken to include the issue of gender equality, post-communist countries still display the following aspects of the legacy of their historical development in the second half of the 20th century:

High Female Employment

This phenomenon was partially caused by economic hardship in families. After 1945, and especially during the 1950s, incomes were so low that one was not enough to cover a family's needs. Women thus had to join the work process for economic reasons. This economic necessity was determined, among other things, by the fact that in the post-war period the economy had to be revived and production needed kick-starting. The communist countries responded to the shortage of labour by engaging women in the work process, even women who were caring for small children. State childcare facilities (nurseries and kindergartens) cared for the children while women were at work (J. Bauerová and E. Bártová 1987). The women's work was then ideologically justified by the necessity for equal rights for men and women.

This situation changed dramatically in many post-communist countries in the early 1990s. During the economic transformation, when many state companies were privatized and restructured, it was women, rather than men, who were made redundant first and their employment rate decreased a lot. In the same period, many childcare facilities were closed – first, because of the lack of money (during communist times, those services were financed in almost all aspects by the state),[1] second, because of the decreased birth rate (after 1990 people started to marry and have children much later, as they wanted to use the opportunity to develop their careers before having children) (Rychtaříková 1996; Němec 2007).

Pay Gap

As in western European countries, the new Member States display differences in men's and women's incomes (Fischlová 2002; Plantenga and Remery 2006). These differences are chiefly caused by the fact that women do lower-paid work and also tend to hold rank-and-file positions in the workplace hierarchy.[2] As a rule it is men who hold better paid, management positions, even in 'feminized' sectors such as education and healthcare.

Generous Social Security System

In the 1950s, socialist Central and Eastern European countries adopted the Soviet model of social security, which was very generous, especially to families with children. For example, in the 1970s Czechoslovakia introduced highly generous pro-population measures supporting families with small children and young couples. As

1 According to Eurostat, the female unemployment rate ranged from 3.8% in Ireland to 19.1% in Poland. Only in Estonia, Ireland, Latvia, Sweden and the United Kingdom were the same or a lower proportion of women unemployed than men. The female employment rate varied between 34% in Malta and 71% in Denmark and Sweden. On average, around a third of working women were in part-time jobs, compared to 7% of men. The proportion of women working part-time ranged from less than 5% in Slovakia to more than 75% in the Netherlands. See 'A statistical view on the life of women and men', Eurostat News Release, March 2006.

2 The already cited Eurostat report states that almost a third (32%) of the managers in the EU25 were women: the highest shares were found in Latvia (44%), Lithuania (43%) and Estonia (38%), and the lowest in Cyprus (14%), Malta (15%) and Denmark (23%). The gender pay gap in the EU25 in 2004 was 15%, meaning that women earned 15% less than men. The gap was around 5% in Malta, Portugal and Belgium, and about 25% in Cyprus, Estonia and Slovakia. See 'A statistical view on the life of women and men', Eurostat News Release, March 2006.

a result, there was a baby boom in the 1970s; its negative impacts will be felt by the generation born in the 1970s at the time when they reach retirement age and – it is reasonable to assume – the pension system crisis culminates (Kučera 1994; Bezděk 2005).

Low Flexibility of Workforce, Including Women

Housing always has been and still is a problem in socialist countries. These countries do not possess a sufficiently flexible housing market and consequently their citizens, including women, are not particularly willing to relocate for work, which creates pronounced regional differences in unemployment rates. The level of foreign mobility of labour is much higher than internal mobility in these countries, including the willingness to relocate for work. According to the latest surveys, Slovaks are the most willing to relocate for work of all the new member countries. Most Slovaks relocate to the Czech Republic for work.[3]

'Old' and 'New' Member States: Commonality of Problems within Different Contexts and Traditions

All these aspects of the legacy borne by the new member countries are very familiar to old EU member countries as well. The only difference lies in the origin of these problems and the reasons why they arose and persist. Women's employment is an interesting example in this context. While socialist countries prided themselves on their high women's employment before 1989, at present it is mostly the 'old' member countries to have met or gone beyond the 60 per cent female employment target defined as one of the goals of the Lisbon Strategy. The new Member States lag behind somewhat in this regard, though less so if full account is taken of the high numbers of women working part-time in certain 'old' Member States such as the Netherlands and the UK.[4] According to Eurostat, statistical data from all EU Member States shows that while nine old and just two new EU member countries have reached the 60 per cent mark for women's employment, ten new and just six old member countries are below this boundary.[5] Whereas women's employment was considered an important ideological component of the former socialist countries, the increase in women's employment in old Member States was caused by – besides emancipation – economic necessity as well: as a rule, one income is no longer enough to support a family in these countries.

Europe's history in the last 50 years, which divided the continent into countries belonging to the 'capitalist' bloc and countries belonging to the 'socialist' bloc, built

---

3 See Euractiv survey, "Workers' Mobility in the Countries of Central and Eastern Europe", available at <http://www.euractiv.cz/cl/81/2854/Mobilita-pracovniku-v-zemich-stredni-a-vychodni-Evropy>.

4 Available at <http://epp.eurostat.ec.europa.eu/cache/ITY_OFFPUB/KS-QA-08-004/EN/KS-QA-08-004-EN.PDF>.

5 Available at: http://europa.eu.int/comm/employment_social/gender_equality/gender_mainstreaming/activity_reports_en.html.

some differences between the two blocs of countries, including the area of gender equality policies. On the other hand, all European countries share this continent's common and long historical development, thanks to which the differences between these countries are not very pronounced and, if they do exist, can be tackled. Proof of this is the relatively easy implementation of Community law into the legal orders of the new Member States, which was a condition of their accession to the EU.[6] In gender equality, all the directives issued in this area had to be transposed into law.[7]

With some degree of generalization it can be said that all these directives were included into the new Member States' legal orders and the requirements of individual directives were satisfied by transposition into the relevant legislation. Even so, it would be wrong to claim that the new Member States (like the old Member States, in fact) implement gender equality absolutely and that these post-communist countries have done away with all forms of gender-based inequality and discrimination.

The debate on gender policy, therefore, concerns both old and new Member States and the enlarged EU undoubtedly requires new impulses and new approaches to this issue, which is still relevant and in certain aspects highly delicate for European states that pride themselves on their high standard of protection of human rights and human dignity. This chapter looks at the operation of the Open Method of Coordination (OMC) in the new Member States. This approach is justified because, it is purported, hard law alone is unlikely to bring about cultural change in the new Member States, which seems to be the biggest challenge regarding gender equality. The OMC is examined here in more detail, as it might prove a useful supporting approach to gender equality. Whereas the OMC is more politically-based and, it may be argued, more connected with so-called positive duties, the *aquis* implemented into national legislations is based on individual defence claims against discrimination (Fredman 2005). The chapter considers the operation of the OMC in two policy areas, the European Employment Strategy (EES) and the social inclusion policy, in five post-communist states, the Czech Republic, Slovakia, Slovenia, Estonia and Poland, and questions how effective the OMC has been in these states in advancing gender equality.

In the following section some principal features of the OMC are identified and discussed with particular reference to the situation pertaining to post-communist Member States. Section 3 then turns to the five states selected for examination and considers both their preparations before the accession to the EU and their post-accession reports on implementing the policy targets into their policies and measures. The chapter then concludes by returning to the question whether the OMC

6 Even though the legal orders of socialist countries were to some extent modified to correspond to the prevalent ideology of the time, they were still derived from centuries of evolution of the law and respect for human rights. After 1989 therefore it was not necessary to rebuild everything 'from scratch' and entirely re-formulate the fundamental principles of statehood and respect for human rights.

7 Since the 1970s EU Directives have dealt with eliminating the pay gap (including inequalities in incomes from social security systems), access to employment, career advancement etc., protection of certain special categories of employees (pregnant employees, persons on parental leave, reconciling work and family life), and access to goods and services (the latest topic). For a fuller discussion see Chapter 2 of this book.

as a relatively new method of approximation of national policies and measures can be deemed suitable from the point of view of the new Member States in the area of gender equality.

OMC – A New Method for Solving Old Problems

At the start of this century the OMC has been considered to be an effective mode of governance, particularly in the area of employment and, later, in the field of social protection as well – pensions and social inclusion (Aybars 2006; Plantenga 2004). The OMC has been assessed as successful when getting Member States to reflect in a common and systematic manner, stimulating a consultative process at Member State level on pension and social inclusion strategies with the social partners and non governmental organizations and also when stimulating a focus on gender issues (Advisory Committee on Equal Opportunities for Women and Men 2005).

The OMC has been applied to those social policy areas which in the last decade have become crucial and problematic for the entire European Community. In particular, employment policy was the first area in which the OMC was implemented as individual Member States were having difficulty finding effective instruments to combat the high levels of employment which stalled economic growth and thus hindered the attainment of the goal set by the EU – to become the most dynamic and competitive economy in the world. Although the Amsterdam Treaty inserted an employment chapter (Title VIII) into the EC Treaty, the provisions included have not provided a legal basis for the adoption of 'hard' measures such as Directives or Regulations as the focus is on the coordination of employment policies.

In subsequent years, the OMC was also implemented in another social policy area closely linked to employment policy, that is, the fight against social exclusion, an issue that has become highly pressing for Europe. This was mainly brought about by the fact that a growing number of socially excluded persons would be a highly alarming social development in the EU which has one of the highest standards of social protection in the world.

OMC has also been extended more recently to two further areas: pensions and healthcare (see Chapter 2), which pose similar challenges for the EU. Pensions and pension reform designed to ensure financial sustainability are another important topic, particularly from an economic point of view, which is gaining in importance as the European population gradually ages. This is also linked to the latest domain that has become a subject of the OMC, that is, healthcare and long-term healthcare. As the population gradually ages, there are changes in healthcare needs and in the requirements for individual medical services in healthcare, with a particularly marked increase in the demand for long-term nursing care for patients with chronic illnesses. In both these areas there are important gender issues to be addressed; however, for reasons of space they are not considered further here.

All the domains in which the OMC has been employed to date are areas in which the European Community does not have sufficient powers under the Treaties to tackle these problems by means of its own legislation; on the other hand, these are highly pressing problems that need to be addressed – that is something that the

Member States all agree on. For that reason the use of the OMC seemed to be a relatively good solution. From the point of view of the new Member States it seems that the OMC may serve as a complement to national law and to national social policy, which can thus to some extent be guided towards essentially common goals.

However, in all the areas in which the OMC has been implemented it has been conceived without taking into consideration the new Member States. Hence, certain specific features of these countries cannot be readily accommodated by existing OMC processes (Cf. De La Rosa 2005). Having said this, the OMC may be a valuable mode of governance for the new Member States whose policies rest on different traditions and who went through a different history during the second half of the twentieth century. In this regard, the softness and relative flexibility of the OMC could be of particular benefit to new Member States. Moreover, each new Member State followed its own path when reforming its policies and social security system in the aftermath of communism.[8] Therefore, all the new Member States are now in a unique situation in terms of their employment and social policies. From this point of view, the possibility provided by the OMC to issue country specific guidelines and use different instruments to achieve common targets seems to offer welcome recognition of the diversity even between new Member States.

The OMC also has potential pitfalls due to its non binding nature. Being a soft instrument it may be practically unenforceable and some countries may not consider it important to reflect the targets and guidelines in their national policies and measures and simply consider it as a window dressing exercise. However, thus far it seems that most Member States including the new ones have made serious efforts to implement the targets and guidelines into their national systems.

From the point of view of gender, OMC seems to be a promising method for new Member States. For them, there is a long way to go to achieve equality and equal treatment within society. It requires more than simply the implementation of relevant EC directives to bring about a real change of the situation in new Member States' societies. For example, there are deeply rooted gender stereotypes to be eradicated from the common way of thinking of both men and women which cannot be done merely through the introduction of legal acts. A well thought out measure which reacts on a real situation in a concrete society, may be much more successful than any type of law or legal instrument. That is because inequality is not simply the product of unequal legal treatment but rather stems from deeper societal attitudes, expectations and practices. OMC could help in this regard especially through promoting the exchange of good practices and through focusing on gender issues as such e.g. by using benchmarking methods.

As regards gender equality, there are also some established limitations to Community equality law (Beveridge 2007). In addition Beveridge argues that 'a major criticism of the 2004 accession was that 'readiness' was conceived to involve gender only or primarily in respect of the equal opportunities *acquis*, rather than as a

8 Many post-communist countries were helped especially during the first years of transition by international funding and expertise coming from e.g. World Bank, EU etc. The EU funded many projects aimed at helping the transition in post-communist countries, including the future Member States of the EU.

cross-cutting issue running through all areas of preparation' (Beveridge 2008). This may support the argument on the utility of having other instruments besides hard law provisions to promote gender equality.

In the new Member States it seems that the legal requirements of EC law in respect of gender equality have been introduced quite easily. However, guaranteeing that gender equality measures are implemented effectively is harder to achieve. There are several reasons for this which are more or less common to all the new Member States. First of all, there are deeply rooted traditions and gender stereotypes which result in low levels of litigation in the area of gender equality and also in the biased attitude of judges and courts.[9] Moreover, the role of gender equality bodies is rather limited in some new Member States, whereas in others such as the Czech Republic they still do not exist. Only in a few states do equality bodies have the power to hear complaints on sex discrimination and provide assistance to victims of discrimination (Estonia, Slovakia, Latvia and Lithuania), although this power is still not used enough.[10]

Many new Member States have adopted a formalistic approach to the whole agenda of gender equality: while they have formally implemented the requirements of EC directives, there will be greater difficulty ensuring that the new measures are implemented and enforced, as will be discussed further below. In addition, the social partners in new Member States, especially trade unions, have lost most of their powers since 1989 (prior to this, private employers in fact did not exist and trade unions played a role as an 'alternative state organization'). Currently, they are not focusing on gender equality matters as their primary concern is to develop a significant role in the legislative process and build an effective representation of their basic collective interests. A persisting problem is that adapting legislation is not enough to prevent equality being violated and to ensure that men and women are genuinely treated equally. For true gender equality to be achieved there has to be a change in the social climate and the behaviour of individual actors in society has to adapt to the spirit of the gender equality policy promoted by the EU.

Bearing the above mentioned pros and cons of the OMC in mind and reflecting on the fact that the implementation of the Community directives appears to have had relatively little impact on the actual situation of women and men in the EU, the question which arises is whether the adoption of the OMC has the potential to resolve at least some of the persisting problems. Could the OMC be more effective in this context than the equality *acquis* or serve as a useful complementary tool, and could it be used to initiate at least some positive changes in the behaviour of society as regards gender equality? There is currently no special OMC on gender equality although gender features prominently in some existing OMC mechanisms, for example employment policy and social inclusion, and is inherent in others such as pensions. These areas, therefore, present an opportunity to analyse the experiences

9 See some recent decisions of the Czech and Slovak courts, commented on by Havelkova (2007).

10 See Report on Gender Equality Bodies by the Network of legal experts on the application of Community law on equal treatment between women and men, 2004.

of new Member States of the OMC and to examine its potential to improve gender equality within these states.

The next section will examine the employment policy and social inclusion policy measures adopted through the OMC guidelines in five selected new Member States. The aim is to understand better the impact of the OMC in some of the new Member States and identify possible positives and negatives of this method used in the areas of employment policy and social inclusion policy in new Member States.

OMC and Selected New Member States – Employment Policy and Social Inclusion from a Gender Perspective

In this section the focus is on employment and social inclusion which are well-established areas of the OMC and may be considered to be particularly important for gender equality. The development and evolution of OMC in these areas is covered elsewhere in this volume and will not be discussed in detail in this chapter and the main documents produced in the context of these two OMC processes are only mentioned in so far as they have a bearing on the issue of gender equality.

For the purposes of this chapter, the following new Member States have been selected: the Czech Republic, Slovakia, Slovenia, Estonia and Poland. The Czech Republic and Slovakia have been chosen because of their proximity and common recent history which has shaped their respective different paths taken in the post-communist years.[11] Slovenia seems to be a country which in recent years has been quite pro-active towards gender equality. Estonia is one of the Baltic countries and is an exemplar of a country with historically high levels of female employment and high representation of women in academic careers and management, whereas, Poland represents a 'conservative' country which considers gender equality as an important challenge.

The area of employment policy was introduced into the EC Treaty in 1997, utilizing a range of 'soft' tools. It was from this process that the OMC emerged and was subsequently endorsed by the 2000 Lisbon Strategy. Under this approach, all Member States regularly prepare their own National plans, following guidelines adopted by the Council. During the accession process, the new Member States started to follow the guidelines of the European Employment Strategy (EES) and in 1999 the Commission initiated a co-operation process on employment with the candidate countries. The objective of the Commission was to ensure that candidate countries defined employment policies that would help to prepare them for membership of the Union and that they progressively adjusted their institutions and policies to the EES to allow the full implementation of the Employment Title of the Treaty as from accession. It was agreed that as a first step candidate countries and the Commission would analyze the key challenges for employment policies in Joint Assessments Papers ('JAPs'). The first JAPs were signed with the Czech Republic, Slovenia, Poland and Estonia in 2000 and early 2001, followed by Malta, Hungary, Slovakia,

11 The Czech Republic and Slovakia, formerly constituent parts of Czechoslovakia, became independent states on 1 January 1993 after splitting the common federation.

Cyprus and Lithuania in late 2001/early 2002 and by Romania, Bulgaria and Latvia in Autumn 2002.

The JAPs helped to identify the main problems of candidate countries and the Commission translated them into areas of action. One of these policy areas was the promotion of gender equality due to the high level of discrimination on grounds of sex prevailing in most of these countries. In its Communication on the progress made by candidate countries on the implementation of the JAPs on employment policies (European Commission 2003) the Commission emphasized that almost all candidate countries had strongly gender-segregated labour markets with substantial gender pay gaps. With regard to childcare, it was stressed that in many of these countries affordable childcare facilities had disappeared and that their re-instatement was needed in order to promote the reconciliation of family and working life (European Commission 2003). The new Member States were encouraged to work on the above mentioned areas and pursuant to the 2003 guidelines all the then new Member States prepared their first National Action Plans (NAPs) by October 2004, within six months of accession.

It should be noted, however, that these new guidelines were already attracting a lot of criticisms due to the 'demotion' of gender equality from one of the four pillars of the whole EES to just one of ten guidelines (Rubery 2003; Rubery, Grimshaw, Fagan, Figueiredo, Smith 2003). Shortly after these first reports were prepared by the new Member States, the Commission made a proposal in February 2005 for a revamp of the Lisbon strategy to focus on delivering stronger, lasting growth and more and better jobs. As a consequence, the EES has been completely revised and from 2005 to 2008 the guidelines are presented in conjunction with the macroeconomic and microeconomic guidelines. New integrated guidelines are the basis for National Reform Programmes for Growth and Jobs (NRPs) which are being adopted every year by the Member States. In the 2005 guidelines (Council of the European Union 2005) equal opportunities is referred to only as a general principle: "Equal opportunities and combating discrimination are essential for progress. Gender mainstreaming and the promotion of gender equality should be ensured in all action taken."

Thus it can be seen that in the three years since their accession the new Member States have witnessed significant changes in the EES to which they have had to adapt. Initially, during the accession process they had to adopt measures pursuant to a certain concept of the EES which was then subject to change. Such a situation has been particularly challenging for the administrations of the new Member States which not only had to adapt to the new context of membership and to the idea of EES as such but also to its process of reform.

Selected New Member States and their Employment Policy: Gender Aspects

Member States submitted their NRPs in October 2005 and in autumn 2006 their first reports on implementing National Reform plans were published.[12] It is quite difficult

12 All reports of Member States are available at: <http://ec.europa.eu/growthandjobs/key/nrp2006_en.htm>.

to compare and analyze the national reports of the new Member States as not all of them have followed the proposed scheme of the plan and of the annual report. Significant differences in form and substance between individual reports may be observed, including differences in their level of reporting.

The country reports from the selected Member States tackle gender equality from two perspectives:

- Reconciliation of family and working life
- Support of women´s employment

Reconciliation of Family and Working Life

The majority of selected countries stressed the adoption of family support measures and harmonizing family and working life in their reports.

The Czech Republic adopted the Action Plan for Support of Families with Children 2006-2009. The program aims at providing more effective financial assistance in maternity and parenthood which is part of the social security system, effective support of different types of families by means of the tax system, changing the opening hours of kindergartens to adjust to the needs of working parents and encouraging employers to operate kindergartens and nurseries at workplaces, train their employees on parental leave and use more flexible forms of employment.[13]

In 2006, the conditions for claiming parental allowance were redefined more in favour of working parents. Children over three years,[14] who are in the personal, all-day and due care of their parent, may attend kindergarten or a similar childcare facility every day for up to four hours, without their parents losing their entitlement to parental allowance. Parental allowance is not a means tested benefit and parents are allowed to work and organize childcare provided by any other adult person, without losing their entitlement to the allowance. Under a new Sickness Insurance Act,[15] fathers taking care of a newborn child will be entitled to draw a so-called 'maternity cash assistance' (70 per cent of daily assessment basis) from the seventh week of their child's life. This could help to increase fathers' participation in childcare.

In Poland unemployed single parents with at least one child younger than 7 years of age may be reimbursed the cost of care provided for such a child. Another benefit is the availability of pre-school education of good quality and at a moderate price. One of the operational goals of the Government's draft programme for supporting education in rural areas is the promotion of pre-school education. The possibility of providing periodical childcare for persons who wish to enhance or change their qualifications is a planned task of the Government's draft "Programme for the Growth and Education of Small Children". The draft also provides for, *inter alia*, supporting families, in particular mothers, in resolving problems related to the upbringing

13 The Czech report 2006 on implementation of national reform program is available at: <http://ec.europa.eu/growthandjobs/pdf/nrp/CZ_nrp_en.pdf>.

14 Parental leave in the Czech Republic is until 3 years of age of a child, whereas parents are eligible for parental allowance until their child is 4 years of age.

15 It is not yet clear when the Act will enter into force – probably in January 2009.

of children, so that they can better combine their professional and private lives. Currently, some projects funded from the ESF are being implemented, regarding the reconciliation of women's social and professional roles, partnership in families and the promotion of labour law anti-discrimination regulations. These projects take the form of information and education campaigns targeting also women who are returning to the labour market after a longer absence, for example, after maternity and/or parental leave.[16]

In Slovenia, in the area of reconciliation of family and working life, the title 'Family-friendly company' shall be conferred on the International Day of the Family starting in 2007 to those companies which meet broad criteria in creating optimal conditions that will allow their employees to reconcile their everyday professional and family obligations. In 2006 an action-programme called 'daddy, get active!' was launched in order to implement awareness-raising campaigns to fight against discrimination in the labour market and, in particular, to promote a more active role of men in family life, to combat stereotypes and cultural obstacles that determine the roles of men and women in family and society.[17]

In Slovakia a document entitled 'Draft Measures to Harmonize Professional and Family Life for 2006 with an Outlook to 2010' has been passed. Its main objective is primarily to support employment and employability of persons with responsibility for family and to reduce the risk that they are exposed to the dilemma 'work versus family' and, at the same time, to increase the support for services to families so that the support has a positive effect on the demographic situation. In the course of 2007 – 2008, new legal provisions for services are being prepared, the objective being to create conditions for provision of services to families, to ensure availability of services for all who need them; equal rights to the providers; equitable remuneration to those performing such services; creation of new jobs for the intermediate labour market and community work.

The elimination of gender stereotypes has been improved through the adoption of projects aimed at the removal of barriers to equality of men and women in the labour market. Moreover, measures aimed at stimulating and increasing the quality of education to meet employers' and the business sector's needs, also provided for the care of minor children during parents' education. Other projects aimed at gender research and gender audit as a means of achieving equality of women and men in the labour market with the objective of gender sensitization of various actors involved (employers, unions, state administration and territorial self-government, education system) and supporting gender-sensitive education.[18]

In addition, non-governmental organizations (NGOs) through the means of subsidies have played an important role in the reconciliation of professional and family life. For example, so-called 'maternity centres' are managed by non-

16 Country report for Poland is available at: <http://ec.europa.eu/growthandjobs/pdf/nrp/PL_nrp_en.pdf>.

17 Country report for Slovenia is available at: <http://ec.europa.eu/growthandjobs/pdf/nrp/SL_nrp_en.pdf>.

18 Country report for Slovakia is available at: <http://ec.europa.eu/growthandjobs/pdf/nrp/SK_nrp_en.pdf>.

governmental not-for-profit organizations founded by parents, mostly by women on maternity leave, for the purpose of self-provision of services to families with minor children in the territory of a municipality in accordance with the state's family policy.

Estonia does not seem to report anything significant on promoting the reconciliation of family and working life. In the report from this country, only the EQUAL funding programme and its implementation is mentioned with a number of given projects funded by EQUAL.[19]

Support of Women's Employment

In comparison to the prominence given to the reconciliation of family and working life, the support of women's employment is not mentioned very much in the national reports. Moreover, when mentioning women´s employment and its support the national reports often refer to the employment of women/mothers and parents.

In Poland, professional integration and re-integration of women is a task under the strategic action entitled 'Activation of persons particularly disadvantaged on the labour market.' The aim is to provide comprehensive assistance to women in the labour market, leading to a higher employment rate for women and the improvement of their professional and social status. This entails, for example, the promotion of flexible forms of employment to facilitate the combination of professional and private lives.

In Slovenia, under the goal of implementing special programmes to promote the careers of women it is stated that: 'Equal opportunities will be created with an array of measures for the removal of obstacles that prevent men and women from playing an equal role in public and private life. The ultimate goal of the equal opportunities policy is gender equality – the equal recognition, power and participation of women and men in all spheres of public and private life.' In 2005 Slovenia adopted a policy document called 'Assistance in the self-employment of long-term unemployed women'. Also among its priorities are: the analysis and research of gender-based discrimination in employment and work and raising awareness about prevention mechanisms; the implementation of special programmes for promoting the employment and work activity of women in the framework of active employment policy measures; and the implementation of special programmes for promoting self-employment of women and for female entrepreneurship.

Some Aspects Deriving from the Selected National Reports

As already mentioned above, it has not been an easy task to analyze the national reports on implementing the new Lisbon Strategy Guidelines and cross-country comparisons have been difficult to make due to strong differences between the

19 The Estonian report argues also that "a remarkable fact is that in the field of natural sciences and technology in Estonia the share of women is the highest in Europe (42.5% as opposed to 31.1% in Europe). See <http://ec.europa.eu/growthandjobs/pdf/nrp/ET_nrp_en.pdf>.

countries under analysis. However, some common aspects of the five reports may be identified.

All the reports pay particular attention to the reconciliation of family and working life. Each of the states analyzed (with the exception of Estonia) is trying to contribute to this important aspect of gender equality. The national reports mention three types of instruments to reach this objective:

- Legislative measures – the Czech Republic, Slovakia and Poland report on legislative measures aimed at supporting the combining of family and working life – through benefits, childcare cost reimbursements, and protective measures in labour legislation.
- Incentives in policy measures, especially in governmental programs – the Czech Republic and Poland try to motivate employers, kindergarten and nursery managers, and the social partners.
- Special projects aimed at responding to country specific needs (often funded by EU projects) – all 5 countries mention these projects, aimed at a wide spectrum of specific needs. These projects are often realized by NGOs.

Some positive and some negative observations can be made following this study of 5 national reports. One very positive initiative mentioned by Slovakia is a focus on eradicating gender stereotypes. Even before the accession this was one of the main problems of acceding countries (see above), but only Slovakia mentions this as one of its priorities when promoting gender equality.

It is also noteworthy that all 5 new Member States examined stress the reconciliation of family and working life. This is very positive because many other consequences flow from difficulties women (and men) face in this area, such as segregation of the labour market, lower rates of accession by women to employment and sometimes even discriminatory behaviour of employers towards women of reproductive age.

On the other hand and on the negative front, Poland in its report includes women and promoting their employment under the title 'persons particularly disadvantaged in the labour market'. Different instruments should be used for promoting employment of women and employment of socially excluded, disabled, elderly etc. Women represent half (in some states more than half) of the labour force and therefore it is not very wise to define women as 'persons particularly disadvantaged in the labour market'.

It is also interesting to note that in the Commission's assessments of the annual reports of the Member States,[20] there was hardly any reference made to gender equality. Instead, most of the recommendations were of a general economic nature. Despite its fairly high profile in the Employment Strategy, gender did not seem to be regarded as an important issue. The Commission divided new Member States into those which are making 'very good' or 'good' progress, those that are 'making progress' and those which are making just 'limited progress.'[21] When assessing developments in

20 See <http://ec.europa.eu/growthandjobs/pdf/1206_annual_report_legal_basis_en.pdf>.

21 See <http://ec.europa.eu/growthandjobs/pdf/1206_annual_report_legal_basis_en.pdf>.

the Member States, the Commission refers more to general evaluations, stressing, for example, the combination of economic growth instruments and employment policy instruments. Gender equality is just mentioned twice in the Commission's most recent assessment of developments in the new Member States discussed in this chapter.

With regard to specific recommendations, Slovakia was defined as a country 'making progress' and it was recommended that it should further focus on addressing the gender pay gap. The Czech Republic and Poland were among the countries defined by the Commission as making just 'limited progress.' The Commission recommended the Czech Republic to modernize its labour market, to focus on the reconciliation of work and family life and to tackle the gender pay gap.

Selected New Member States and their Social Exclusion Policy: Gender Aspects

The social inclusion policy of the EU went through a similar development process to the EES. Global objectives were adopted by the European Council in Nice – promoting access to employment and resources, preventing risks, acting to protect the most vulnerable as well as mobilizing all actors – and monitoring indicators were agreed upon at the Laeken European Summit (European Council 2001). The first National Action Plans were submitted in June 2001.

In 2005 the European Commission issued a communication which was presented as a common program for social inclusion proposing a streamlined OMC on social protection and social inclusion (European Commission 2005). A close interaction was required between the social protection and social inclusion OMCs with a focus on providing a high level of social protection and social cohesion and policies for employment and growth. The objective of guaranteeing 'access to all to the basic resources, rights and social services needed for participation in society, while addressing extreme forms of exclusion and fighting all forms of discrimination leading to exclusion' was mentioned among the objectives with the aim of poverty eradication and social exclusion (European Commission 2005: para. 2.2.1.). According to the Commission's Communication, there were three overarching challenges of which one is to 'promote social cohesion and equal opportunities for all through adequate, accessible, financially sustainable, adaptable and efficient social protection systems and social inclusion policies.' Prior to the establishment of these objectives the Commission had already established a cooperation process with accession countries which led to the signature of a number of Joint Memoranda on Social Inclusion (JIMs) at the end of 2003. These JIMs foreshadowed the National Action Plans on social inclusion, which were submitted at the beginning of 2005.

As regards gender equality and gender mainstreaming which were envisaged as an important element of social inclusion, in the summary of all the JIMs it is reported that

> only a few countries have incorporated a gender mainstreaming strategy into their respective development plans or strategies (Cyprus, Estonia, Latvia) to be used as the tool for the integration of women's issues into all government policies. Others have integrated

> the gender dimension in a number of employment and social programs and are planning to oblige all central administration bodies to implement gender mainstreaming principles in all sector policies in their respective future NAPs (Lithuania and the Czech Republic). Finally, in other new Member States the elaboration of the JIMs increased awareness on this issue and gave further political impulse to the existing policies on women's access to the labour market and in general on equal opportunities for women and men (Hungary, Malta, Poland, Slovakia and Slovenia).[22]

The Commission added that the new Member States, in order to promote gender mainstreaming, will need to create a context combining legal provisions, political will and the formulation of clear goals, build a capacity including training and expertise all along the process and establish adequate institutional mechanisms, keeping in mind that the ultimate institutional mechanisms are new ways of working, planning and implementing policies.[23]

National Inclusion Reports

As of 2005, the new Member States started to produce National Reports on Strategies for Social Protection and Social Inclusion, so there is currently just one set of these reports from the 5 new Member States examined in this chapter.[24] Not all of these countries mention the gender aspect of the national social inclusion policy.

In the Czech national report[25] it is stated that the method of gender mainstreaming was used as a tool for enforcing the policy of equal opportunities. In the report, women are mentioned among disadvantaged persons in the labour market because of the discriminatory behaviour of employers and prejudices concerning age, motherhood and family duties. Reintegration into the labour market after maternity leave and parental leave is difficult and modern forms of work organization are not yet widely used. With regard to the harmonization of family and working life which is mentioned in the National Inclusion Report, it is stated that the unattractiveness of part-time work and low level of use of other forms of work reduces the possibility for parents to keep in contact with their professions which makes the return to employment more difficult. Another problem seems to be the practical non-existence of affordable and available childcare services for children up to the age of three. Such care is provided by a network of nursery schools which are widely used, but greater adaptation of these services to the needs of families with children would assist a greater reconciliation of professional and family roles. On the other hand,

22 See Summary of Joint Inclusion Memoranda: Commission Staff Working Paper Social inclusion in the new Member States – a synthesis report of the joint memoranda on social inclusion, SEC (2004)848, available at: <http://ec.europa.eu/employment_social/social_inclusion/docs/sec_04_848_en.pdf>.

23 ibid.

24 All National Reports on Strategies for Social Protection and Social Inclusion for 2007 are available at: <http://ec.europa.eu/employment_social/social_inclusion/naps_en.htm>.

25 National Report on Strategies for Social Protection and Social Inclusion for 2006-2008 Czech Republic available at: <http://ec.europa.eu/employment_social/social_inclusion/docs/2006/nap/czech_en.pdf>.

after-school care centres and clubs for younger schoolchildren are very widespread and used.

In the Estonian national report [26] there is just a small paragraph regarding equality between men and women. It is stated in general terms that special measures intended for women or men and the strategy of mainstreaming are applied and administrative capacity will be increased through exchange of information, training for target groups and preparation guidelines. Lack of day care and nursing services is reported as one of the substantial reasons for the absence of working age people from the labour market. Moreover, poverty is reported to be more likely to occur in female-headed households. Women are predominantly in low paid jobs given the gender-based segregation of jobs in the labour market and the difference in women´s and men´s wages. The Estonian report also identifies, as a priority for 2006-2008, the prevention and alleviation of poverty and social exclusion of families with children.

In the Polish report[27] women's lower economic activity rates and the gender pay gap are mentioned as major obstacles to equality between men and women. It is also reported that the differentiation of women results to a great degree from historical and cultural determinants and the traditional idea of their role in the family and society. Moreover, some legal solutions, in theory aimed at protecting women on the labour market, reduce their attractiveness as employees. Consequently, as the Polish report suggests this is not just a problem of the labour market but is related to traditional way of thinking embedded in society and rapid change therefore cannot be expected to happen.

The Slovenian report[28] is the only document among those examined which enumerates a list of concrete measures that have been adopted such as the setting up of a Council for the Implementation of the Principle of Equal Treatment and the involvement of the social partners and NGOs in the formulation of solutions and proposals on equal treatment. In addition, a Resolution on a National Programme for Equal Opportunities for Women and Men for 2005-2013 has been adopted and the Slovak Government issued the periodical plan for its implementation. Moreover, several calls for tender have been published by the Office for Equal Opportunities in order to support the activities of NGOs.

The Slovak report[29] only mentions gender equality or gender mainstreaming in its annex and includes projects designed for the elimination of obstacles to equality between men and women with an emphasis on reconciliation of work and family life. The activities relating to this measure involved 5381 persons, 506 employers creating family-friendly jobs and 233 employers participating in the programmes of family-friendly policies and the policies for equal opportunities in the workplace. Five projects on the monitoring or research on equal opportunities between women

26 National report from Estonia is available at: <http://ec.europa.eu/employment_social/social_inclusion/docs/2006/nap/estonia_en.pdf>.

27 See the National report <http://ec.europa.eu/employment_social/social_inclusion/docs/2006/nap/poland_en.pdf>.

28 Available at: <http://ec.europa.eu/employment_social/social_inclusion/docs/2006/nap/slovenia_en.pdf>.

29 ibid.

and men in the labour market are underway. The Slovak report also refers to legislative changes in parental allowance. The new legislation unified the amount of parental allowance for the parent who, personally and properly, takes care of his/her own child and for the parent involved in gainful employment. This could create opportunities for the rise of more flexible childcare services and positively influence the options open to the parents in making provision for qualified childcare, while facilitating training and participation of the parent in the labour market. In order to strengthen family-friendly policies, the Slovak Government adopted a document entitled 'A proposal for measures to reconcile work and family life for the year 2006 with an outlook by the year 2010.' The main objective is to increase employability and employment of persons with family obligations, while reducing the risk of individuals being subject to discrimination in the labour market owing to their family care obligations. The measures should contribute to the elimination of the work versus family dilemma.

Some Aspects Deriving from the National Reports

When reading the national reports on social inclusion, some similarities with the EES national reports as well as differences and even discrepancies can be identified. In general, it seems that the structure of the social inclusion reports is clearer in comparison to that of the reports on employment policy. Member States have used a common structure when reporting on social inclusion policy and there is more concrete data and information in the reports on social inclusion policies.

In many cases, the reports merely state what the current situation is without mentioning concrete measures which have been adopted or concrete actions which have been taken. Moreover some of the reports refer to changes in measures which do not seem to advance the objectives in question and/or do not appear to introduce any change whatsoever.[30] In some cases, the social inclusion national reports seem to diverge and to some extent contradict the national reports on employment policy. For instance, the Czech EES report provides some examples of measures aimed at reconciliation of family and working life while in the report on social inclusion it is said that reconciling family and working life is very difficult in the Czech Republic because of the lack of measures in favour of this.

In addition, some overlaps and discrepancies between the two sets of reports can be observed. There are some states which report the same information twice in both national reports whereas other states include a particular topic only in one report and omit to mention it in the other report. For example, the Slovakian government only included measures on parental allowance in the national report on social inclusion whereas the Czech Republic has included its information on that type of benefit in its national report on employment policy.

30 The Czech Republic is illustrative. The changes regarding parental allowance mentioned in the report will not necessarily contribute to the reconciling of family and working life, especially if not accompannied by other measures: in the Czech Republic 98% of parents claiming this benefit are women who usually spend the whole period of three years of parental leave staying at home with children.

The above mentioned problems could be caused either by a lack of clarity of the OMC guidelines and targets or by a lack of competence on the part of the Member States in relation to the reporting process. While the latter may play a part it seems that these problems are not confined to the new Member States and that the old Member States share similar problems. This seems to suggest that the problem lies in the definition of objectives in the OMC documents which at times are too vague or broad and thus lack clarity.

OMC – an Appropriate Method for Gender Equality from the Perspective of the New Member States?

From the information provided in this chapter several conclusions may be drawn. Gender equality remains one of the most challenging objectives to achieve for the whole EU. New Member States are facing similar problems to the old ones although some of the problems are more intensified.

While EC law and national legislation on gender equality have an important role in promoting gender equality, without the adoption of measures aimed at cultural and ideological change they are insufficient to bring about major social change. It is necessary therefore to adopt some additional instruments in order to make further positive steps towards real gender equality in European societies. In this context, OMC processes seem to provide a good opportunity for the new Member States to identify more effective policy measures to those required to implement the *acquis communitaire*, for example, through benchmarking and exchange of good practices. However, in the area of gender equality the method of benchmarking is seldom used (the only exception being the target on female employment) and the guidelines regarding gender equality are rather general. One solution could be to define the method of benchmarking regarding gender equality more clearly to improve its effectiveness.

Finally, it should be considered further whether the OMC as a method for promoting gender equality can be effective. From the point of view of the new Member States this question may, it seems, be answered positively. However, a clearer definition of the current policies to be adopted and way of reporting should be developed. The inclusion of the gender aspect into the two OMC policies analyzed has the potential to bring about positive changes in government policies which are central to the pursuit of equality and which shall complement the national legislation adopted in order to implement EC gender equality directives. However, experience to date of national reporting seems to invite further reflection and points to the need for better and stricter evaluation. One possible proposal could be the participation of e.g. social partners in the reporting process (De La Rosa 2005).

Better and more concrete rules for reporting from the Member States could be defined in the future. Gender mainstreaming should run throughout these OMC processes due to the cross-cutting nature of the gender equality issues and their importance to these processes.

Based on the experience of the new Member States discussed in this contribution, it seems that, as regards gender equality, the OMC offers some potential but at the same time should be better coordinated in order to make it an effective instrument of European gender equality policy.

References

Aybars, A.I. (2006), 'Open Method of Coordination, Welfare States and Gender Equality' *University of Ulster*. Ulster, <http://eucenter.wisc.edu/Conferences/WorkWelfareMay06/Idil_Govconf.pdf>.

Advisory Committee on Equal Opportunities for Women and Men (2005), Opinion on the Evaluation of the Open Method of Coordination in Order to Prepare the Streamlining in the field of Social Protection, May 2005, <http://ec.europa.eu/employment_social/gender_equality/docs/2005/opinion_streamlining_en.pdf>.

Armstrong, K.A. (2005), 'The Open Method of Coordination and Fundamental Rights: A Critical Appraisal, Draft Paper for Discussion at the 'Fundamental Rights and Reflexive Governance' Seminar, Columbia Law School, NY, 4th November 2005, <http://eucenter.wisc.edu/OMC/Papers/Rights/armstrong.pdf>.

Bauerová, J. and Bártová, E. (1987), Proměny ženy v rodině, práci a ve veřejném životě *Nakladatelství Svoboda*. Prague.

Beveridge, F. (2007), 'Building Against the Past: the Impact of Mainstreaming on EU Gender Law and Policy' *European Law Review* 32(2): 193-212.

Beveridge, F. (2008), *Gender, the Acquis and Beyond* In: Currie, S. and Dougan, M. (eds.) (Oxford: Hart, forthcoming).

Bezděk et all (2005), Závěrečná zpráva – podklady k duchodové reformě, <http://www.mpsv.cz/cs/2228>.

Council of the European Union (2005), Decision on guidelines for the employment policies of the Member States, 2005/600/EC of 12 July 2005.

Czech Statistical Office (2005), Women and men in data, *Czech Statistical Office*. Prague, <http://www.czso.cz/csu/2005edicniplan.nsf/engp/1416-05>.

De La Rosa, S. (2005), 'The Open Method of Coordination in the New Member States – the Perspectives for its Use as a Tool of Soft Law', *European Law Journal* 11(5): 618-640.

European Commission (2003), Communication from the Commission to the Council, the European Parliament, the European Economic and Social Committee and the Committee of the Regions, of 30 January 2003, entitled 'Progress on the implementation of the Joint Assessment Papers on employment policies in candidate countries' COM (2003) 37, <http://www.europa.eu/scadplus/leg/en/cha/c11912.htm>.

European Commission (2005), Communication from the Commission to the Council, the European Parliament, the European Economic and Social Committee and the Committee of the Regions, *Working Together, Working Better: A New Framework for the Open Coordination of Social Protection and Inclusion Policies in the European Union* COM(2005) 706.

European Commission (2006), Communication from the Commission to the Council, the European Parliament, the European Economic and Social Committee and the

Committee of the Regions, *Road Map for Equality between Women and Men 2006-2010*, COM(2006) 92.

European Council (2001), Laeken Presidency Conclusions, 14 and 15 December 2001.

Eurostat, (2006) 'A Statistical View of the Life of Women and Men in the EU 25', <http:// ec.europa.eu/pis/portal/docs/PAGE/PGP_PRD_CAT_PREREL/PGE_CAT_PREREL_YEAR_2006/PGE_CAT_PREREL_YEAR_2006_MONTH_03/3-06032006-EN-BP1.PDF>.

Fischer, G. and Tholoniat, L. (2006), 'The European Employment Strategy in an Enlarged EU', ZAF No. 1. Kohlhammer-Institut für Arbeitsmarktforschung, Nürnberg.

Fischlová, D. (2002), Analysis of Differences in the Wages of Men and Women, RILSA, Prague.

Fredman, S. (2005), 'Changing the Norm: Positive Duties in Equal Treatment Legislation', *Maastricht Journal of European and Comparative Law* 12: 369-397.

Havelková, B. (2007), 'Burden of Proof and Positive Action in the Czech and Slovak Constitutional Courts – Milestones in Implementing EC Equality Law', *European Law Review* 32(5): 686-704.

Kučera, M. (1994), *Populace české republiky 1918-1991.* Acta demographica XII. ČDS, Praha: Sociologický ústav AV ČR.

Larsen, T.P., Taylor-Gooby, P., Kananen, J. (2005), 'European Policy Coordination and the OMC', University of Kent, <http://www.kent.ac.uk/wramsoc/conferencesandworkshops/conferenceinformation/espanetconference/europeanpolicycoordination.pdf>.

Němec, D. (2007), 'Komparace demografického vývoje Maďarska a Polska v období transformace', Research Center for Competitiveness of Czech Economy, WP No. 5.

Plantenga, J. (2004), 'Investing in Childcare. The Barcelona Childcare Targets and The European Social Model', conference presentation, "Child Care in a Changing World", 21-23 October, Groningen, The Netherlands, <http://www.childcareinachangingworld.nl/downloads/introduction_janneke_plantenga.pdf>.

Plantenga, J. and Remery, C. (2006), *The Gender Pay Gap: Origins and Policy Responses. A Comparative Review of 30 European Countries*, <http://ec.europa.eu/employment_social/publications/2006/ke7606200_en.pdf>.

Rubery, J., Grimshaw, D., Fagan, C., Figueiredo, H., and Smith, M. (2003), 'Gender Equality Still on the European Agenda – But For How Long?', *Industrial Relations Journal* 34(5): 477-497.

Rubery, J., Figueiredo, H., Smith, M., Grimshaw, D., and Fagan C. (2004), 'The Ups and Downs of the European Gender Equality Policy', *Industrial Relations Journal* 35(6): 603-628.

Rubery, J. (2005) 'Gender Mainstreaming and the Open Method of Coordination: Is the Open Method too Open for Gender Equality Policy?' in Zeitlin, J. and Pochet, P. (eds) with Magnusson, L. *The Open Method of Coordination in Action. The European Employment and Social Inclusion Strategies* (Brussels: PIE-Peter Lang).

Rychtaříková, D. (1996), Současné změny charakteru reprodukce v České republice a mezinárodní situace. *Demografie* No. 2. Prague.

Trubek, D. and Trubek, L.G. (2005), 'Hard and Soft Law in the Construction of Social Europe: The Role of the Open Method of Coordination', *European Law Journal* 11(3): 345-364.

Chapter 8

Gender Equality and Mainstreaming in the Re-articulation of Labour Market Policies in Denmark and Italy

Samantha Velluti

This chapter examines whether the European Employment Strategy (EES) may effectively promote gender equality in the context of the re-organization of European labour markets. By adopting a gender audit approach it identifies synergies and conflicts between measures aimed at encouraging the adaptability of businesses and their employees to structural, economic and industrial change and measures aimed at promoting gender equality in the labour market. In particular, the chapter examines the implementation of the EES as a 'New Governance' tool and uses a comparative analysis approach to evaluate how effective it is to implement and enforce social policy measures. The countries selected are Denmark and Italy, representing Scandinavian and Southern European social policy systems.

The chapter seeks to answer the following question: given that gender mainstreaming is considered one of the most important objectives of the EES how have gender and equal opportunities issues been mainstreamed in the modernization of European labour markets at national level? The findings of the study underpin a generalized analysis of the effectiveness of the EES and its impact on macro-economic labour market policies at national level. The study also illuminates the impact of the Open Method of Coordination (OMC) on the constitutional and institutional structures of the Member States and, more generally, on EU social governance. This in turn helps us to understand to what extent the EES is a new mode of policy-making in the social policy field. More specifically, the significance of this chapter lies chiefly in subjecting the theoretical assumptions of how the EES operates (for example, distribution of competence between the EU and the Member States and within the state between thc ccntral government and the regional and local policy-makers) to further critical analysis in order to evaluate the effectiveness of the EES in the wider context of EU social governance.

The chapter also shows that, while the 2003 and 2005 simplification and streamlining of thc EES with the Broad Economic Policy Guidelines has reduced the visibility of the gender equality dimension to the EES, the problems regarding the implementation of gender equality go beyond the governance debate and are linked to the complexities of conceptualizing gender equality. In particular, the legal construct of equality and the social construct of gender are based on different premises: while equality is based on likeness or similarity gender is based on difference (Barbera 1991).

The chapter is structured as follows. Section 1 provides an overview of the reform of the EES with a focus on the changes affecting adaptability and equal opportunities measures. Section 2 focuses on the joint study of adaptability and equal opportunities in order to assess to what extent measures aimed at modernizing European labour markets foster the promotion of equal opportunities between women and men at work through collective bargaining and, more broadly, the involvement of the social partners (employer and employee organizations). The EES assigns an important role to the social partners in ensuring good governance of employment policies and in the implementation of the strategy, particularly in promoting 'flexicurity' measures in the context of adaptability. Prior to the reform of the EES and the Lisbon Strategy, the Employment Guidelines assigned the social partners a prominent role across all the then four Pillars of the EES including the Equal Opportunities Pillar (Council of the European Union 2002). The simplification of the Employment Guidelines and their inclusion in the Integrated Guidelines has entailed a decrease in importance of the social partners in the strategy with Member States regaining centre stage in the implementation of the EES (Council of the European Union 2005).

Section 3 provides a comparative study of Denmark and Italy. This analysis allows us to evaluate the effectiveness of the EES and, in particular, to assess how the EES operates in two Member States with different economic and social structures which nevertheless share similar problems. Section 4 brings together the main arguments put forward throughout the chapter and makes some suggestions for strengthening the synergy between adaptability and equal opportunities in the context of the EES.

The Importance of Linking the Modernization of Work Organization to Equal Opportunities Policies

The Ups and Downs of Gender Mainstreaming in the EES

In the first year of implementation of the EES in 1998, the employment coordination process centred around four key areas named 'pillars': employability, entrepreneurship, adaptability and equal opportunities. The 'Equal Opportunities' pillar included policies aimed at fostering gender equality, reducing gender gaps and promoting gender mainstreaming. Four guidelines were formulated referring to tackling gender gaps, reconciling work and family life, facilitating the return to work and promoting the integration of people with disabilities into working life (Rubery et al 2003). In 1999, at the end of this first cycle, a mainstreaming approach to equal opportunities was adopted for the fourth Pillar, with the aim of strengthening the integration of equal opportunities issues into the employment framework and reducing gender pay gaps.

Subsequently, the employment guidelines under the fourth equal opportunities pillar were developed on the basis of four principles (EGGSIE 2007). The first referred to the need to adopt a gender mainstreaming approach. The guidelines included promotion of equal access to active labour market policies among women and men in unemployment, assessment of the gender impact of tax and benefit systems and application of the principle of equal pay for work of equal value. The second principle required Member States to tackle gender gaps. Guidelines included the reduction of the unemployment gap through supporting female employment growth (possibly in line with a national target), action to reduce sex segregation, initiatives to diminish the gender differential in income and measures to further women's advancement in employment. The third principle required Member States to encourage the reconciliation of work and family life. The fourth principle referred to facilitating reintegration into the labour market.[1]

At the Lisbon Summit, the European Council re-emphasized the importance of the gender dimension to employment: 'Member States should strengthen their efforts to include and make visible a gender perspective across all the pillars' (European Council 2000) and quantitative targets for higher employment rates were agreed: 70 per cent for all in employment and 60 per cent for women, to be reached by the year 2010. In 2001, the Stockholm European Council added other quantitative targets: intermediate targets of 67 per cent (total) in employment and 57 per cent (for women) by the year 2005 and an additional employment target of 50 per cent for older men and women (55-65 years old) by 2010 (European Council 2001).

Following the 2002 Barcelona Spring European Council, which called for a strengthening of the EES (European Council 2002), the Commission issued a series of Communications. In the Communication *Taking Stock of Five Years of the European Employment Strategy* (European Commission 2002) the Commission reviewed the experience of five years of the EES and broadly outlined a re-design of the EES for the future. The most significant change introduced was a streamlining of the European Employment Strategy with other key policy coordination processes including the broader economic policy guidelines and the internal market strategy (European Commission 2002a) and the adoption of three overarching and interrelated objectives: full employment, quality and productivity at work and social cohesion and inclusion and the disappearance of the four pillars. Moreover, the guidelines were simplified and reduced to ten (Council of the European Union 2003). Employment Guideline 6 referred to gender equality and emphasized, again, the integrated approach of combining gender mainstreaming and specific policy actions. This approach should focus on the reduction of gender gaps (chiefly gender pay gap) and reconciling work and family life. Moreover, it included the goals that by 2010 Member States should provide childcare to at least 90 per cent of children between three years old and the mandatory school age and at least 33 per cent of children under three years of age. This review was followed by another major revision of the EES and in 2005 the Brussels Spring European Council adopted Integrated Guidelines for Growth and Jobs for the period of 2005-2008. Reduced from ten to eight, the Employment Guidelines are now part of a package of 24 guidelines of the Lisbon Strategy (corresponding to Integrated Guidelines 17-24). The Guidelines are presented in conjunction with the macroeconomic and microeconomic guidelines (previously Broad Economic Policy Guidelines) and for a period of three years and

1 From 2001 this last principle was no longer included under the pillar of equal opportunities.

the National Action Plans (NAPs) are replaced with the National Reform Programmes (NRPs).[2]

Gender equality is no longer included as a specific guideline although gender mainstreaming and the promotion of gender equality are included as a general principle. For example, Integrated Guideline 17 refers to the employment target of 60 per cent for women and Integrated Guideline 18 addresses the reduction of gender gaps and the introduction of reconciliation policies as a means to promote a lifecycle approach to work (EGGSIE 2007). However, due to the disappearance of a specific gender equality guideline, the visibility of gender and the attention paid both to gender equality policies and gender mainstreaming in the national reports has declined (Fagan et al. 2006).

The loss of focus and the increasing invisibility of gender is also mentioned by the Joint Employment Report for 2006-2007: "Through the European pact for gender equality Member States were asked to include a perspective of gender equality when reporting on implementation. In spite of this, the promotion of female employment and systematic gender mainstreaming of policies are rarely emphasized" (Council of the European Union 2007: 4). The disappearance of the equality guideline in the EES explains why the NRPs give less importance to the gender equality dimension of employment policies, particularly gender mainstreaming.

Understanding Adaptability in a 'Flexicurity' Context in the EES

Prior to the reform of the EES, the 'Adaptability' pillar, as the title expressly stated, encouraged adaptability of businesses and their employees to structural, economic and industrial change. Measures adopted under this pillar were developed and implemented at workplace level. The three main interdependent elements of the pillar were: partnership, creation of a new working environment at enterprise level and adoption of policies which promoted the development of workers' capacities. In particular, the 'Adaptability' pillar aimed at promoting policies that pursued the modernization of work organization including flexible working arrangements and also measures that contributed to the strengthening of lifelong learning strategies, high skills of workers and quality at the workplace. More precisely, the 'Adaptability' pillar covered two sets of policies: on the one hand, policies that contributed to making firms productive and competitive in the context of new technology and, on the other hand, measures that improved the quality of jobs, ensuring a proper balance between flexibility and security.

The Role of the Social Partners

The objective of establishing a balance between flexibility and security has been included in the EES since its inception in 1998. Flexibility and security were included in the third pillar, 'encouraging adaptability of business and their employees', from 1998 to 2002 and emphasis on their importance has been confirmed in subsequent

2 Both NAPs and NRPs are available at: <http://ec.europa.eu/employment_social/employment_strategy/national_en.htm>.

years. The social partners were invited to take an active role in establishing this goal. They were asked to negotiate (and, as of 2000, also to implement) agreements to modernize the organization of work, including flexible working arrangements, with the aim of making undertakings productive and competitive (as of 2002, also adaptable to industrial change) and achieving the required balance between flexibility and security.

In 2001, the task of the social partners was broadened, as they were asked to report annually which elements of work organization were covered by negotiations, what the level of implementation was, and what the influence on employment and labour market functioning was (Council of the European Union 2001). Moreover, from 2001, the part of the modernization of work organization for which the Member States are held responsible was reformulated so that the notion of security for workers in atypical contracts should not only meet business needs but also the aspirations of workers. Member States would have to examine their legislation in cooperation with the social partners or based upon the negotiated agreements between the social partners. The social partners also became more involved in supporting the adaptability of enterprises, with a specific focus on making agreements about lifelong learning.

From Adaptability to Flexicurity

In 2003 the adaptability pillar underwent drastic changes, also affecting the formulation of flexibility and security. The distinction in the pillar between guidelines concerning the modernization of work organization and guidelines concerning the adaptability of enterprises disappeared, and, more importantly, the need for a balance between flexibility and security was replaced by the less restrictive and less balanced formulation of 'the need for both flexibility and security':

> Member States will facilitate the adaptability of workers and firms to change, taking account of the need for both flexibility and security and emphasising the key role of the social partners in this respect (Council of the European Union 2003:18).

Moreover, Member States were encouraged to examine overly restrictive elements in their employment legislation which affected labour market dynamics and the employment of target groups. In addition, the pillar suggested that Member States should address labour shortages and bottlenecks, for example by promoting occupational and geographic mobility and simplifying mobility, by improving the recognition and transparency of qualifications and competencies, and simplifying the transferability of social security and pensions rights.

For 2004, the guidelines remained the same, whereas in 2005 another major change was introduced in order to anticipate, trigger and absorb economic and social change. In this respect, emphasis was given to employment-friendly labour costs, modern forms of work organization and well-functioning labour-markets that allow more flexibility combined with employment security to meet the needs of both companies and workers. Although this implicitly refers to the need for a balance between flexibility and security, the actual formulation of Integrated Guideline 21 merely mentions the promotion of flexibility combined with employment security. It also reduces the broad term of security to the more specific term of employment security. Moreover, the former *key role* of the social partners is now seen only as a *role*: 'Guideline No 21: Promote flexibility combined with employment security and reduce labour market segmentation, having due regard to the role of the social partners' (Council of the European Union 2005: 23).

In 2006 'flexicurity' was placed high on the European political agenda and balancing flexibility and security has become a priority in the context of the EES. Following the evaluation of Member State practices early in 2006, the Commission stressed the importance of establishing further conditions of 'flexicurity'. In the conclusions of the Austrian Presidency later that year the European Council endorsed the joint initiative by the Commission, the Member States and the social partners to identify a set of common principles on 'flexicurity' (European Council 2006) and the following year the Commission issued a Communication on *Flexicurity* (European Commission 2007).

The first time the Commission referred to striking a balance between flexibility and security was in the 2002 Joint Employment Report. The notion of a balance between flexibility and security was considered central to the adaptability pillar (European Council 2002). Flexibility was defined as the capacity for firms to adjust to market demand and was distinguished by the Commission into external and internal flexibility. External flexibility was defined as the flexibility of companies to 'hire and fire', whereas internal flexibility implied the reorganization of the existing work force, for instance, in terms of working time, working methods, training, and mobility. These forms of flexibility were believed to complement each other and to bring both advantages and disadvantages to workers and firms. Security was seen from both a static and a dynamic perspective. The former focused on a stable employment relationship and the availability of a safety net in case of unemployment. The latter focused on non-discrimination between different forms of working contracts and arrangement and the acquisition and preservation of employability. In 2006, the Commission again addressed flexibility and security; however this time it explicitly referred to the term 'flexicurity' which has become one of the key concepts in the European debate on labour markets. The Commission states that the core of adaptability lies in finding the right combination of flexibility and security and the reduction of labour market segmentation. It calls for creating efficient conditions of 'flexicurity', which, according to the Commission, are:

> Sufficiently flexible work contracts, coupled with effective active labour market policies to support labour market transitions, a reliable and responsive lifelong learning system, and modern social security systems combining the provision of adequate income support with the need to facilitate labour market mobility ... (European Commission 2006: 6).

Since then the 'flexicurity' concept is considered as being one of the most viable ways to achieve modernized EU labour markets fit to adapt to changes resulting from increasing global competition, the ageing of the population, and lifestyle choices (European Commission 2006).

The 2007 Communication on Flexicurity ended with the statement that flexibility and security can be mutually reinforcing and serve the interests of both the employer and the employee. This implies that an integral approach to flexibility and security was deemed possible. However, the Commission's Communication made no reference to striking a balance and it did not put forward any design for combined flexibility and security policies. In this context it seemed somewhat surprising that flexibility was considered to bring benefits to workers while it was defined by the Commission as the capacity for firms to adjust to market demands.

From the above we can see that the level of integration of flexibility and security has changed over time and that policy suggestions included in the guidelines mostly address flexibility and security as separate issues. Moreover, the guidelines and proposed measures concerning adaptability are extensive, covering many different terrains and involving various actors (Bekker 2007). This does not contribute to the clarity of the notion of balancing flexibility and security and thus might hinder a coherent implementation by the Member States. In the adaptability pillar the flexibility measures mostly concerned internal and external numerical flexibility and functional flexibility. This contrasts with scholars who consider 'flexicurity' as a deliberate policy strategy to deal simultaneously with flexibility and security in a coordinated manner (Wilthagen, Tros and van Lieshout 2004) and the need for an integrative approach (Madsen 2006).

Injecting a Gender Perspective in Adaptability Measures

Studies have often analyzed adaptability as a gender-neutral issue and likewise the promotion of equal opportunities has been mostly conceived as an extra-work organization issue. European labour markets, however, have become increasingly feminized particularly in the 'third sector jobs' and thus the traditional 'gender contract' on which the organization of work is based is no longer adequate for the adaptability of undertakings and the labour force to the new economic, structural and industrial changes. The traditional 'gender contract' consists of a set of implicit and explicit cultural and *quasi*-legal rules governing gender relations which allocate different values, responsibilities and obligations to women and men not only at the workplace but also with regard to education and family welfare issues. Furthermore, the European Union (EU) is confronted not only with external challenges posed by new technology but also with internal ones, chiefly, changing demographic patterns caused by low fertility and birth rates and an ageing population. In addition, most Member States have become immigration countries and participation rates in the labour market are still relatively low compared with the United States.[3] This explains why increasing employment rates for women, bringing the representation of women and men in certain economic sectors and occupations into balance and increasing career opportunities for women have also become important for improving the competitiveness of European labour markets.

---

3 See EC Commission, Employment in Europe 2001, Recent Trends and Prospects, <http://ec.europa.eu/employment_social/publications/2001/ke3801762_en.pdf>.

The above analysis highlights the importance of linking the modernization of work organization to equal opportunities policies. The new changing patterns and the implications for economic and social policies described above have compelled the EU Institutions to adopt and implement new strategies and action programmes in order to promote structural reforms at national level. The role of the social partners is particularly important in this context because collective bargaining may be a useful tool for challenging organizational cultures, breaking down occupational segregation and reducing gender pay gaps by encouraging a more equal distribution of paid and unpaid work. Indeed, collective agreements cover a wide range of equal opportunities policies (Bercusson and Dickens 1996).

Changes in the Conceptualization of Gender Equality Policies

The Impact of Globalization on Gender Equality Policies

'Flexibilization' processes of European labour markets and more specifically of working patterns such as the new forms of employment contracts and working-time arrangements involving part-time, casual, fixed-term, tele-working, self-employed, independent or homeworkers, to name but a few, fostered the adoption of policies which promote equality. At the same time, the increased variety of legal instruments and atypical working contracts has entailed a greater need for protection against discrimination. There is an important gender dimension to the debate on the effects of globalization on employment patterns and chiefly on atypical work as men are disproportionately represented in standard employment relationships and increasing numbers of women in the labour force work under 'atypical conditions'.

The persistent gender pay gap is one of the main consequences of the differences and inequalities which women face on the labour market owing to the increased difficulty of reconciling their professional and private lives, and the unequal division of domestic and family responsibilities which remain very marked. Women earn an average of 15 per cent less than men for every hour worked and thus women's earnings remain, on average, significantly below those of men across the Union (European Commission 2007b). It was at the 1994 Essen Summit that equal opportunities between women and men were defined as being a 'paramount task' of the EU and its Member States and a requirement for the further development of the Internal Market (European Council 1994). The promotion of equal opportunities has since then been considered pivotal in EU economic planning and policy. To this end, the regulations on the Structural Funds for 2000-2006 increased the funding for gender mainstreaming initiatives and programmes and the *Framework Strategy for 2001-2005* (European Commission 2000) provided further funding for promoting gender equality. 2006 saw the adoption of a new regulation for the Structural Funds (Regulation 2006 and Council of the European Union 2006) and of the Community strategic guidelines on cohesion for the period 2007-2013 which provide specific measures and the integration of a gender perspective in all actions (Council of the European Union 2006a: Article 16). Their implementation will primarily be the task of the Member States, in the form of National strategic reference frameworks and operational programmes. The remit of the European Rural Development Fund also includes the principle of equality between men and women (Article 8, Council of the European Union 2005a) in rural development support policy. In addition, the Community's 'PROGRESS' programme (Council of the European Union, 2006a) contains a section dedicated to gender equality which will support the implementation of Community policy on equality between women and men in the areas of employment and social solidarity.

The EES may be considered to be a product of globalization and in this context a new form of EU social governance seeking to promote gender mainstreaming within adaptability policies and rejecting a gender neutral approach to the modernization of work organization. Globalization has fostered the promotion of different living standards and life-styles. Economic constraints have led to a situation whereby men are no longer the only breadwinner of the family and there are many dual-earner households. Moreover, women's participation in the labour market has become very important due to an ageing population. A report on low fertility, families and public policies (Bagavos and Martin 2000) posits that low levels of fertility across all Member States are not so much a consequence of women entering the labour market but the result of an asymmetric division of family responsibilities (see also Guerrina in this volume). If policy-makers enabled women to better reconcile work and family life and men took on a greater share of the household tasks couples wanting to have children would realize their plans more readily (Eurostat 2002). The report added that the process of modernization does not necessarily engender low fertility figures. The example of Scandinavian countries illustrates that people will choose to become parents if the efforts undertaken to raise employment go hand in hand with policies incorporating a gender equality perspective. It also shows that the exercise of a pro-natalist choice and the creation of a better environment for children will only be possible through modernized family policies and alternative childcare policies (Bagavos and Martin 2000). Finally, the report added that fertility and female unemployment have a reverted proportional relationship: higher levels of female unemployment are most likely to cause low levels of fertility and vice versa, high female occupational levels will increase fertility levels. Scandinavian countries have been able to modernize gender relationships and the concept of the family without undermining the importance of the latter.

Another issue which has risen up the policy-agenda in recent times as a consequence of the socio-economic changes brought about by globalization, such as for instance the feminization of the labour market, is the need to increase women's representation in the decision-making process where there is still an under-representation of women. Gender balance in decision-making is one of the five core priorities identified by the *Framework Strategy for 2001-2005* (European Commission 2000) and its importance has been confirmed in the Commission's *Roadmap for Equality* (European Commission 2006a). A *de facto* gender-balanced working environment can only be achieved if changes to society's cultural and political perspectives on gender roles are made. Adopting and implementing awareness strategies and initiatives represent a first step in this direction (Council of the European Union 2000). To this end, the action programmes adopted by the Commission in the framework of gender mainstreaming are to be welcomed.

Moreover, since the year 2000, the Broad Economic Policy Guidelines (European Commission 2002a) have addressed the impact of globalization with the inclusion of various recommendations concerning not only labour market policies but also social cohesion and employment policies including the EES and, in particular, the promotion of appropriate wage developments, the modernization of labour markets and the promotion of a stronger knowledge-driven economy. In addition, the Broad Economic Policy Guidelines emphasized the importance of linking adaptability measures to equal opportunities and assigned an important role to the social partners in the framework of growth and stability oriented macro-economic policies. In particular, social partners are called upon to promote appropriate wage developments taking into account productivity differences such as, for example, skills, qualification or geographic areas, when determining wage levels and finally to pursue policies aimed at reducing gender pay differences due to *de facto* discrimination.

Furthermore, the Broad Economic Policy Guidelines pointed out that modernization of welfare systems must ensure that structural change does not compound the existing social problems, such as unemployment, social exclusion and poverty. Hence, the Broad Economic Policy Guidelines stressed that more efforts had to be made on equal opportunities policies by improving incentives in tax and benefits systems and by promoting policies to reconcile work and family life (see also Guerrina in this volume).

While priority is still largely given to guaranteeing the macro-economic objectives of the Lisbon Strategy there has also been an emphasis on the adoption of policies which strengthen the European Social Model. Particular emphasis has been given to gender pay gaps and to reconciling work with family life. In 2006, the Commission launched a formal consultation among the social partners on the possible thrust of Community action regarding the reconciliation of professional, private and family life, including the promotion of flexible working arrangements, the development of crèche and care services and the possible revision of existing provisions regarding maternity leave and parental leave (European Commission 2006b). However, a close examination of the integration of the EES with the Broad Economic Policy Guidelines in the NRP highlights the link between the EES and the overall growth and macroeconomic policy and indicates the limits placed on the commitment to gender equality. The general macroeconomic rationale for promoting female employment is to raise the fiscal base and reduce the share of the population dependent upon state welfare payments (Fagan et al. 2006).

While some positive results for gender equality can be expected in the form of childcare provision, there is also a risk of negative impacts, for example, those pension reforms that make it even more difficult for women to obtain full pension entitlement or the promotion of flexible employment that fails to offer job security or career opportunities (Fagan et al. 2006). Furthermore, the macroeconomic emphasis on reducing public expenditure has negative implications both for the development of services to support families and for women's employment opportunities given that they are disproportionately employed in the public sector (Fagan et al. 2006).

Hence, globalization processes have exacerbated certain gender equality problems in employment and working patterns and while emphasis has been placed on the adoption of measures to tackle them, the overall growth and macroeconomic rationale indicates how the commitment to gender equality remains limited by the prevailing economic objectives of the Lisbon Strategy.

The Implementation of "Adaptability" and "Equal Opportunities" Policies in Denmark and Italy

The Economic and Employment Context of Denmark and Italy

Since the launch of the EES both countries have had relatively stable economies and for different reasons suffered from a tightening of the labour market, that is, a shortage in labour supply (European Commission 2006c) which, combined with an ageing population, emphasized the need to avoid an increase in wages and prices and posed Denmark and Italy with the long-term challenge of increasing the active labour force.

At the same time, however, large differences exist between the two countries, particularly in terms of labour market performance, industrial relations system and the employment situation. In Italy, both labour and productivity growth have increased less than the EU average (European Commission 2007c). Even though the overall and female employment rates have increased significantly as a consequence of new flexible work arrangements (63 per cent) the female employment rate continues to be well below the EU average (45-46 per cent against 63.8 per cent) with a highly segregated labour market. In addition the gender gap and gender pay gap remain substantial (European Commission 2006c). Furthermore, Italy is confronted with highly asymmetric regional economic and employment trends, due to the situation in the *Mezzogiorno*. Differences in activity rates are very high: 58 per cent in the North, 55.1 per cent in the Centre and 36.3 per cent in the South of Italy. There are also strong differences in unemployment rates: 6.5 per cent in the Centre/North and 19.2 per cent in the South (ISTAT 2005). Finally, the critical state of public finances in Italy (NRP 2006-2008) explains the low levels of expenditure on the implementation of the EES.

The labour market reforms enacted in the last decade (Italy 1997; Italy 2003) have led to an increase in employment, although employment data may have been somewhat boosted by flows of previously under-recorded informal labour, especially newly regularized immigrant labour. Moreover, the recent pension reform (Italy 2004) should help raise participation rates among older workers in future years.

The labour market reforms have made it easier and cheaper to adjust enterprise labour forces via temporary contracts, and tax incentives have facilitated their conversion to permanent contracts. Thus employers have been more willing to take on low-skilled or inexperienced employees on flexible contracts, which have allowed them to gain work experience and build up skills. However, despite recognition that women account for most of the recent growth in employment and that a further large increase in the female labour supply will be required to improve the overall employment rate, there is no specific strategy towards women's labour supply and their specific needs (Villa 2003). In general, there is an assumption that the measures will produce some positive impact on female employment without any strategic emphasis on a gendered understanding of the labour market or on a gender perspective on policy.

In particular, this process of reform has not been accompanied by parallel changes in the social security system and it has been gender-blind as scant consideration has been given to care work and to the distribution of care not only between women and men but also between individual and collectively provided care work. Also, little attention has been given to gender equality in respect of unpaid work at household level. Women, therefore, whose employment situation in comparison with that of men is relatively more precarious, have not benefited greatly from the labour market reform of recent years.

Labour market policies in Denmark have been extremely successful since the mid 1990s with unemployment decreasing dramatically, leading many scholars and experts to talk about a 'Danish job miracle'. The overall employment rate continues to be the highest rate in the EU with 75 per cent and just over 70 per cent for women (Denmark NRP, 2005). It is, therefore, well above the Lisbon targets for 2010 also with regard to women. The Danish labour market model combines traits of the liberal labour market model with strong elements of the Scandinavian welfare state model and is often referred to as the 'flexicurity triangle' (Larsen 2005; Madsen 2006). It supports a flexible labour market while at the same time maintaining a social safety net in the case of unemployment, combined with active labour market initiatives aimed at getting the unemployed back to work.

The Danish version of 'flexicurity' would seem to be more coherent with regard to equal opportunities as it apparently affects both men and women equally. However, increasing maternity leave to twelve months, without extending and making paternity leave compulsory for men, initially has had an adverse effect on those women who aim to have a professional career, as the cost incurred by the employer during the maternity leave period appears to have had a negative effect on the employment possibilities of women (Jepsen 2005). However, in response this has led the social partners to agree on the establishment of a common fund to compensate employers for the financial loss incurred during their employees' maternity leave. The contribution to the fund is irrespective of the number of women working in the firm or sector and is a solidarity measure across the various sectors of the Danish economy.

Moreover, this woman friendly approach has not corresponded with tackling the distribution of work in the family sphere, which contributes to the persistence of lower wages for women as women voluntarily opt for part-time work. This in turn explains why in Denmark there is still a certain level of gender pay gap, 14 per cent for the private sector and 13 per cent for the public sector (Emerek 2006).

Family Structure and Welfare in Denmark and Italy

With regard to gender roles in family welfare and, in particular, in employment law there are great differences between Denmark and Italy. Italy was and is still based on a family-breadwinner model or, more precisely, a family-values oriented model. The family is seen as the main provider of welfare to its members. Bettio and Villa (1996) have identified a Mediterranean path to the emancipation of women which differs markedly from that of Northern countries. The combination of low female participation rates, high unemployment rates and low fertility rates is underpinned by the role of the family which determines the wealth and welfare of all its members. Moreover, the cultural dimension of family making is a key factor for developing work or career plans which explains the highly gender segregated Italian labour market (both vertically and horizontally).

Denmark is based on a social democratic welfare regime characterized by egalitarianism, solidarity, universalism, generous benefit levels and a comprehensive social citizenship (Aybars, in this volume). In contrast to Italy, Denmark's welfare regime is more woman-friendly and it is not centered on the family but is rather a de-familialized and service-oriented one taking direct responsibility for the care of children combined with generous income support for working women (Kjeldstad 2001).

The different approach to gender issues is clearly reflected in the development of equal opportunities policies and in gender equality law discussed below. However, if we consider the NAPs and the NRPs in the two periods of 1998-2002 and 2003-2008 there is a difference in the visibility and commitment to gender equality. The removal of the Equal Opportunities Pillar and the subsequent removal of the gender equality guideline have meant that the majority of Member States, including Denmark and Italy, have paid less attention to gender equality issues. In the following section these two periods will accordingly be considered separately.

Gender Equality and Gender Mainstreaming between 1998-2002

Italy

In the context of Italian gender equality legislation the *Equal Treatment* Directive (Council of the European Union 1976) was implemented through the setting up of specific institutions and bodies with representatives of the social partners (Italy 1977). These included a National Committee at the Ministry of Employment which gained responsibility for legislative regulation (Italy 1991)[4] and a National Commission based in the Office of the President of the Council of Ministers. A Department of Equal Opportunities was set up with a Decree of the President of the Council of Ministers in 1997 (Italy 1997a). At company level, the first Bilateral Commissions on Equal Opportunities were set up in 1986 in a number of large Italian companies and the social partners involved agreed to implement measures aimed at promoting positive action measures for women. Moreover, from the end of the 1980s equal opportunities and positive action issues started to be included in national collective agreements for specific employment categories, leading to the creation of an appropriate Joint Commission.

Since the end of the nineties, there has been an emphasis on positive action measures and gender mainstreaming even though no definition of the latter can be found in official documentation apart from a repetition of the ones by the

4 Under Act No. 125/91 the National Committee also had the power to monitor the implementation of the law, to draw up behavioural codes, to promote research into male and female unemployment and to assess the funding of positive action plans.

Council of Europe (1998) and the European Commission (1996). Moreover, gender mainstreaming has almost exclusively involved those institutions and bodies which are already responsible for adopting and implementing gender equality measures and certain sections of political parties and trade unions. In turn, the limited development of a gender mainstreaming culture has meant that its practice has been directionless without a clear understanding of what gender mainstreaming is meant to do either procedurally or substantively at national and regional/local levels of policy-making. There is also a lack of adequate monitoring procedures and gender impact assessments on policy proposals. In turn these factors explain why gender mainstreaming policies in Italy have been fragmented and not very effective.

In the 2001 Italian NAP measures mainly centered on financial and fiscal incentives aimed at creating a more favourable environment for job creation. In particular, the Italian 2001 NAP had three main objectives: to foster economic and employment growth in the South of Italy with fiscal incentives and investment in infrastructure; to adopt measures aimed at extending the applicability of flexible labour contracts defined as 'coordinated and continuing cooperation schemes;' and to promote the modernization of public service and the PES. However, data on quantitative achievements of the programmes was insufficient, particularly in relation to the overall or long-term objectives. In addition, the 2001 Assessment Report on Implementation (ARI) (European Commission 2001) outlined the delay and/or further postponement of measures announced in recent years: the re-organization of the PES at local level was still very slow, the Employment Information System (SIL) was not operative; and the announced reform of the benefit system which was urgently needed had not been put into effect. In general, measures remained unspecified and were not implemented in a comprehensive and coherent way. With regard to adaptability, lifelong learning policies were enacted through innovative training schemes at all levels of industry agreed by social partners, who also managed the newly created inter-professional funds.

However, the process of increasing flexibility in the labour market promoted by the government was criticized by some of the social partners, mostly trade unions. As regards equal opportunities, most policies remained mainly programmatic and no detailed information was given on the few measures outlined in the Italian NAP. In the context of Objectives 1 and 3 of the ESF the Department of Equal Opportunities was given a coordinating function in matters concerning equal opportunities for men and women and it monitored the implementation of gender equality measures of central and regional administrations. Female regional and provincial 'Equality Advisers' sat on all the main regional monitoring committees and participated in local social partnership boards in order to promote gender mainstreaming across the Italian territory. However, the NAP did not explain how the coordinating role of the Department of Equal Opportunities was to operate in practice.

The *Master Plan of the employment services* represented a first step towards a more comprehensive approach to gender equality with the inclusion of indicators by gender. However, the NAP failed to explain in detail what these indicators were and how they were to be put into effect. Finally, in accordance with Act No. 125/1991 (Italy 1991), the procedures for financing positive actions in the work place were improved.

In particular, the National Equality Committee of the Minister of Labour selected forty-eight projects to enhance positive action measures. A brief analysis of the causes of gender segregation was given but apart from a general description of the budget allotted to these measures no detailed breakdown with explanatory notes was made available. A *National Plan for Female Employment* announced in the year 2000 was still in the process of being implemented by the Department of Equal Opportunities. With regard to policies aimed at reconciling work with family life, the government adopted further measures to support families and working mothers by strengthening the enforcement of Act No. 53/2000 (Italy 2000) on parental and training leave schemes and, in particular, by adopting a *Unified Code of Regulations in the matter of maternity and leaves* which simplified and streamlined the existing legal framework. This measure, however, was mainly programmatic describing in general terms the financial measures enacted.

The government's response to the Council recommendation on pursuing active labour market policies and on implementing specific measures to narrow the wide gender gaps in employment and unemployment (Council of the European Union 2001) was considered disappointing in the ARI and the measures adopted to enhance female employment were considered to be marginal improvements particularly because of the gender-neutral approach employed in the newly adopted flexible working arrangements. With regard to the document submitted by the subsequent government, the ARI criticized the lack of a gender dimension in the adoption of measures aimed at increasing both female and youth employment rates. The NAP was also criticized for the lack of a gender dimension in the context of positive action measures and for containing insufficient measures regarding part-time work and the issue of undeclared work.

The main focus of the 2001 NAP was on the "Employability" and "Adaptability" pillars. In particular, the Italian government referred to its White Paper on the Italian Labour Market (Italy 2001) which aimed at, *inter alia*, completing the modernization of the PES, reviewing the benefit unemployment system, continuing the process of improving flexibility in the organization of work and facilitating the introduction of further atypical contracts and measures to combat undeclared work through new fiscal measures. The report also focused on territorial fragmentation and the need to establish a strong partnership among all different levels of decision and policy-making through the development and implementation of territorial employment pacts (Gualini 2004),[5] in particular, Regional and Local Action Plans for Employment in line with Guideline 11 and pursuant to the principle of horizontal subsidiarity.

As regards equal opportunities policies, the NAP was criticized for the absence of concrete measures for gender mainstreaming which confirmed that the conceptual framework for developing a gender dimension to the field of employment remained weak. Moreover, the NAP failed to provide more information on equal opportunities policies. The only reference made was to Council Directive 2000/78/EC (Council of the European Union 2000a) and how it was going to be implemented at national level. The situation in 2002 remained the same and the NAP was still mainly programmatic.

---

5 In Italy, the first TEPs were adopted and implemented before the development of the EES.

The only significant initiative was the involvement of various Ministries such as the Ministries of the Economy, Education and Research, Equal Opportunities, Innovation and Technology and Public Affairs in the drafting of the NAP.

Denmark

The Danish 2001 NAP listed a number of new measures in the gender equality field. In particular, with the adoption of the *Equal Opportunities Act* in June 2000 (Denmark 2000), the application of the mainstreaming approach to gender equality was established by statute.[6] Since then 'all new relevant legislation is subject to equality screening'. Moreover, the government launched a major equal pay campaign in 2001. A large number of firms were invited to participate in the establishment of a network of firms with a view to monitoring equal pay measures and using job evaluation to ensure better assessment of employees' qualifications. In this new context the social partners in the municipal and county labour markets initiated a project with the purpose of providing guidance and awareness, in order to fight against gender-biased stereotypes. Moreover, the Ministry of Labour launched a project aimed at fighting occupational segregation in both the public and private sectors and to this end it set up a working group to study gender segregated labour markets.[7] Finally, a new *Knowledge Center for Equal Opportunities* ensured a network of information services for women at the workplace.

The Danish 2001 NAP also gave a detailed description of the results achieved by the government. In particular, even though there was still a segregated labour market the number of female managers continued to increase and 1/3 of young managers were women. Moreover, the degree of coverage for children under 10 years in day care facilities and school clubs increased by 1 per cent and in the year 2000 it amounted to 81 per cent. In this context, the Ministry for Social Affairs in co-operation with the National Association of Municipal Authorities and the National Union of Childcare and Youth Workers initiated a joint project with a view to ensuring pedagogical quality in the day care institutions. The only disappointing figures were the ones relating to men's and women's use of parental leave, which remained the same as the previous NAP.

The 2002 NAP was less detailed and also less programmatic than the previous one and it confirmed the further implementation of all the measures enacted since the adoption of the 2000 *Equal Opportunities Act*. However, the implementation of the measures, especially those regarding gender gaps and gender mainstreaming, was still at an embryonic phase. Hence, it was not possible to fully evaluate the

---

6 Under this Equal Opportunities Act, Ministries, state institutions and enterprises are required to submit a report every second year about their equality work. These reports are considered to be a central element in the implementation of gender mainstreaming in public planning and administration. The first report was submitted by the Minister of Equal Opportunities in September 2001 and formed part of the annual reports to the Danish Parliament.

7 See also Danish EQUAL programme approved by the Commission in March 2001. The project looked at gender distribution in occupations with growing employment; within the job hierarchy; and/or in selected female occupation.

effectiveness of these measures. Moreover, gender pay gap issues apart, the information on the social partners' role in the field of equal opportunities and, in particular, in reconciling work with family life (Guideline 18) was insufficient and it did not allow for an effective assessment. In addition, the 'Adaptability' and the 'Equal Opportunities' pillars were not treated in a comprehensive and coherent way. However, in comparison with the Italian NAP, where equal opportunities policies received little attention and where adaptability was still entirely considered as a gender-neutral matter, the Danish NAP represented a great step forward in the strengthening of gender equality policies. Finally, adaptability measures were all implemented on the basis of a partnership approach with the inclusion of the county and municipal sector as well as the social partners pursuant to Horizontal Objective D of the Employment Guidelines.

Denmark has a long tradition of gender mainstreaming in the public employment service and there are equality advisers in all public offices. A new framework for a more efficient and transparent labour market has been set up following the employment service's structural reform which merged employment services and municipalities, creating new job centres.

Active labour market policies apply to all unemployed persons, irrespective of whether they are receiving unemployment benefits, social assistance or sickness benefits and focus on individualized measures. As such, women should benefit from the policies on a more or less equal footing to men. As the ninety-one new local job centres will all have an anchor person for equality and a connection to the new centre of equality consultants, this may result in more efficient gender mainstreaming.

Comparative Evaluation

The evaluation reports of Denmark and Italy provide important information on the impact of the EES at different levels of policy-making. With regard to Italy, the analysis showed how this country is particularly affected by high levels of unemployment due mainly to the peculiarities of the Italian labour market such as, for example, inefficient transition between school and jobs for young people and lack of participation of women in the labour market. In addition, there is also a very high level of early retirement of older people from the market, widespread undeclared labour and serious geographical imbalance and internal segmentation. According to the 2002 Italian Impact Evaluation Draft Report of the EES (Italy 2002) and to interviews conducted with representatives of the Italian government and the social partners in Brussels and Italy the strategy, while representing a major incentive for the adoption of active and preventative measures and the creation of *ad hoc* committees (Ferrera and Gualmini 2002), has not contributed greatly to solving the major structural problems in the Italian labour market. This is due in part to delays in the implementation and even to the non-implementation of some of the Employment Guidelines and the still mainly centralized system of regulation but also partly to the fact that the EES does not consider Italy's structural problems which cannot be solved exclusively with supply-side measures but also require demand-side policies that take into account the adoption of macroeconomic policies.[8]

The Danish evaluation report (Denmark 2002) indicated that employment policies have been implemented in accordance with the principles and objectives of the EES.[9] This explains why the overall objectives of the strategy have already been met. As in the Italian case, the strategy has definitely been a source of inspiration for policy developments but it has not entailed a major institutional rationalization. Representatives of the Danish Government argue that it is 'hard to detect an explicit change of policy' since the launch of the Luxembourg Process.[10] Danish social partners have been to a great extent satisfied with the strategy particularly because it assigned them with important functions in the implementation of the EES and because the strategy maintained intact their traditional role in the Danish labour market. In particular, the Confederation of Danish Trade Unions (Landsorganisationen i Danmark, LO) maintained that the EES did not introduce any new strategies in Denmark. However, it welcomed the strategy for bringing employment and labour market issues within the European context.[11] Finally, the Danish Government suggested strengthening the quality side of the strategy and defining a more detailed and selected list of indicators to support the evaluation of the NAPs which would also take into account differences between the various Member States.[12]

Gender Equality and Gender Mainstreaming between 2003-2008

Following the disappearance of the Equal Opportunities Pillar and the subsequent removal of the gender equality guideline both Denmark's and Italy's 2003 and 2004 NAP and 2005/2006 NRP reports seemed to have adopted an instrumental approach to gender equality and focused on gender equality issues only incidentally, that is, only in the context of the macroeconomic objectives of the Lisbon Strategy, even though during this period gender equality measures have been adopted in both countries. In particular, equality policy is concentrated on breaking down the gender-segregated labour market and creating a better harmony between working and family life in order to reduce the wage gap between men and women and there is no gender awareness in the implementation of adaptability measures.[13] This section,

---

8 Interview with Dr. Paolo Sestito, economic adviser of the Italian Ministry of Labour and member of the Italian Committee for the Drafting of the National Action Plan for Employment, 3 January 2003. See also Sestito (2002).

9 Interview with Mr. F. Pedersen and Ms. L. Henriksen, consultants of the Danish Ministry of Employment, online questionnaire, 12/07/2002.

10 Idem.

11 Interview with Mr. P. Karlsen, LO representative, Brussels, 17 July 2002, who was directly involved in the drafting of the 2001 NAPs.

12 Idem.

13 See Danish NAP 2003: s. 1.2. and Part II-3; Danish NAP 2004: Part II.6; Danish NRP 2005: 41; Danish NRP 2006: 50 and Annex 7, para. 7.1; Italian NAP 2003: Part VI; Italian NAP 2004: 19-22; Italian NRP 2005 (where there is no reference to gender equality) and Italian NRP 2006: Part 5.

therefore, is going to look at the main policies adopted in the two countries provided in other official national documents.

Italy

The measures adopted in Italy between 2003-2008 are very few and do not introduce a notion of gender mainstreaming tailored to the Italian situation or any particularly significant change in the direction of Italian gender equality policies.

In recent years a series of programmes have been issued by the Ministry of Labour and the Ministry of Equal Opportunities respectively, aimed at promoting the presence of women at different levels and positions within organizations, strengthening female self-employment and developing *ad hoc* positive action projects. However, these programmes are a mere repetition of existing legislation and are purely programmatic in nature without outlining any clear objective and action for the future.

The only measure adopted in the field of equal opportunities worthy of mention is Law Decree 198/2006 (Italy 2006) which provides for a 'Code for Equal Opportunities between women and men' (a) establishing a Committee for Women's Self-Employment with the role of promoting female self-employment, for example, by establishing a network between the government at ministerial level and the associations of small and medium enterprises and craftsmanship and by fostering research and raising awareness on female self-employment; (b) promoting the adoption of a comprehensive programme of positive action measures including those for promoting female self-employment with the involvement of different actors such as Equal Opportunities Committees and Councillors at national, regional and local levels, Equality Advisers, social partners and private and public employers. This is implemented through a partnership approach ensured by the Equal Opportunities Network which operates at decentralized level. However, the rationale of this law is to reform Italy's public service and simplify Italian legislation in the field of equal opportunities rather than aiming at introducing new gender equality measures.

Moreover, the recent pension reform (see above) does not have any gender perspective or awareness and only addresses 'technical' issues of retirement age and post-employment benefit in a strictly macroeconomic and gender-neutral context (Italian NAP 2003: 23-24).

Denmark

With regard to Denmark, the most significant measure adopted by the Government is the launch of a new gender equality strategy (Denmark 2002) following the adoption of the 2000 Equality Act which included gender mainstreaming among the existing gender quality measures and made it compulsory to adopt a gender mainstreaming approach in the adoption of all legislative measures. This new strategy was based on an inter-ministerial gender mainstreaming project encompassing both ministerial departments and related agencies and institutions. The main objectives are to ensure that gender and gender equality perspectives become a natural and integrated part of key ministerial core tasks, and that ministries are able in their work to perceive society's gender equality challenges in the context of their own policy areas.

The overall responsibility for the inter-ministerial gender mainstreaming project was vested in an inter-ministerial steering committee, whose members are executives from all ministries. The individual ministries implemented initiatives and were responsible for their own policy areas. The Department of Gender equality has set up an inter-ministerial network for employees engaged in the gender mainstreaming project in the individual ministries. The network gave professional support and expertise to the employees working actively to implement the gender mainstreaming strategy.

The implementation of this strategy has helped to provide the necessary tools and methodologies for analyzing and assessing bills for gender equality impact (on a par with economic and administrative impacts, impact on trade and industry and environmental impact); analyzing and evaluating budgets in relation to gender equality impacts; analyzing, assessing and preparing other types of activities and initiatives from a gender equality perspective, for example, health campaigns, guidelines for trade and industry's social responsibility, guidelines for primary and secondary schools, and so on; generating gender-segregated data, material and statistics and making them easily accessible to employees in their daily work; and producing new knowledge, that is, being able to analyze and process material and data from the point of view of gender and gender equality. In addition, it has helped to set up and develop an organizational and management structure in each ministry for implementing gender mainstreaming. The mainstreaming approach used by the government aims at changing the focus of equal opportunities in Denmark from one which considers the underprivileged, that is, women, to one which considers both women and men.

The adoption of the inter-ministerial gender mainstreaming action plan for 2007-2011 (Denmark 2007) confirms the commitment to developing and strengthening further the gender mainstreaming strategy at inter-ministerial level. The main objective for this period is to improve the ability of ministries to assess from a gender perspective parliamentary bills and the allocation of resources through the development of benchmarks and to this end to increase the availability of gender-segregated data. In this context the Ministry for Gender Equality has issued a document with a list of initiatives considered as examples of good practice.

Moreover, in 2003 the LO adopted an internal gender mainstreaming strategy as part of its equal opportunities' policy for 2003-2007 (LO 2003) with the aim of a) improving women's representation in the organization top ranks; b) improving the training of women; c) creating mainstreaming tools and guidelines; d) mapping of reasons behind gender wage gaps; e) fighting against a gender segregated labour market; and f) working towards identifying a 'family-friendly workplace'. Among other things, LO's mainstreaming project entails that all recommendations for the day-to-day management and the General Council shall contain a separate recommendation on gender. This recommendation shall define more closely whether there is a gender aspect to the main recommendation, and if so, what gender-specific consequences and implications this is likely to have at organizational and political levels. LO and its affiliated unions aim to ensure that gender becomes an integral part of all relevant statistics and all other types of analyses prepared or ordered by the trade union movement. The political responsibility for the coordination of equal opportunities' measures is vested with the LO's General Council.

In addition, the General Council is presented with a set of "accounts" documenting trade union policy and organization in relation to equal opportunities. These accounts include an overview of representation by gender in LO and its affiliated unions, the registration of the number of participants in skills development on gender and mainstreaming, mainstreaming projects and other equal opportunities projects and results. These accounts are submitted every year during a four-year period and they may be compared to EU Scoreboards in that they are tools to monitor the implementation of policy objectives and measures. The first accounts were produced in 2005 (LO 2005). The 2005 accounts included a table with information about LO's mainstreaming strategy and, in particular, which affiliated unions, cartels and members of the LO had been implementing it as a political strategy, as an integrated part of everyday activities and had a dedicated budget for carrying out mainstreaming activities. Examples of mainstreaming included the inclusion of mainstreaming activities in a separate budget by two affiliated unions and by LO, the creation of a module on mainstreaming in the training course for union representatives and the establishment of a regional equal opportunities' network by another two affiliated unions. Moreover, 2005 was the year in which the LO obtained equal representation of both women and men among LO's elected representatives.

In 2006 the Law of Equal Pay for Men and Women (Denmark 1976; Emerek 2006) was amended and now includes the obligation to provide enterprise statistics, broken down by gender. This is restricted to enterprises with a minimum of 35 employees, and groups where a minimum of 10 women and 10 men hold the same job. However, the most important policy document of recent years, the Welfare Agreement (Denmark NRP 2006 and 2007), does not discuss pay or equal pay as part of future welfare policy.

Comparative Evaluation of Italy and Denmark in the Period between 2003-2008

An analysis of the main policies adopted in the two countries provided in official national documents other than the NAPs and NRPs in the period under examination confirms the different approach to gender equality and gender mainstreaming of both the government and the social partners due to different understandings and meanings assigned to gender equality and to different models underlying their welfare systems. With regard to gender roles in family welfare, Italy was and is still based on a family-breadwinner model or, more precisely, a family-values oriented model whereby legislation (including employment law) protects women from being discriminated mainly with regard to what is considered to be their essential family role as against Denmark's welfare regime which is not centered on the family but is rather a de-familialized and service-oriented one taking direct responsibility for the care of children combined with generous income support for working women.

In Italy few gender equality measures were adopted and they did not introduce a notion of gender mainstreaming tailored to the Italian situation or any particularly significant change in the direction of Italian gender equality policies. The measures adopted were in the form of non-binding instruments, mainly programmatic, repeated existing legislative measures and were mostly positive action measures. The focus was largely on the underprivileged, that is, women rather than on conceptualizing gender equality as a policy/principle/right affecting equally women and men.

The analysis of Denmark's legal and policy measures, by contrast, illustrated how this country remains strongly committed to gender equality and how in recent years both the government and the trade unions have been developing a gender mainstreaming strategy, the most significant measure being the obligation to include a gender mainstreaming approach in the adoption of all legislative measures which has been strengthened further by the inter-ministerial gender mainstreaming action plan.

Conclusion

The globalization phenomenon and the introduction of new technologies have compelled Member States to shift from a system based on management by regulation to a system of management by objectives (Biagi 2000). Economic change has also required the modernization of work organization and a rethinking of gender equality policies at all levels of decision and policy-making. In this context, the role of the state and law has changed and new forms of partnership and cooperation between the state, territorial authorities and the social partners have developed. In turn, these changes have paved the way towards new and more flexible forms of employment in order to adapt to this new economic and social scenario. Furthermore, the feminization of European labour markets has also led to the adoption and implementation of structural reforms with a stronger gender perspective.

In this context, to what extent has the EES contributed to the modernization of work organization and to the promotion of a gender dimension to workplace and employment policies? The EES may have an important role in promoting better working conditions for both sexes within an adaptable working environment. However, the study showed that the EES has not initiated the promotion of equality policies. The EES and, more broadly, coordination processes such as the OMC may have an important function of promotion and brokerage in the context of adaptability and gender equality. This function is made operational through periodic monitoring and supervision and peer pressure and also by fostering an open ended learning process via the exchange of best practices. The latter are particularly important in the field of equal opportunities since the concept covers considerable ground. They are equally important in the context of adaptability which requires the ongoing modernization of working patterns. The exchange of best practices helps Member States and other policy makers to find more appropriate solutions in an area which is subject to continuous change. Hence, soft law measures may play a key role in introducing change both at EU and national levels of policy-making. First, they may subsume and systematize changes occurring outside the legal dimension. Second, non-binding measures may represent a valuable tool to bring sensitive policy areas into the remit of the Community.

The chapter showed that between 1998 and 2002 the EES helped to make the commitment to gender equality more visible by including equal opportunities between women and men as the then fourth pillar of the Employment Guidelines and by including gender mainstreaming as one of the guidelines of the EES (Guideline 19). During this earlier period gender equality was one of the main objectives of both governments' agendas. However, the study showed that even though the EES includes significant learning-promoting mechanisms there is not enough comprehensive statistical data and information available to confirm that changes at national level are directly linked to the implementation of the EES.

Nevertheless, the study of the first years of implementation of the strategy showed that the EES may have provided the basis and the operational framework for introducing new adaptability policies with a gender dimension. In particular, the EES may have fostered a learning process through which Member States, regional and local authorities could exchange best practices and develop and use benchmarking tools for adopting more effective policy measures.

Following the disappearance of the Equal Opportunities Pillar and the subsequent removal of the gender equality guideline both Denmark's and Italy's NAP and NRP reports seemed to have adopted an instrumental approach to gender equality and focused on gender equality issues only incidentally, that is, only in the context of the macroeconomic objectives of the Lisbon Strategy even though gender equality measures have been adopted in both countries.

Hence, gender mainstreaming and gender equality have lost visibility in the format of the new Integrated Guidelines. As stated by Fagan et al. (2006: 586) "this new format has made it even more apparent how much political and capacity building is needed if gender equality is to be mainstreamed into employment policy as well as economic and social policies". There is a need, therefore, for some reform to the Integrated Guidelines to reinforce the gender dimension of employment policies.

At the same time, the current situation of gender equality and gender mainstreaming confirms the fact that problems concerning the implementation of concrete measures for ensuring the mainstreaming of gender issues and for promoting equality cannot be explained solely as a consequence of the redesign of the EES. The comparative analysis of Denmark's and Italy's labour markets and welfare and family regimes showed that a combination of factors such as, for example, the economic and social situation, cultural and societal norms and governments' political will determine the positive or negative development of gender equality measures.

References

Bagavos, C. and Martin, C. (2000), *Low Fertility, Families and Public Policies*, Synthesis Report, Annual Seminar, Seville, Spain, 15-16 September 2000.

Barbera, M. (1991), *Discriminazione ed Uguaglianza nel Rapporto di Lavoro*. (Milano: Giuffrè).

Bekker, S. (2007), 'Flexibility and Security in the Adaptability Pillar of the European Employment Strategy' (March 2007). Social Science Research Network, <http://ssrn.com/abstract=957769>.

Bercusson, B. and Dickens, L. (1996), *Equal Opportunities and Collective Bargaining in Europe, 3* (Loughlinstown, Dublin: European Foundation for the Improvement of Living and Working Conditions, Luxembourg: OOPEC).

Bettio, F. and Villa, P. (1996), 'A Mediterrenanean Perspective on the Break-down of the Relationship between Participation and Fertility' Discussion paper No. 5, University of Trento.

Biagi, M. (2000), 'The Impact of the European Employment Strategy on the Role of Labour Law and Industrial Relations', *International Journal of Comparative Labour Law and Industrial Relations* 16(2): 161.

Council of Europe (1998), *Gender Mainstreaming: Conceptual Framework, Methodology and Presentation of Good Practices, Final Report of the Activities of the Group of Specialists on Mainstreaming*. EG-S_MS(98)2. (Strasbourg: Council of Europe).

Council of the European Union (1976), Directive on the Implementation of the Principle of Equal Treatment for Men and Women as Regards Access to Employment, Vocational Training and Promotion, and Working Conditions (76/207/EEC).

Council of the European Council (2000), Decision of 27 November 2000 Establishing A Community Action Programme to Combat Discrimination (2001-2006), (2000/750/EC), OJ L 303/23.

Council of the European Union (2000a), of 27 November 2000 Establishing a General Framework for Equal Treatment in Employment and Occupation (2000/78/EC), OJ L 303/16.

Council of the European Union (2001), Decision of 19 January 2001 on Guidelines for Member States' Employment Policies for the Year 2001 (2001/63/EC).

Council of the European Union (2001a), Recommendations of 19 January 2001 on *The Implementation of Member States' Employment Policies* (2001/64/EC).

Council of the European Union (2003), Decision of 22 July 2003 on Guidelines for the Employment Policies of the Member States (2003/578/EC).

Council of the European Union (2005), Decision of 12 July 2005 on Guidelines for the Employment Policies of the Member States (2005/600/EC).

Council of the European Union (2005a), Council Regulation (EC) No. 1698/2005 of 20 September 2005 on Support for Rural Development by The European Agricultural Fund for Rural Development.

Council of the European Union (2006), Council Regulation (EC) No 1083/2006 of 11 July 2006 laying down general provisions on the European Regional Development Fund, the European Social Fund and the Cohesion Fund and repealing Regulation (EC) No 1260/1999.

Council of the European Union (2006a), Council Decision of 6 October 2006 on Community Strategic Guidelines on Cohesion (2006/702/EC).

Council of the European Union (2007), *Joint Employment Report 2006/2007*. Brussels.

Denmark (1976), Equal Pay Act, Act No. 32/1976, <http://ligeuk.itide.dk/>.

Denmark (2000), Equal Opportunity Act, Act No. 388 of 30 May 2000, as amended by section 4 of Act No. 440 of 7 June 2001, Act No. 146 of 25 March 2002, section 2 of Act No. 373 of 6 June 2002 and section 1 of Act No. 396 of 6 June 2002, <http://ligeuk.itide.dk/>.

Denmark (2001), Minister of Finance, *Agreement on Future Prosperity, Welfare and Investments in the Future*, <http://www.fm.dk>.

Denmark (2002), Danish National Institute of Social Research, *Impact Evaluation of the European Employment Strategy- Denmark, Synthesis Report*, February 2002, available on the website of the European Commission DG Employment and Social Affairs.

Denmark (2002a), The Danish Inter-ministerial Gender Mainstreaming Project Action Plan 2002-2006. The New Gender Equality Strategy, <http://ligeuk.itide.dk/>.

Denmark (2007), The Danish Inter-Ministerial Gender Mainstreaming Project Action Plan 2007-2011, <http://ligeuk.itide.dk/files/PDF/Mainstreaming/mainhandlingsplan2007-2011eng.pdf>.

EGGSIE (2007), *Gender Mainstreaming of Employment Policies. A Comparative Review of Thirty European Countries* European Commission, Directorate-General for Employment, Social Affairs and Equal Opportunities, Unit G1, <http://ec.europa.eu/employment_social/gender_equality/docs/2007/gend_mainstr07_en.pdf>.

Emerek, R. (2006), 'The Gender Pay Gap: The Danish Case – Thematic Report' European Commission's Expert Group on Gender, Social Inclusion and Employment report for the Equal Opportunities Unit, DG Employment.

European Commission (1996), Communication to the European Parliament and the Council: Incorporating Equal Opportunities for Women and Men into all Community Policies and Activities COM(96) 67 final.

European Commission (2000), Communication from the Commission to the Council, the European Parliament, the Economic and Social Committee and the Committee of the Regions Towards a Community Framework Strategy on Gender Equality (2001-2005), COM(2000) 335 final.

European Commission Staff Working Paper (2001), *Assessment of the Implementation of the 2001 Employment Guidelines*, Supporting Document to the Joint Employment Report 2001, COM(2001) 438 final.

European Commission (2002), Communication from the Commission to the Council, the European Parliament, the Economic and Social Committee and the Committee of the Regions - Taking stock of five years of the European Employment Strategy, COM(2002) 416 final.

European Commission (2002a), Communication from the Commission on Streamlining the Annual Economic and Employment Policy Coordination Cycles COM(2002) 487 final.

European Commission (2002b), *Broad Economic Policy Guidelines for 2000*; European Commission, DG for Economic and Financial Affairs, *Broad Economic Guidelines for 2002*, European Economy, No. 4/2002.

European Commission (2006), Green Paper on Modernising Labour Law to Meet the Challenges of the 21st Century, COM(2006) 708 final.

European Commission (2006a), Communication from the Commission to the Council, the European Parliament, the European Economic and Social Committee and the Committee of the Regions, 'A Roadmap for equality between women and men 2006-2010', COM (2006) 92 final.

European Commission (2006b), Communication from the Commission, First-Stage Consultation of European Social Partners on Reconciliation of Professional, Private and Family Life, SEC(2006) 1245.

European Commission (2006c), Employment in Europe 2006, <http://ec.europa.eu/employment_social/employment_analysis/eie/eie2006_summary_en.pdf>.

European Commission (2007), Communication on *Common Principles on Flexicurity* COM (2007) 359.

European Commission (2007b), Report on Equality between Women and Men – 2007, COM (2007) 49.

European Commission (2007c), Report *The EU economy: 2007 review Moving Europe's productivity frontier*, <http://ec.europa.eu/economy_finance/publications/publication10130_en.pdf>.

European Council (1994), Essen Presidency Conclusions, 9 and 10 December 1994.

European Council (2000), Lisbon Presidency Conclusions, 23 and 24 March 2000.

European Council (2001), Stockholm Presidency Conclusions, 23 and 24 March 2001.

European Council (2002), Barcelona Presidency Conclusions, 15 and 16 March 2002.

European Council (2006), Brussels Presidency Conclusions, 23 and 24 March 2006.

Eurostat (2002), 'Women and Men Reconciling Work and Family', *Population and social conditions, Statistics in focus, No. 9/2002.*

Fagan, C. et al (2006), 'The Subordination of the Gender Equality Objective: The National Reform Programmes and "Making Work Pay" Policies', *Industrial Relations Journal* 37(6): 571-592.

Ferrera, M. and Gualmini, E. (2002), 'La Strategia Europea sull'Occupazione e la Governance Domestica del Mercato del Lavoro' in Dell'Arringa C. (ed) *Impact Evaluation of the European Employment Strategy*. (Rome: ISFOL Papers).

Gualini, E. (2004), *Multi-level Governance and Institutional Change: The Europeanization of Regional Policy in Italy* (Aldershot: Ashgate).

ISTAT (2005), Permanent survey of the labour force, III Quarter 2005.

Italy (1977), Legge 9 dicembre 1977, n. 903 'Parità di trattamento tra uomini e donne in materia di lavoro', pubblicata nella *Gazzetta Ufficiale* n. 343 del 17 dicembre 1977.

Italy (1991), Legge 10 Aprile 1991, n. 125 'Azioni Positive per la realizzazione della parita' uomo-donna nel lavoro', pubblicata nella *Gazzetta Ufficiale* n. 88 del 15 Aprile 1991.

Italy (1997), Legge 24 giugno 1997, n. 196 'Norme in materia di promozione dell'occupazione', pubblicata nella *Gazzetta Ufficiale* n. 154 del 4 luglio 1997 – Supplemento Ordinario n. 136.

Italy (1997a), Decreto del Presidente del Consiglio dei Ministri No. 405 del 28 Ottobre 1997 'Regolamento recante istituzione ed organizzazione del Dipartimento per le pari opportunità nell'ambito della Presidenza del Consiglio dei Ministri', pubblicato nella *Gazzetta Ufficiale* n. 278 del 28 Novembre 1997.

Italy (2000), Legge 8 marzo 2000, n. 53 'Disposizioni per il sostegno della maternità e della paternità, per il diritto alla cura e alla formazione e per il coordinamento dei tempi delle città', pubblicata nella *Gazzetta Ufficiale* n. 60 del 13 marzo 2000.

Italy (2001), Ministero del Lavoro e delle Politiche Sociali, 'Libro Bianco sul Mercato del Lavoro in Italia – Proposte per una Societa' Attiva e per un Lavoro di Qualita', Rome, October 2001.

Italy (2002), *Impact Evaluation of the European Employment Strategy, Italian Employment Policy in Recent Years: Impact Evaluation, Final Report, Draft*, <http://europa.eu.int/comm/employment_social/news/2002/may/eval_en.html>.

Italy (2003), Decreto Legislativo del 10 settembre 2003, n. 276 'Attuazione delle deleghe in materia di occupazione e mercato del lavoro, di cui alla legge 14 febbraio 2003, n. 30', Gazzetta Ufficiale N. 235 del 9 Ottobre 2003.

Italy (2004), Legge 23 agosto 2004, n. 243 'Norme in materia pensionistica e deleghe al Governo nel settore della previdenza pubblica, per il sostegno alla previdenza complementare e all'occupazione stabile e per il riordino degli enti di previdenza ed assistenza obbligatoria', pubblicata nella *Gazzetta Ufficiale* n. 222 del 21 settembre 2004.

Italy (2006), Decreto legislativo 11 aprile 2006, n. 198, 'Codice delle pari opportunità tra uomo e donna, a norma dell'articolo 6 della legge 28 novembre 2005, n. 246', pubblicato nella Gazzetta Ufficiale n. 125 del 31 Aprile 2006.

Jepsen, M. (2005), 'Towards a Gender Impact Analysis of Flexicurity' in Bredgaard, T. and Larsen, F. (eds.) *Employment Policy from Different Angles* (Copenhagen: DJØF).

Kjeldstad, R. (2001), 'Gender Policies and Gender Equality', in Kautto, M. *et al* (eds), *Nordic Welfare States in the European Context* (London: Routledge).

Larsen, F. (2005), 'Active Labour Market Policy in Denmark as an Example of Transitional Labour Market and Flexicurity Arrangements. What Can be Learnt?' in Bredgaard, T. and Larsen, F. (eds.) *Employment Policy from Different Angles* (Copenhagen: DJØF).

LO (2003), Resolution on Equal Opportunities in the Trade Union Movement – Adopted at LO's 35th ordinary Congress in 2003, <http://www.lo.dk/upload/LO/Documents/E/equal.PDF>.

LO (2005), LO's equal opportunities accounts for 2005, <http://www.lo.dk/upload/LO/Documents/2/2007%200301%201301%20%20Ligestillingsrapport_3738.pdf>.

Madsen, P.K. (2006), 'Flexicurity: A New Perspective on Labour Markets and Welfare States in Europe. The Case of Denmark' Danish National Centre for Labour Market Research (CARMA), Aalborg University.

Regulation (2006), (EC) No. 1081/2006 of the European Parliament and of the Council of 5 July 2006 on the European Social Fund and repealing Regulation (EC) No 1784/1999.

Rubery, J., Grimshaw, D., Fagan, C., Figueiredo H., and Smith M. (2003), 'Gender Equality Still on the European Agenda – But For How Long?', *Industrial Relations Journal* 34(5): 477-497.

Sestito, P. (2002), *Il Mercato del Lavoro in Italia* (Rome-Bari, Laterza).

Wilthagen, T., Tros, F. and van Lieshout, H. (2004), 'Towards 'Flexicurity'? Balancing Flexibility and Security in EU Member States', *European Journal of Social Security* 6(2): 113-136.

Chapter 9

Is the OMC a Provider of Political Tools to Promote Gender Mainstreaming?

Amparo Serrano Pascual

European institutions are playing an important role as vectors of integration of the principles of gender equality in a large number of Member States in the European Union (EU). However, the nature of this process is not as well known and there is no true consensus on its implications in terms of social cohesion and equal opportunities in studies conducted so far.

European institutions' hegemonic form of governance for social issues is the open method of coordination (OMC). Without entering into the discussion of whether this is an innovative mode of regulation of the social question (Szyszczak 2006), it is submitted that this method encompasses forms of governance that are particularly suited to promoting gender mainstreaming. Its ability to disseminate concepts that underpin political debates (agenda setting) and, therefore, its potential influence on determining rules for reading and interpreting the *real* situation puts the OMC in a good position to restructure the asymmetrical power relations between the sexes. As Fairclough states: "...political struggles have always been partly struggles over the dominant language" (2000, 3).

The aim of this chapter is to discuss the potential, as well as the dangers, inherent in the OMC, and in particular the European employment strategy (EES), to promote gender mainstreaming. One of the key issues examined is the extent to which the OMC is in a better position than previous governance tools to foster the gender mainstreaming paradigm.

This chapter is structured as follows. First, it discusses what gender mainstreaming means, especially the way gender inequality is perceived in this intervention paradigm. A key aspect of this paradigm is its emphasis on the transformation of politically constructed gender assumptions, which reproduce and uphold asymmetrical power relations. That is why it is important to produce alternative regulation models aimed at combating the political origins of the problem. This is the analytical framework for discussing the regulatory nature of the supranational level, the OMC (part 2). The OMC represents an important departure from traditional legal instruments and it is applied in those areas where traditional legislative processes are especially weak. Three main potentialities of the OMC will be identified in the promotion of GM: the provision of political and strategic opportunities, discursive framing and the establishment of methodological conditions to encourage a reflexive stage (part 3). This chapter will end with some concluding reflections on the main weaknesses of this strategy and the role EU institutions have/could have to promote gender equality.

Gender Mainstreaming as a New Policy Paradigm

Gender mainstreaming entails a paradigm shift in thinking and acting compared to previous policies designed to achieve gender equality (Beveridge *et al.* 2000; Rees 1998; Verloo and Pantelidou Maloutas 2005; Woodward 2003). Unlike previous intervention paradigms, gender mainstreaming requires intervention aimed at combating the causes rather than the symptoms of gender inequality, in other words dealing with the issue by tackling androcentric views. It requires the adoption of a perspective that will radically transform the asymmetrical power relations reproducing this situation and break away from the convictions of these discourses and the implicit evidence at work and in institutions; in other words the very ways in which people reason about gender need to be questioned. Therefore, gender mainstreaming entails a pluralist and transversal approach tending to enable citizens to take on different gender identities and still be entitled to equal citizenship rights (Behning and Serrano Pascual 2001). It implies the rethinking of how gender is underpinned in institutions and knowledge. In this respect, it is essential to have a holistic approach, which does not just attack the economic and legal questions of inequality, but above all the political and ideological questions that feed it. As demonstrated in a previous study (Magnusson *et al.* 2003), it is difficult to tackle issues such as equal pay or job segregation, where social values and ideological assumptions on the sexes are brought to bear, with intervention paradigms, such as equal opportunities or positive discrimination, and they require a perspective aimed at deconstructing the power relations produced in contemporary discourses on gender.

Gender power relations are based on and supported by the symbolic structures of the androcentric definition of reality (Bourdieu 1998; Butler 1990). These authors point out how symbolic power is exercised mainly via channels of communication and knowledge. In order to deconstruct these asymmetrical gender-based power relations, Bourdieu stresses the need to challenge the *doxa* (social beliefs that are taken for granted, which are seen as normative, unquestionable and beyond criticism). Some of the social assumptions that are the basis of this gendered perception of reality are:

a. Dichotomous thinking: implicit hierarchical dichotomy between men and women, logic/rationality and emotions, public and private. This two-fold interpretation establishes rhetorical contrasting poles for making sense of the "reality" of gender.
b. Symbolic reliance on the male model. The male model defines the standards.[1]

1 "Man" is the general word to refer to a human being. But man is also used to refer to a male human being. To refer to a female human being we need to add "wo"-man.

c. Essentialist approach: reification of masculinity and femininity. The reality of these concepts is taken for granted. Men's and women's behaviour is the result of a supposed "natural essence", which determines behaviour. Naturalization implies "...the appeal to a certain kind of givenness, an appeal to a world which has a structure and order independent of our interactions with it, a structure which we cannot modify and which conditions our lives and agency" (Alsop *et al.* 2002: 14). Naturalization renders this political construction of gender *invisible.*

These assumptions appear as universal, out of time, but they are socially constructed (Butler 1990). In order to de-naturalize these assumptions, we need to understand gender as relational, constructed and involving power redistribution issues. These assumptions are not neutral, but serve to reproduce asymmetrical power relations between what has been socially constructed as men and women.

In this framework, gender mainstreaming, in contrast to other intervention paradigms, means:

a) Denaturalizing gender: addressing the ideological foundations of social inequalities rather than the symptoms

In order to combat the roots of gender inequality, we need to make these self-evident assumptions explicit (visible) and challenge the givenness and invisibility of gender. Part of this givenness is the social construction of the role of men and women in society as well as their abilities. Visibility favours accountability (Beveridge *et al.* 2000). These assumptions also lead to policies that help to reproduce the asymmetrical power relations between the sexes. Policies play a crucial role in the construction of gendered institutions and identities. Consequently, we need to deconstruct policies and practices resulting from androcentric conceptions and question policy assumptions on the private and public division of work (Woodward 2003). Gender mainstreaming, therefore, implies a rethinking of how the gender contract is underpinned in institutions and structures, the degendering[2] of the current definition of reality. Consequently, the integration of gender awareness (visibility) in re-designing policies and institutions before the policy is made and questioning gendered models and policy paradigms that are taken for granted are crucial aspects for gender mainstreaming. In this respect, instruments such as gender impact

2 De-gendering is the breaking down of convictions in discourses, of the ways in which meaning is structured to reproduce asymmetrical power relations between the sexes. Foucault suggests how knowledge can be understood as a means of appropriation of sovereignty, which is why he insists on deconstruction processes of ideas, discourses and concepts that standardize and organize meaning. These concepts integrate moral theories on how things should be. Consequently, it is important to concentrate analytically and politically on studying the constructed object rather than the universal subject. The focus of intervention should be the social construction of gender, and not lean so much towards women (femininity versus masculinity: private versus public, etc.). In these social construction processes, discourses form the basis of classifications of individuals, oppositions to truth and skill, differences between people, statistical categories, etc.

assessment, aimed at identifying the impact of a policy initiative or analyzing the gender dimension of institutions, are particularly important for suitable gender mainstreaming implementation. Another crucial aspect is the development of gender segregated statistical indicators, and others that are more qualitative, so that we can view the asymmetrical situation between the sexes.

b) A comprehensive approach

Policy on gender equality tends to focus on only some specific areas, such as family policy or positive discrimination, but all policy fields have an impact on gender. Women's equality should be understood as a gender issue, rather than a women's issue, which affects all policy areas and involves transforming structures, systems and practices. The action is not focused on changing behaviour and women's attitudes. Instead it is aimed at intervention in the deconstruction of the symbolic gender order through the *visibility* of power relations between the sexes and, therefore, an intervention targeted at different political levels (women's empowerment movement), social levels (redefining the public and private division of labour) and ideological levels (tackling gender assumptions and expectations). The goal of the gender mainstreaming approach is a new gender contract based on equal access and equal sharing, not only of employment opportunities, but also of domestic and family-care responsibilities (Behning and Serrano Pascual 2001).

c) The need to reverse the idea of what is problematic and what should remain constant

It is important to change male-streamed perspectives. Male standards remain the unquestioned norm and women's behaviour is interpreted as a deviance from this norm. For instance, we need to modify the principle of trying to help women fit into male institutions. This policy trend contributes to the view of women as a deficit carrier. Gender mainstreaming implies a change of emphasis so that policy processes appear as the main object of change, and not women. As highlighted by Bustelo *et al.* (2004) policies are often guided by stereotyped conceptions of gender and do not challenge patriarchal constructions of society. This form of constructing gender is based on assumptions taken for granted rather than being socially constructed, and it is an obstacle to tackling the roots of the problems, adding fuel to the perception of gender relations as unchangeable. Consequently, a de/reconstruction of policies is needed.

Two issues are particularly relevant in the social and historic construction of the problem of social exclusion and gender inequality: the tension between the *processes of naturalization versus the processes of problematization* and between the processes of *risk socialization versus risk individualization* (Serrano Pascual and Crespo 2007). The former defines issues where political intervention is possible, whilst the latter shares out social responsibilities, so that several social institutions can find a solution to them. In the first focus, the rhetorical use of "naturalization" consists of appealing to something given, which cannot be changed and which conditions our lives (Alsop *et al.* 2002, 14). Conventional and contingent issues become natural and unquestionable, thus making socio-historical and political processes look as if they are governed by an unchanging and eternal nature.[3] Compared with naturalization, problematization encompasses two issues. On the one hand, it involves highlighting the unfair and, therefore, unjustified nature (unlawful, and, therefore, susceptible to review) of a certain social condition/situation. On the other, it involves the *moral and political need* to be combated. If naturalization involves *depoliticization*, in other words, omitting any connection with issues of power and oppression, problematization facilitates politicization (collective regulation) of a certain issue. *Problematized* issues become visible and, therefore, structure the space of *public* intervention. The second issue, the allocation of risk focuses on the way in which responsibilities towards exclusion and inequality are shared out among the different social institutions (individuals, state, companies and family).

The visibility (problematization) of gender assumptions and the distribution of social responsibilities vis-à-vis the problem are essential elements in the implementation of a suitable gender mainstreaming strategy. However, the dominant perspective has been to put forward several actions aimed at transforming *women*'s behaviour and attitudes, without questioning *men's* conduct or that of *institutions*. Central issues which mainstreaming strategies need to cover are to ensure that all the parties involved (individuals, companies, state, family) are mobilized to fight unequality and, in this respect, target the intervention at areas traditionally considered to be exempt from the scope of political intervention, such as questions of intimacy or the organizational model of firms (for instance, the culture of long working hours), etc. A method of regulation of this type of issues based on financial sanctions (such as the economic and monetary union processes) or legal sanctions (such as European directives) will not suffice to tackle this type of more ideological and normative factor. The OMC can be used to deal with the more political and structural questions.

The OMC: a New Form of Social Governance?

The OMC[4] which is used to regulate European employment issues was integrated into the Lisbon European Council. It includes a new governance model whose

---

3 Naturalization is an important political/discursive device that makes it possible to justify social differences rhetorically. For example, gender differences can be explained by biological laws (female or male behaviour governed by hormones, genes, etc.), social differences by social laws ("there have always been rich and poor people"), political differences and citizenship access by economic laws (such as the globalization discourse, which allows production transformations to be justified and thus naturalized). Using anthropological universalisms also forms part of naturalization, which allows certain behaviours to be justified by appealing to a supposed human nature. Economicism and psychologization contribute to this naturalization to a large extent. Hormones, history, new economic demands and human nature all seem to be outside the scope of potential political intervention.

4 The term "open" in the group of "open method of coordination" concepts has three main meanings. Firstly, it refers to the non-mandatory basis of this regulation. Although the aim is to promote common objectives and indicators, the way they are performed is open pursuant to

aim is to solve the political and institutional blockade European institutions find themselves in. This method complements, and, in some cases, replaces, traditional European modes of regulation based on harmonizing legislative proposals (European directives). It consists of a regulation targeted at convergence in terms of results, but it gives Member States the possibility of opting for the instruments they consider suitable to meet these objectives.

This method of coordination has become very popular in recent years and has spread to a large number of areas (social inclusion, social policies and education, Lisbon, 2000; the struggle against exclusion, Nice, 2000; social protection, Stockholm, 2001; and environmental issues, Gothenburg, 2001) as it allows decentralized autonomy and self-regulation. These methods of coordination can be understood in the global context of the emergence of new modes of social regulation, whose common characteristic is semantic opposition to more centralized or bureaucratic regulations that were typical in the past. It mobilizes and multiplies alternative resources for promoting self-regulation, such as benchmarking procedures, exchange of good practices, empowerment strategies, partnership promotion, etc. (Walters and Haahr 2005). The aim is to encourage an optimization logic of "social performance" in the EU. This mode of regulation fosters reflexive negotiation in procedures and methods, as well as in the contents of proposals, and it appeals for the plural participation of a large number of political and social players to establish them. This reformulation of the modes of regulation consists of a de-formalization and de-substantialization of normative resources, which means they are subjected to a gradual reinvention process, pursuant to multiple registers, i.e. economic, political, legal and emotional. This mode of regulation is essential in the construction of the European project, as there is agreement on the mechanisms and ways to negotiate social precepts, rather than the latter's contents. This mode of regulation is an alternative solution to the difficulties faced by legislative regulation, which is considered to be excessively rigid, not just due to new ideologically produced conditions (see the discourse on flexibility) but also due to normative, ideological and economic diversity in the EU (*inter-normativity* process). This regulation model could, therefore, be called a deliberative "invention" of a normative order, which explains the contingent and constantly reviewed nature of its proposals.

This is a procedural regulation (dissemination of procedural routines) rather than a substantive one, consisting of the establishment of a series of "rituals" for the dissemination of epistemic paradigms structured around concepts. As a result, European powers in social and employment questions are extended and increased, on the one hand and their methods of regulation are diversified, multiplied and transformed, on the other (Goetschy 2006). The number of political instruments in the hands of European institutions is growing. Consequently, besides less frequent

---

national political elections and social situations. Secondly, it is understood as the opposite to bureaucratic, in other words, open to discussion and can thus be adapted to possible changes in the economic or social situation or to results of assessments of prior policies. Thirdly, it is "open" because it promotes the participation and cooperation of several social players who belong to various geographical, social and administrative, etc., levels under the "partnership" principle (multi-level governance).

use of directives, other methods of regulation have been added, such as the "open" method of coordination, peer group pressure, promotion of social dialogue in Europe and the redistribution policy of structural funds. The legal perspective is thus replaced or complemented by a mode of governance characterized by an absence of formal sanctions, which appeals to the Member States' willingness to cooperate ("soft regulation").

This mode of governance is inspired by new business management ethics (better practices, benchmarking, peer group review, partnership, contract, self-improvement) (Walters and Haahr 2005, 19) and makes more and more use of autonomous spaces in order to reinforce effectiveness. Formal methods of subordination are replaced by collective methods of coordination and reaching a negotiated consensus. The idea is to encourage European institutions to transform into "organizations that learn" in the broad sense of the term.

This is how the majority of the instruments that have become popular in the new organizational management methods of companies have come about. This colonization of metaphors from the business world is seen in their particular course of action. In other words, this method of regulation mainly consists of four principles:

a. *Principle of subsidiarity*: objectives are defined *centrally*, but implementation is *decentralized.* These objectives, proposed by European institutions, consist of general principles, rather than specific proposals. These general proposals are transposed by the Member States into national policies and in some cases into regional policies.
b. *Principle of partnership*: Related to the above, decentralization of the implementation involves the participation of many actors, not just national and regional ones, but also social partners and other representatives of civil society based on a principle of partnership (multi-level governance), whose aim is the involvement of a large variety of levels and players in the decision-making processes and thus to adapt a broad range of political perspectives and social interests. The idea is to mobilize different levels and actors to achieve a set of agreed aims.
c. *Principle of evaluation (benchmarking).* A series of indicators is established, which quantify objectives in order to quantitatively *measure* the progress made by the different Member States towards achieving these objectives and a period is defined in which these targets have to be met. The use of graphs and comparative tables to view the data contributes to a strategy of *self-control* and self-government (Walters and Haahr 2005). European institutions thus promote a competitive logic among the Member States, subjecting them to an ongoing "competitive self-improvement process" (Walters and Haahr 2005, 131). A constant method of progress assessment and systematic comparison (diachronic among countries and synchronic over time) is established in order to control Member States' progress.
d. *Principle of mutual surveillance.* A system of constant review by the peer group (other Member States) and of the Commission (Joint Report) is established, as well as the mutual exchange of so-called "good experiences".

To sum up, the nature of European regulation in the social and employment domain is not based on exogenous coercions (legalizations, economic sanctions), but rather on endogenous pressures (persuasion, dissemination of concept paradigms of the social question), which lead to spaces where the social question can be formulated and reorganized. Its regulating power comes from being able to participate in a policy to produce subjects. As Walters and Haahr state (2005: 13): "power works in terms of the ways we govern ourselves: it encourages us to adopt such subjectivities as the active job seeker, the empowered citizen, the discerning consumer, etc." Therefore, the main regulating nature of the OMC lies in its symbolic potential, in its capacity to put forward new intervention paradigms, and, at the same time, new ways of problematization and naturalization, alternative forms of distributing social responsibilities, thus contributing to a rethinking of anthological concepts and dominant assumptions in social policies. The concepts disseminated by EU institutions help to construct Member States political problems and aspirations.

Strengths and Weaknesses of the OMC to Promote the Gender Mainstreaming Paradigm Shift

Bearing the OMC's particular mode of regulation in mind, it would have three main potentialities: the provision of political opportunities and strategic resources for empowering social movements, its persuasive capacity and the possibility of providing instruments that push Member States towards reflection and visibility of social assumptions about gender.

a) Provision of Political Tools to Some Women's Movements?

The OMC can promote a deliberative problem solving process (Zeitlin 2004). In the search for political and scientific legitimacy, EU institutions are relying on a large number of scientific and political experts ("expertocracy"), as well as social actors, pursuant to a government model that has been described as *multi-level governance*, in which a range of different voices would take part in devising social responses. Some gender expertise actors (EP Committee on Women's Rights and Gender Equality, gender experts and the European Women's Lobby) participate partly in the EU framing of gender inequality (Lombardo and Meier 2006, 160). This situation could, therefore, encourage a governance project, in which women´s movements would have a say in developing social responses. Women's participation in defining the terms of the problem of gender inequality, as well as in the visibility of patriarchal institutions, is crucial if gender mainstreaming is to be implemented properly.

Moreover, the concepts promoted by the EES can serve as political resources in the hands of civil society, so that asymmetrical power relationships can be challenged. The EES may assist in the *empowerment* of certain social groups. Empowerment of women's representatives and greater involvement of women's voices are key aspects for an adequate implementation of gender mainstreaming (Beveridge *et al.* 2000; Verloo and Pantelidou Maloutas 2005). The key question is, therefore, the extent to which supranational institutional regulation has empowered women's groups nationally. Although very few studies have been conducted to analyze how this possibility has been put into practice, the conclusions of some comparative analyses show that for some groups in civil society, the EES is providing *political tools* to promote certain items on their agendas. In some cases, EU institutions provide *strategic resources* for women's movements, trade union women's departments and so on, which can use EES concepts to promote certain items on the agenda, such as a more ambitious equal opportunities agenda. Some women's groups use the EU as an arena for expressing their demands in feminist policy (Cichowski 2002). Gender mainstreaming guidelines, for instance, have been useful in enabling calls for government action in this area. The EU's commitment to gender equality opens up opportunities for pressure groups nationally, which they have used to lobby for more attention (Rubery 2003). In Spain, Greece and Italy, trade unions use references to the EES strategically in political debates and in the media (Mailand 2005). The EES has helped actors to give gender equality more priority and to make a commitment to addressing gender equality in the workplaces (López Santana 2004). Therefore, the gender movement is playing an essential role in the process of providing a strategic framework for the representation of the gender equality problem (Verloo and Pantelidou Maloutas 2005).

In some cases it has facilitated the participation of specific groups in civil society (see the emphasis on partnership). The OMC has also led to the creation of opportunities for women and NGOs to act as political actors and experts. Social players are supposed to participate in the implementation and preparation of NAPs. In some countries, women's departments have gained in importance. In countries such as France several attempts have been made to achieve a better balance in accessing key posts in the political world (Lemière and Silvera 2001). In Belgium, for instance, de Troyer and Krzeslo (2003) highlight that although the EES has contributed to making reducing pay gaps a priority nationally, this was due to the involvement of women's organizations and women's departments in trade unions. But the top-down approach devised at EU level and in the drafting of NAPs does not allow women's movements to be included in most cases. Therefore, an important weakness of the EES has been the limited extent to which a wide range of actors has been genuinely involved. The participation of other civil society groups is rather limited and selective (with the possible exception of some influential lobbies). Zeitlin (2004) points out the need for review openness and participation in OMC processes and to ensure a broad participation by diverse actors.

In relation to *institutional innovation*, the EES may actually contribute *to establishing institutions.*[5] This has happened in some countries, such as Greece, Spain and the United Kingdom (Zervou 2001; Escobedo 2001; Walby 2001) with the implementation of gender mainstreaming. But in other cases gender mainstreaming has been used to replace previous infrastructures and actors that promoted gender equality since, rather than being limited to a specific group of gender experts, gender mainstreaming has been interpreted as a task for all the actors involved in policy design (Behning and Serrano Pascual 2001; Mósesdóttir 2005). This situation may

5 For an interesting description of the main forms of institutional innovation promoted by the EES in different member states, see Rubery (2003).

even weaken gender departments, but this may be particularly dangerous, since effective gender mainstreaming implementation requires suitable understanding of gender relations.

Fagan *et al.* (2005, 573) point out that institutional innovations (inter-ministerial and steering committees, women's departments and units within government ministries, equality advisors in the ministries) in relation to gender mainstreaming have been important in EU Member States, particularly in the ten new Member States in the period before the accession. In countries such as France, improving women's participation in policy-making and the creation of "equality advisers" have played a crucial role (Lemière and Silvera 2001). Rubery (2003) argues that the role of the EES in reinforcing enabling institutions seems to be particularly important in Southern countries where the strategy was very underdeveloped. However, it also seems to be these countries where institutional innovation has been very vulnerable, jeopardizing important improvements when changing the political complexion of government (Rubery 2003). Fagan *et al.* (2005) highlight how a large part of these institutional institutions has stopped operating, both in countries with an important egalitarian tradition (Finland and Denmark) and in countries where this strategy was more incipient (Greece and Portugal), which reinforces, yet again, the frailty of this institutional design. Other authors (Behning and Serrano 2001; Mósesdóttir 2005) emphasize the fact that women's opinions are barely represented among social partners. In turn, several authors (Fagan *et al.* 2005; Mósesdóttir 2005) stress the scarce efficiency of these institutions when there is no firm political commitment from national representatives to this problem. As a result, a clear political intention is a fundamental condition for an adequate implementation of this strategy.

Another important aspect for achieving an adequate implementation of gender mainstreaming in all decision making processes is to ensure the involvement of all parties responsible for policy implementation. The OMC may promote interactions and cooperation among different spheres of interventions and facilitate the establishment of a *holistic intervention* that deals with the various dimensions of gender inequality transversally (Rubery 2003). It can enhance *policy dialogues* among diverse social players and raise the level of political deliberation. The participation of a wide range of actors in policy formulation, implementation and evaluation (multi-level governance) is essential to keep those involved responsible and accountable for carrying out their commitments (Zeitlin 2004). The EES seems in some cases (France, Austria) to have stimulated cooperation among different levels. However, in most cases, NAPs consist of individual approaches without a horizontal approach (Magnusson *et al.* 2003).

Drafting NAPs is often merely a bureaucratic exercise in which only a small number of civil servants is involved with no obvious media involvement, as it is not given very much publicity. The vague and ambiguous nature of the concepts means that NAPs are often simple continuations of previous policies. Consequently, we still need to ascertain whether epistemic communities exceed the bounds of a small group of civil servants in charge of the implementation and production of NAPs.

b) OMC: Discursive Framing?

The adoption of concepts proposed by EU institutions has an important impact on the terminological construction employed to designate the problem of gender inequality, and on proposing common frames of reference (creation of epistemic communities around gender inequality). These supranational bodies influence the main lines along which the debate has been conducted and the way in which problems are described. The OMC has been defined as a reflexive reform strategy (Zeitlin 2004), which can be particularly adequate for the aims of gender mainstreaming.

A certain vocabulary (gender mainstreaming, activation, life long learning and active ageing) has spread into national discourses, encompassing certain issues with a problematic status. Changes in policy thinking can be promoted, for instance, to establish a causal linear relationship between equality and economic growth. It can enhance a normative reformulation of social problems. For example, the focus on the activity rate promoted by the EES explains why inactivity increasingly appears as the main reason for the majority of the problems. It has also helped to disseminate certain concepts in the discourse, which contribute to problematizing gender inequality in countries such as Spain (Guillén and Álvarez 2004). More attention is given to the issue of women's integration in the labour market and the inclusion of women as a target group of employment policies. In countries such as Spain, Austria, Czech Republic, Estonia and Slovenia the EES has served to increase sensitivity about gender inequalities (Caprile and Escobedo 2003; Leitner 2003; Zeman *et al.* 2003; Laas 2003; Cesen 2003). Therefore, the EES has served to facilitate the integration of equal opportunities issues in the national political agenda (Fagan *et al.* 2005).

It also helps to give certain political decisions more power. The EES has led to political support for some areas, for instance women's labour market participation in countries such as the Netherlands (Zijl *et al.* 2002). As the authors state, the EES emphasis on women's labour market participation has enabled the Department of Emancipation of the Dutch Ministry of Social Affairs and Employment to foster a Dutch target for women's economic participation as an official government position. The issue of reconciling work and caring has become a priority in most EU countries. That is why one of the main areas of emphasis in the NAPs has been the development of good infrastructures to facilitate the integration of women in the labour market (Behning and Serrano Pascual 2001). As Mósesdóttir (2003) points out, the EES has encouraged Member States towards the dual breadwinner model.

The EES may well assist in *raising awareness* of the situation of specific groups in the labour market, so that certain types of issues and situations can be regarded as problematic rather than taken for granted. The EES may serve as a catalyst in some areas and push certain issues/reforms higher up the political agenda. EU institutions have important power to portray certain situations as problematic. This can lead to situations that are often taken for granted (for instance, the issue of the "private" division of tasks) becoming problematized and to raising awareness about the situations of certain groups in society. For instance, Nordic countries, and to a lesser extent the Netherlands and Germany, have emphasized the importance of integrating men into the efforts to achieve gender equality and the need to change male and female attitudes (bilateral perspective focusing on both men and women

(Mósesdóttir and Erlingsdóttir 2006, Schippers 2001). In these countries, men are also targeted by reconciliation policies of work and family life. In the Netherlands, the so-called "combination scenario" (men and women share paid and unpaid work on an equal footing) has been developed to facilitate this reconciliation for both men and women (Zijl *et al.* 2002). Such measures have also been targeting men in Finland and Denmark, but it is not clear to what extent this is due to the EES (Sjorup *et al.* 2006). Moreover, although the EES has encouraged Member States to have a dual breadwinner model, no dual caring model has been promoted (Mósesdóttir 2003).

Another additional problem is the way gender mainstreaming has been understood in the EES as a means to promote the integration of women in the labour market and in particular in knowledge-based society sectors. Therefore, one of the key objectives is to enhance women's participation in the labour market. Gender mainstreaming is mainly understood in terms of activation, focusing primarily on removing barriers likely to impede women's access to the labour market (supporting women's entrepreneurship, provision of childcare and family leave to facilitate the reconciliation of work and family life, reviewing tax and benefit systems, women's training and employability, the increase in women's share in certain occupational groups, positive action to facilitate access to the labour market, and so on). Activation has been the key policy to integrate women in the labour force. One of the few targets (together with the provision of childcare) established by EU institutions regarding women's equality is increasing the female employment rate to 60 per cent by 2010. Other policies have been introduced in countries such as Spain or France consisting of financial incentives for firms to encourage the recruitment of members of the underrepresented sex (Escobedo 2001; Lemière and Silvera 2001). As a matter of fact, the employment gender gap has been reduced since the EES. However, the predominant emphasis of the EES on increasing women's employment rate without taking into consideration the qualitative aspects of labour market integration, could encourage other forms of inequality (for example increasing pay gaps and gender segregation). The concentration of women in poor-quality jobs could be partially the result of this way of understanding gender mainstreaming. The exclusive emphasis on quantitative aspects of integration could, therefore, have negative consequences for qualitative aspects. As Rubery *et al.* (2001) state, female employment grew in the EU in some cases due to the fact that women accept lower quality jobs rather than because of a decrease in gender inequalities. Consequently, this quantitative approach might serve to reproduce the problem of gender inequality rather than solve it.

This activation approach is based mainly on economic factors, focusing on the need for additional labour which allows the economy to function. These policies are characterized by the tendency to see women as a population surplus (supply of additional labour and potential contributors to manpower) rather than in terms of equality. They focus exclusively on women's role in the labour market rather than taking a broader approach to individual rights (Behning and Serrano 2001). But we need an understanding of women's and men's social rights which focuses on citizenship rather than on employment-related issues (Mósesdóttir 2005).

c) Provision of Methodological Conditions to Promote a Reflexive Stage

The EES may enhance policy learning through policy exchange between Member States and by providing the methodological prerequisites for a reflexive stage. The main tools for achieving this have been, firstly, the opportunity to appeal to experts and stake holders (expertocracy), secondly, the use of benchmarking and, thirdly, the spread of an evaluation culture. The OMC can promote an important exchange of practices and ideas, which enhance an intensive learning process. More participation from professional experts might facilitate a reflexive deliberation. That could be particularly important in the case of GM, whose meaning has been so unclear and misunderstood at a national level.

The process of pressuring Member States to converge towards commonly defined goals could involve being explicit about the main targets and the tools needed to reach them as well as monitoring of the process through common indicators. Indicators can serve as diagnostic tools for self-corrective action by national and local actors (Zeitlin 2004). It could, therefore, enhance the development of more sophisticated and common statistical tools for evaluating the effectiveness of employment policies. Fagan *et al.* (2005: 569) state that gender mainstreaming mechanisms have been established in some EU Member States, but they are politically weak, and although statistical indicators to monitor gender impacts have improved, they are still underused nationally.

More emphasis is placed on evaluation and on the need to promote suitable indicators (for instance, the impact of the EES on spreading practices such as gender impact assessment). Most Member States have developed statistics, including data broken down by gender, and promoted research on gender equality, thus enhancing debates on this issue. The role of EU institutions in promoting the monitoring of equality has been particularly important in Southern countries. In some countries, such as the Netherlands, the EES has encouraged statistical monitoring and the cooperation required to obtain good statistical information among all administrative parties (Zijl *et al.* 2002). In Spain and Poland, inter-ministerial cooperation and coordination, consultation with social partners, as well as evaluation and follow-up, have improved as a result of the EES (Mailand 2005).

The development of gender sensitive statistics and research on gender impact makes differences visible and increases awareness of gender inequalities. Gender audits and gender assessments are often the channels countries such as Germany, the Netherlands and Austria use to implement gender mainstreaming. In Austria, for instance, gender experts and suitable structures have been designed to accompany the gender mainstreaming process (Leitner 2001). In Germany, an inter-ministry working group has been set up at the executive level for the improvement of equality (Töns and Young 2001). In some of the 10 new EU Member States, a gender impact assessment system has been established in individual ministries and public services (Fagan *et al* 2005). In Finland, a project to incorporate the gender approach in central administration processes (in the drafting of government proposals, budget control and information planning) was mentioned in NAP 2000, but no reference is made to concrete measures to implement it (Roivas 2006). Gender mainstreaming has been integrated in the new Equal Opportunities Act (2004) and, therefore, all public actors are supposed to include a gender dimension in their planning and administration (Roivas 2006). A pilot project has been launched in Denmark to integrate a gender dimension in the core activities and attitudes of public employment services (PES) (Sjorup *et al.* 2006).

However, these potentialities are very relative. The increasing use of quantitative rather than qualitative indicators in these evaluative practices hinders the strategy's efficacy (Magnusson *et al.* 2003). Although women's employment has risen, a large proportion of this increase is due to the integration of women in low quality jobs, thus reinforcing gender inequalities (Webster 2006). As a result of this quantitative way of measuring success, labour integration is seen as the main tool to fight all problems, gender inequality included. But the extent to which employment offers opportunity for gender equality depends on the quality of the jobs. From a gender mainstreaming perspective, it is essential to consider the quality of the jobs as well (Fagan *et al.* 2005). Real progress on gender mainstreaming demands radical changes in the behaviour of firms or distributional issues, but these aspects are beyond the scope of the EES.

Moreover, the debate runs the risk of becoming confined to aspects that might be of use for the operations of the economy, but not necessarily for the wellbeing of workers. A "political" assessment of these policies requires a qualitative approach to evaluation to complement previous types, and analysis of the wide-ranging purposes that policies may entail. Producing statistics will simplify and typify reality, as it will be codified into synthetic categories (Greenwood 1998). This may lead to reproducing an essentialist view of gender that makes women and men more similar than they actually are. Furthermore, it will favour a construction of the problem, since it involves a selection process of relevant aspects of the problem. Lack of cooperation amongst the various departments involved, which has been the case in Spain (Escobedo 2001), Greece (Zervou 2001) and Italy (Barbera and Vettor 2001), also represents an obstacle for an efficient implementation of gender mainstreaming.

Conclusion

Gender mainstreaming implies an understanding of gender as relational, constructed and involving issues of power distribution (Woodward 2003). The OMC is in a good position to make gender visible and to promote a degendering perspective aimed at problematizing and denaturalizing certain assumptions about gender that reproduce asymmetrical power relations between the sexes and this governance model can ensure that different social, economic and institutional players take responsibility and get involved. However, the way in which this method is being implemented in the EES seems to be reproducing power relations rather than challenging them. Some of the main weaknesses are, firstly, that the sole focus on labour market policy does not address the fundamental roots of gender inequality based on assumptions and expectations about gender. A second aspect is the failure to address the "sacred" aspects of the problem (organizational aspects and men's and women's long working hours, distributional aspects: low numbers of men caring for dependents, etc).

Another important obstacle is that these policies essentialize gender and tend to reproduce gender stereotypes. They support traditional gender roles, with women having a secondary earner status. Rather than recognising diversity between women in terms of values and interests, but also in terms of performance, these policies tend to see women as a problem without making the link between the structural and political causes of inequality. Fourthly, and related to the previous point, there is an exclusive emphasis on quantitative dimensions rather than qualitative ones. Women are considered as a supplier of additional labour. Fifthly, it is focused on socializing women and changing their choices and attitudes. The male norm remains the standard. Women have a problematical status, without addressing the male dominated nature and structure of policies. The problem is defined as women not having access to or not being able to attain male standards. These standards are not questioned, only female behaviour is.

Another problem is that there is no truly horizontal approach. Moreover, the main understanding of the problem is economic (integration in the labour market) and psychological (lack of self-esteem, need to change attitudes towards technical fields, etc.), rather than political, which in turn reproduces, rather than solves, the problem. Perceiving women as a potential reserve army may be why they take on unqualified precarious jobs in the labour market. Consequently, although the asymmetrical social and sexual division of productive and domestic, or public and private, activities is overcome, this division is going to be reproduced with new terms in the public field, without even questioning the sexual division of work in the private sphere (Webster 2006).

Finally, this strategy can involve many different paradoxes. For example, developing statistics broken down by gender is fundamental in order to visualize the problem. But, on the other hand, these same statistics can further an essentialist view of gender. Another is when this method requires the involvement of all administrative and political levels, and therefore actors not specialized in gender issues take on a central role. However, a correct implementation of this concept requires in-depth knowledge of this subject. Another potential paradox is that although a more general perspective is required, it may become more diluted and thus weakened by this more general nature. Finally, despite the fact that the beginning of gender equality has been presented as favourable towards economic growth, both principles can contradict each other when a specific growth model is followed. Extending child care is a central objective in Member States in order to reconcile family and working life, but, on the other hand, the regulation process and economic harmonization that has been promoted in recent years is encouraging budgetary austerity, which could lead to the dismantling of public services and, therefore, to a deterioration in the quality and quantity of these services (Webster 2006).

These problems with the EES are partly the result of the nature of the mode of regulation encouraged by the OMC. In particular, we consider three aspects to be particularly relevant: it lacks room for manoeuvre to change institutions and asymmetrical power relations, the ambiguous and polysemic nature of their concepts (gender mainstreaming as a *floating signifier*) and the imbalance between this project's economic and social dimensions. These three aspects are, however, inter-related.

The first issue illustrates one of the most important weaknesses of the Open Method of Coordination. This method basically aims to achieve a standardization of ideas, visions and political concepts, rather than of institutions and laws. As a result, although this kind of regulation can disseminate political perspectives or ideological models, it has, on the other hand, very little power to achieve convergence of the available means or instruments in each country (institutions and rules). Indeed, the same intervention model can have very different consequences depending on the dominant system of regulation and on the political will of national governments. In other words, an appropriate social policy not only requires the adoption of the right political perspectives (if possible), but also the implementation of the requisite instruments.

The ambiguous meaning of GM is a second obstacle, as understanding of the concept, varies considerably from equating it to "equal opportunities" and "equality" to "affirmative action" and "equal treatment".[6] Lombardo and Meier (2005) argue that the EU concept of gender mainstreaming is an empty signifier as it is focused on procedures to achieve this goal without addressing what the goal means. In our opinion, the feature that characterize the concept of GM is also its floating nature (a *floating signifier,* Levi Strauss), a notion that is essential and vague and whose precise identity is the result of the *rapport de forces* among different voices. Levi Strauss highlights this notion's excess of meaning: it is invoked in rituals, but fails to define its meanings. As occurs with other concepts proposed by European institutions, these notions are characterized by their polysemy and ambiguity, which explains why the concept is instrumentalized for very different purposes. This polysemy helps to construct a hybrid discourse, which, as we have seen with the activation concept (Serrano Pascual and Crespo Suárez 2007), uses registers that appeal to the empowerment of the subject, while advocating intervention models that often do not offer more decision-making power than respectful submission to the rules of the game. It is this paradox that enables the EU discourse to present itself as socially inspired and geared towards a concept of the promotion of individuals, while also defining a field of possible practices in which politics is reduced to the management of labour transitions.

Moreover, the different interpretations of gender mainstreaming could contradict each other, especially when an instrumental interpretation of gender mainstreaming (women as suppliers of labour force) is hegemonic in this political construction of gender inequality (Behning and Serrano 2001; Mósesdóttir 2005). Lombardo and Meier (2005) demonstrate how competing policy frameworks are mobilized within the EU, which could hinder the implementation of gender mainstreaming. The dominant interpretation in the EES has been to promote the labour integration of women. However, this exclusive emphasis on the quantitative dimension of labour integration can have contradictory effects from a gender perspective. The extent to which employment offers opportunity for gender equality depends crucially on the

6 Woodward (2003) discusses the definitional and conceptual confusion of the concept of gender mainstreaming and identifies different ways of using the concept. Lombardo and Meier (2005) point out that the concept of gender mainstreaming is an open signifier that can be filled with both feminist and non-feminist context (2005: 21).

quality of the jobs. The emphasis on quantifying progress through benchmarking and quantitative indicators is useful to raise awareness of this problem and make this a central issue in the political agenda. However, it can also mislead the debate, by focusing the intervention on changing numbers and on gender rather than transforming the structural and ideological situation in which asymmetrical power relations are produced (Lombardo and Meier 2005). This perspective explains why intervention has been centred on transforming women's attitudes and behaviour or intervening therapeutically to give women self-confidence, rather than on deconstructing gender norms. The focus is on changing women's behaviour and encouraging women to "perform" like a man without questioning men's behaviour (Mósedóttir 2005). Therefore, this approach reproduces assumptions about who is responsible for what, rather than problematizing the gender distribution of power relations.

The ambiguous and polysemic nature of the concepts promoted by European institutions is, in the case of GM, particularly problematic due to its complexities. Some authors stress the fact that underpinning the concept with a theoretical and intellectual framework makes the exercise of understanding it particularly complex, thus creating additional problems for horizontal implementation (Woodward 2003). Others authors (Lombardo and Meier 2005) instead discuss this "understanding" of obstacles as a political rather than a technical problem, the result of the *rapport de forces* within the EU.

This brings us to a third aspect, which characterizes one of the main weaknesses in this process. This asymmetrical power relation explains the persistence of ideological assumptions. The main focus is on women's behaviour as subject to change and the male concept of work (full-time employment in technical and managerial positions). The concept of valued work, skills, positions, organizational practices, etc., remains untouchable (invisible) (Webster 2001; Behning and Serrano Pascual 2001). Crucial aspects to promote gender equality (working time, sharing of caring, the quality of jobs, etc.), such as organizational models, behaviour of employers, families, etc., are beyond the scope of EU institutions. Moreover, the primacy of market rules, which have characterized the current situation, is not positive for the equal opportunities policy (Löfström 2003). The hegemony of this economics-driven discourse encourages dilution of any political analysis of the interventions proposed.

Consequently, as a result of the previous point, this so-called supranational space for the "battle of ideas", which is implicit in the concept of multi-level governance, may transform into a place where the hegemonic "voices" are reproduced as a monologue, given the asymmetrical power relation existing between these social groups. The scarce participation of women's social movements explains the hegemony of economic rather than political representations of the problem of inequality, which directs the terms of the debate towards the discussion of women's "behaviour" and "attitudes", rather than the social and political context in which these attitudes emerge. Therefore, rather than promoting the participation of many voices, this exercise can be transformed into a project of de-politization of gender inequality.

The solutions needed to tackle this situation are not simple, and it is not clear in the most relevant literature what the most suitable way of emphasizing the effectiveness of the open method of coordination would be, and conclusions that are only apparently paradoxical have been arrived at. Whilst some authors (such as Zeitlin 2004; Beveridge *et al.* 2000) point towards the need to make the process more open, others (such as Rubery 2003; Webster 2006) insist that the process is excessively open.[7] The open method of coordination probably requires both processes, more openness to make it easier for the voices of women's groups and other social movements to participate and more firmness and clarity in objectives and responsibilities towards the process in order to further the involvement of the governments of the Member States in issues such as socio-political equality and social inclusion.

References

Alsop, R., Fitzsimons, A. and Lennon, K. (2002), *Theorizing Gender* (Cambridge: Polity Press).

Barbera, M. and Vettor, T. (2001), 'The Case of Italy', in Behning, U. and Serrano, A. (eds.) *Gender Mainstreaming in the European Employment Strategy* (Brussels: ETUI), 259-272.

Behning, U. and Serrano Pascual, A. (2001), (eds) *Gender Mainstreaming in the European Employment Strategy* (Brussels: ETUI).

Beveridge, F., Nott, S. and Stephen, K. (2000), 'Mainstreaming and the Engendering of Policy-Making: a Means to an End?' *Journal of European Public Policy* 7(3): 385-405.

Bourdieu, P. (1998), *La domination masculine* (Paris: Editions du Seuil).

Bustelo, A., Lombardo, E., Meier, P. and Pantelidou Maloutas, M. (2004), 'Women Political Participation and Gender Mainstreaming: Possible Partners', Paper presented at the Second Pan-European Conference. Standing group on EU Politics. Bologna, 24-26 June 2004.

Butler, J. (1990), *Gender Trouble: Feminism and the Subversion of Identity.* Routledge.

Caprile, M. and Escobedo, A. (2003), 'Overcoming Barriers to Equal Pay in Spain: Monitoring Gender Mainstreaming' in Magnusson, L., Mósesdóttir, L. and Serrano Pascual, A. (2003), (eds) *Equal Pay and Gender Mainstreaming in the European Employment Strategy* (Brussels: ETUI), 199-247.

Cesen, T. (2003), 'Overcoming Barriers to Equal Pay in Slovenia: Monitoring Gender Mainstreaming' in Magnusson, L., Mósesdóttir, L. and Serrano Pascual, A. (2003) (eds) *Equal Pay and Gender Mainstreaming in the European Employment Strategy* (Brussels: ETUI), 369-401.

Cichowski, R. (2002), 'No Discrimination Whatsoever: Women's Transnational Activism and the Evolution of EU Sex Equality Policy' in Naples, N.A. and

7 The title of two contributions (Zeitlin 2004: "Opening the OMC"; Rubery's 2003: "Gender Mainstreaming and the OMC: is the Open Method Too Open for Gender Equality Policy") summarizes the positions in existing literature concerning the evaluation of the OMC. In the first case, Zeitlin (as well as Beveridge et al. 2000) emphasizes the need to ensure more actors participate to increase the efficiency of the OMC, while Rubery points out the need to strengthen the OMC's tools and sanctions.

Desai, M. (eds) *Women Activism and Globalisation: Linking Local Struggles and Transnational Politics* (New York: Routledge), 220-238.

de Troyer, M. and Krzeslo, E. (2003), 'Overcoming Barriers to Equal Pay in Belgium: Monitoring Gender Mainstreaming' in Magnusson, L., Mósesdóttir, L. and Serrano Pascual, A. *Equal Pay and Gender Mainstreaming in the European Employment Strategy* (Brussels: ETUI), 167-199.

Escobedo, A. (2001), 'The Case of Spain', in Behning, U. and Serrano, A. (eds.) *Gender Mainstreaming in the European Employment Strategy* (Brussels: ETUI), 231-258.

Fagan, C., Rubery, J., Grimshay, D., Smith, M. Hebson, G. and Figueiredo, H. (2005), 'Gender Mainstreaming in the Enlarged European Union: Recent Developments in the European Employment Strategy and Social Inclusion Process' *Industrial Relation Journal* 36(6): 568-591.

Fairclough, N. (2000), *New Labour, New Language?* (London and New York: Routledge).

Foucault, M. (2000), *Surveiller et punir* (Paris: Editions Gallimard).

Goetschy, J. (2006), 'Taking Stock of Social Europe: is There Such a Thing as a Community Social Model?', in Jepsen, M. and Serrano Pascual, A. (eds), *Unwrapping the European Social Model* (Bristol: Policy Press).

Greenwood, A.M. (1998), 'Incorporating Gender Issues in Labour Statistics' STAT Working Paper, no. 99-1.

Guillén, A. and Álvarez, S. (2004), 'The EU's Impact on the Spanish Welfare State: The Role of Cognitive Europeanization' *Journal of European Social Policy* 14(3): 285-299.

Laas, A. (2003), 'Overcoming Barriers to Equal Pay in Estonia: Monitoring Gender Mainstreaming' in Magnusson, L., Mósesdóttir, L. and Serrano Pascual, A. (2003) (eds) *Equal Pay and Gender Mainstreaming in the European Employment Strategy* (Brussels: ETUI), 401-453.

Leitner, A. (2001), 'The Case of Austria', in Behning, U. and Serrano, A. (eds.) *Gender Mainstreaming in the European Employment Strategy* (Brussels: ETUI), 143-166.

Leitner, A. (2003), 'Overcoming Barriers to Equal Pay in Austria: Ambivalent Experiences with Gender Mainstreaming' in Magnusson, L., Mósesdóttir, L. and Serrano Pascual, A. (2003), (eds) *Equal Pay and Gender Mainstreaming in the European Employment Strategy* (Brussels: ETUI), 279-311.

Lemière, S. and Silvera, R. (2001), 'The Case of France', in Behning, U. and Serrano, A. (eds.) *Gender Mainstreaming in the European Employment Strategy* (Brussels: ETUI), 183-202.

Löfström, A. (2003), 'Overcoming Barriers to Equal Pay in Sweden: Monitoring Gender Mainstreaming' in Magnusson, L., Mósesdóttir, L. and Serrano Pascual, A. (2003) (eds) *Equal Pay and Gender Mainstreaming in the European Employment Strategy* (Brussels: ETUI), 247-279.

López Santana, M. (2004), 'How Soft Pressure from Above Affects the Bottom: Europeanization, Employment Policy and Policy (Re)formulation- The Spanish Case', University of Michigan, <http://eucenter.wisc.edu/OMC/Papers/EES/lopez.pdf>.

Lombardo, E. and Meier, P. (2005), 'Implementing Gender Mainstreaming in the EU: a Battle of Policy Frames?' Contribution to ECPR Joint Sessions of Granada, 14-19 April 2005; Workshop on 'The Future of Gender Equality in the European Union'.

Lombardo, E. and Meier, P. (2006), 'Gender Mainstreaming in the EU. Incorporating a Feminist Reading?' *European Journal of Women Studies* 13(2): 151-166.

Magnusson, L., Mósesdóttir, L. and Serrano Pascual, A. (2003), (eds) *Equal Pay and Gender Mainstreaming in the European Employment Strategy*. Brussels: ETUI.

Mailand, M. (2005), *Implementing the Revised European Employment Strategy - North, South, East and West,* First working paper of the research project: Danish employment policy in a European perspective, [website] <http://www.sociology.ku.dk/faos/fnotat58.doc>.

Mósesdóttir, L. (2003), 'Moving Europe Towards the Dual-breadwinner Model' *Five Years'Experience of the Luxembourg Employment Strategy.* Brussels: ETUI.

Mósesdóttir, L. (2005), Policies and Performances. The case of Austria, Denmark, Finland, the Netherlands, Spain, Hungary and Iceland, [website] <http://www.bifrost.is/wellknow/Files/Skra_0007770.PDF>.

Mósesdóttir, L. and Erlingsdóttir, R.G. (2006), 'Gender Mainstreaming the Transition to the Knowledge Based Society', in Mósesdóttir, L., Serrano Pascual, A. and Remery, C. *Moving Europe Towards the Knowledge-based Society and Gender Equality. Policies and Performances* (Brussels: ETUI), 261-287.

Rees, T. (1998), *Mainstreaming Equality in the European Union. Education, Training and Labour Market Policies* (London: Routledge).

Roivas, S. (2006), 'The Role of the European Employment Strategy in the Transition Towards the Knowledge-based Society', in Mósesdóttir, L., Serrano Pascual, A. and Remery, C. *Moving Europe towards the Knowledge-based society and gender equality. Policies and Performances* (Brussels: ETUI), 157-189.

Rubery, J. (2003), 'Gender Mainstreaming and the Open Method of Coordination: is the Open Method Too Open for Gender Equality Policy?' [website], <http://eucenter.wisc.edu/Conferences/OMCnetOct03/rubery.pdf>.

Rubery, J., Grimshaw, D. and Figueiredo, H. (2001), *Gender Equality and the European Employment Strategy: An Evaluation of the National Actions Plans for Employment 2001.* Expert Group on Gender and Employment Report to the Equal Opportunities Unit, DG Employment, [website] <http://www.mbs.ac.uk/research/europeanemployment/projects/gendersocial/index.aspx>.

Schippers, J. (2001), 'The Case of the Netherlands', in Behning, U. and Serrano, A. (eds.) *Gender Mainstreaming in the European Employment Strategy* (Brussels: ETUI), 101-116.

Serrano Pascual, A. and Crespo Suárez, E. (2007), 'The Government of Activation Policies by EU Institutions' *International Journal of Sociology and Social Policy* 27(9/10): 376-387.

Silvera, R. (2003), 'Overcoming Barriers to Equal Pay in France: Monitoring Gender Mainstreaming', in Magnusson, L., Mósesdóttir, L. and Serrano Pascual, A. *Equal Pay and Gender Mainstreaming in the European Employment Strategy* (Brussels: ETUI), 311-345.

Sjorup, K., Reinicke, K. and Roivas, S. (2006), 'What do the partner countries' employment, gender-equality and KBS policies represent?', in Mósesdóttir, L., Serrano Pascual, A. and Remery, C. *Moving Europe towards the Knowledge-based society and gender equality. Policies and performances* (Brussels: ETUI), 193-221.

Szyszczak, E. (2006), 'Experimental Governance: The Open Method of Coordination' *European Law Journal* 12(4): 486-502.

Töns, K. and Young, B. (2001), 'The Case of Germany', in Behning, U. and Serrano, A. (eds.) *Gender Mainstreaming in the European Employment Strategy* (Brussels: ETUI), 117-142.

Verloo, M. and Pantelidou Maloutas, M. (2005), 'Differences in the Framing of Gender Inequality as a Policy Problem across Europe' *The Greek Review of Social Research* 117 *Special Issue.*

Walby, S. (2001), 'The Case of United Kingdom', in Behning, U. and Serrano, A. (eds.) *Gender Mainstreaming in the European Employment Strategy* (Brussels: ETUI), 203-230.

Walters, W. and Henrik Haahr, J. (2005), *Governing Europe. Discourse, Governmentality and European Integration* (New York: Routledge Advances in European Politics).

Webster, J. (2001), *Reconciling Adaptability and Equal Opportunities in European Workplaces.* Report for DG-Employment of the European Commission [website] <http://ec.europa.eu/employment_social/gender_equality/docs/documents/reconcil_webster.pdf>.

Webster, J. (2006), 'Comments', in Mósesdóttir, L., Serrano Pascual, A. and Remery, C. *Moving Europe towards the Knowledge-based society and gender equality. Policies and Performances* (Brussels: ETUI), 221-229.

Woodward, A. (2003), 'Mainstreaming and Equal Pay: A Logical Partnership?', in Magnusson, L., Mósesdóttir, L. and Serrano Pascual, A. (eds) *Equal Pay and Gender Mainstreaming in the European Employment Strategy* (Brussels: ETUI), 65-89.

Zeitlin, J. (2004), 'Opening the OMC: a Reflexive Reform Strategy' Presentation to conference on *The EES: Discussion and Institutionalisation*, Brussels, 30-31 August 2004.

Zeman, F., Straka, J. and Bittnerová, D. (2003), 'Overcoming Barriers in The Czech Republic: Monitoring Gender Mainstreaming' in Magnusson, L., Mósesdóttir, L. and Serrano Pascual, A. (2003) (eds) *Equal Pay and Gender Mainstreaming in the European Employment Strategy* (Brussels: ETUI), 345-369.

Zervou, M. (2001), 'The Case of Greece' in Behning, U. and Serrano, A. (eds.) *Gender Mainstreaming in the European Employment Strategy* (Brussels: ETUI), 299-321.

Zijl, M., van der Meer, M., van Seters, J., Visser, J. and Keuzenkamp, H. A. (2002), *Dutch Experiences with the European Employment Strategy* (Amsterdam: Universiteit van Amsterdam).

Chapter 10

Gender and the OMC: Conclusions and Prospects

Fiona Beveridge and Samantha Velluti

The developments that have taken place in recent years such as the adoption of the Community Framework Strategy on Gender Equality, the Roadmap and the Gender Pact, the creation of an *ad hoc* independent body such as the European Institute for Gender Equality, the adoption of the goods and services equality Directive extending gender equality law beyond the area of employment, and the recast Directive, are all evidence of the EU's ongoing commitment to gender equality (Beveridge, in this volume). The introduction of Article 13, widening equality concerns to a broad basket of grounds of discrimination, increased attention to citizenship and political participation, the enlargement of the EU, and increased focus on social and economic problems as possible impediments to growth bring about new challenges for gender equality policy. Further challenges will emerge if the Treaty of Lisbon successfully completes its ratification process, bringing the Charter of Fundamental Rights into play, while demographic change and the prospect of economic downturn may also exert considerable pressure on social policy.

The turn towards gender mainstreaming has brought with it an additional set of questions: what is meant by gender mainstreaming in practice; whose activities should change to accommodate a mainstreaming approach and how; what resources are required for mainstreaming to operate successfully; and what implications does mainstreaming have for the future development of the EU.

The past decade has also witnessed dramatic changes in the EU's methods of regulation with the development of regulatory techniques which depart from the traditional instruments of the Community Method, the OMC being the 'paradigm' of this 'New Governance'. The creation of OMC processes appears to offer a response to broader policy concerns of the EU as a polity, such as efficiency, effectiveness and democratic deficit, as well as enabling the EU to stimulate policy development in areas where traditional competences are weak. Many of the OMCs which have developed cover matters which are central to the pursuit of gender equality and are therefore highly relevant to a discussion of the future of gender equality policy. Besides offering new modes of policy-making at both EU and national levels and new opportunities for policy transfer between Member States, the OMC processes have opened up new sites for political intervention to promote gender equality. Potential exists to use OMC processes to pursue new approaches to gender equality, which in turn may lead to a re-focussing of Community gender policy, the development of fresh policy perspectives, new tools, and new approaches to implementation. The experimental nature of the OMC may assist in enabling such innovation.

The chapters in this book have offered a range of perspectives on the interface between gender equality policy and the operation of the OMC and, collectively and separately, illustrate many of these possibilities. Though they focus primarily on the EES and social inclusion OMCs, many of the insights offered are of wider relevance to studies of OMC as a regulatory innovation, as well as to gender equality policy and mainstreaming studies. In this chapter some observations and comments are offered. These are based initially around the four key themes examined in Chapter 2: gender and the nation state; visions of gender equality; strengths and limitations of 'soft' approaches; and actors. This chapter concludes by assessing the contribution of the EES and gender mainstreaming to the pursuit of gender equality. It discusses the limitations to the current approach to gender mainstreaming and the OMC and identifies future prospects for gender equality in the EU.

Gender and the Nation State

Several of the chapters have helped to focus attention on the importance of individual nation state policies and activities in relation to gender equality. Aybars, for instance, identifies the importance of both gender equality and welfare state legacies of Member States in determining the impact of the gender recommendations of the EES. Both the recommendations adopted by the European Council and the response of states to these recommendations reflect the diversity which exists within the EU and the EES does not seem to lessen this diversity: rather it leaves sufficient scope for states to continue to reinforce and reproduce national social preferences. O'Connor offers a similar conclusion, arguing that on childcare provision 'progress is dependent on national historical policy legacies.' This has clear consequences for the progress of gender equality as an outcome, despite the clear targets on participation rates and childcare established under the Lisbon strategy.

There are two concerns here. One concern is that the level of diversity between Member States may be such that the purported policy learning and transfer simply does not take place, despite the definition of broad common objectives. Instead, OMC processes may be the propeller for the adoption of measures and initiatives at national level without ensuring any convergence of results but rather resulting in more nationally distinct and diverse policies, ultimately inducing greater diversity rather than convergence. While in some areas this divergence may be seen as acceptable, or even a strength, it is questionable how appropriate it is in relation to gender equality, supposedly a 'core value' of the EU (Beveridge, in this volume). The actual impact of OMC processes is difficult to assess, as others have suggested, since cause and effect are hard to attribute. Moreover, as is evident in Koldinská's chapter, the quality of Member States' OMC reports is questionable and leaves considerable room for states to present the picture they choose (see also O'Connor's chapter).

This raises a second, related concern, that the OMC may simply be 'too soft' to ensure effective policy co-ordination. Put simply, by placing emphasis on the development of national solutions to Community problems, OMC processes may enable Member States to avoid any substantial or significant changes in the orientation of national policies which are unacceptable to them. Developing a trans-national system of target-setting, benchmarking and peer review with limited enforcement powers may allow Member States to reduce the possibility of unexpected and unwanted consequences, that is, of real structural changes in the areas where the OMC is implemented (Chalmers and Lodge 2003). Thus the OMC may represent a functional and strategic response of the Member States keen to preserve their sovereignty and decision-making powers over specific sensitive and nationally diverse policy areas in the face of growing externalities from and for other EU policies.

This may be of little concern to those who maintain that the OMC is a form of competence creep. More precisely, those who argue that the use of soft coordination processes is some kind of pre-stage towards hard law, instrumental to future expansion of the powers of the EU, will see OMC purely as a window-dressing exercise and may be little concerned with its current effectiveness except in this context. However, this is problematic for gender equality: the development of, for instance, the EES through the OMC necessarily requires that the commitment to gender equality at EU level is mirrored at Member State level, and that commitment may be undermined by the persistence of broad divergences in understandings or in the observation of gender equality norms between Member States. If this is true of EES and gender equality it also suggests a wider problem wherever OMC processes interact with the promotion of 'core values' of the EU.

Koldinská argues that while diversity across the EU has widened substantially since the 2004 enlargement, the enlarged EU presents some common problems across 'old' and 'new' Member States. The difference lies chiefly in the variety of historical, political and socio-economic origins, traditions and root-causes of these problems and, in particular, why they arose and persist. The pluri-dimensional nature of these shared problems represents a significant regulatory conundrum for the EU institutions and the experimental and flexible nature of the OMC seems *prima facie* an appropriate policy instrument to achieve some level of convergence. However, Koldinská questions whether existing OMC processes may be a workable instrument for the new Member States given that the OMC has been conceived without taking into consideration the specific features of the new Member States although she does not exclude this possibility. Both Koldinská and O'Connor identify that sufficient leeway or lack of clarity exists in the reporting requirements and guidance that national initiatives which may seem central to the promotion of, say, female employment can easily be left out of the National Reform Programmes (NRPs) on employment but included in the social exclusion report (or *vice versa*). These findings suggest the need for stricter monitoring and evaluation processes based around more clearly-defined reporting requirements to direct the attention of Member States to the key policy objectives.

This is echoed by both Fuszara and Serrano Pascual, who ultimately seem to question whether OMC is suited to all Member States. Their contributions raise the suggestion that there may be some minimum pre-conditions which need to exist if OMC is to operate effectively – a certain level of political support and stability for the goals and targets identified and a certain capacity to conduct and sustain the discursive processes on which OMC in part rests. In particular, Serrano Pascual argues that the OMC requires more openness to make it easier for the voices of women's groups and other social movements to participate and a clearer definition of objectives and responsibilities in order to further the involvement of the governments of the Member States in issues such as socio-political equality and social inclusion.

A related issue is the extent to which OMC processes have been extended within Member States beyond a high-level executive coterie, to involve a broad range of stakeholders. Many of the contributions to this volume point to the failure of Member States to conduct effective consultation with non-governmental groups or to bring non-state parties into the discursive processes associated with OMC (O'Connor, Fuszara, Serrano Pascual). Serrano Pascual, however, argues that although the participation of non-governmental actors has been disappointing in the EES, chiefly because of its heavy reliance on a top-down approach, the quest for more openness should not result in the depoliticization of key issues. This point is related also to the 'soft' character of the OMC process, through the suggestion that there may be a trade-off between openness and effectiveness, with greater openness helping to conceal governmental responsibility for failure.

Velluti's chapter, as a counterpoint, is a reminder of the central role which the social partners play in many Member States in the negotiation and implementation of social policy and of the need to keep this in mind in relation to gender equality. Successful invocation of OMC processes must, in the EES and elsewhere, take account of the unique position of major political players in national policy-making arenas, whether they are social partners, professional regulatory bodies (for instance in relation to health) or private bodies (e.g. in relation to pensions). Failure to involve these key players in the discursive aspects of OMC processes will undermine what is otherwise regarded as one of this method's key advantages, its iterative character. However 'openness' in this regard should not be confused with a lack of clarity over responsibility for the more persuasive elements of OMC such as target-setting, performance monitoring and accountability for progress.

Visions of Gender Equality

Different visions, understandings and ideals of gender equality coexist within the EU, which vary depending on the particular type of cultural, political, socio-economic structure and welfare model. Aybars' analysis of welfare regime typology highlights how gender equality arrangements differ across Member States with distinct welfare legacies and as a consequence why there are different forms of gender inequalities. The strong differences in welfare regimes and in national institutional settings explain why the process of Europeanization has not led to convergence but rather to diversity although the EES has provided a framework for addressing gender equality issues.

This is particularly the case since the 2004 EU enlargement, as is evident from the contributions of both Koldinská and Fuszara. In Central Eastern Europe, after the collapse of communism there was a reaction to the economic and social values that underpinned that system which often manifested itself in a resentment of any form of intervention based on labour legislation. In addition, in most Central Eastern European countries there was (and remains) a strong conviction that a liberal–democratic political system combined with a market economy and a minimum *laissez-faire* state would automatically ensure democracy, the rule of law and, consequently, individual equality. This explains why, even though the new Member States complied with accession negotiations and implemented the EU gender *acquis*, gender discrimination remains significant and gender equality concerns are not high on the agenda of most new Member States. The reliance on OMC to promote gender may be particularly problematic in this type of context, where state support is relatively low.

The failure of the EU to clearly articulate its gender equality *vision* leaves a vacuum at both EU and Member State levels when OMC processes are pursued, to be filled by whatever *version* of gender equality seems to fit best. O'Connor and Aybars, in their accounts of EES, refer to the continuous re-alignment of priorities under the Lisbon process and the consequent rise and fall in the stress laid on gender equality. The lack of coherence in reporting requirements noted earlier, by which national initiatives might be reported as an employment measure, a social exclusion measure, or both (or possibly, it can be assumed, not reported at all, particularly if deemed unsuccessful) is symptomatic of this lack of vision. At Member State level, O'Connor further notes that some types of initiatives – those which fit neatly with economic priorities without challenging them – may be easier to implement than those which require the redefinition of the division of responsibilities in society or the reconceptualization of equality which are more challenging. This is likely to be exacerbated by the absence of a strong vision of what is required.

As noted in Chapter 2, the absence of a clear vision of a gender equal society "allows Member States extreme freedom in presenting their policies as promoting gender equality" (Rubery 2005: 404). Yet without that vision, the peer review process falls down, since there is no standard or goal against which to measure progress. O'Connor in fact argues that in gender terms little has been achieved in the EES context: while there is a demonstrable increase in labour market participation, assessment of the relationship between this and gender equality is impossible without further analysis of the quality of the jobs created.

Guerrina, Serrano Pascual and O'Connor also point to another problem; that of the ambiguous and rather limited role ascribed to gender mainstreaming within the OMC areas. The focus on activation policies and on quantified targets for employment in the EES, for instance, may have limited the potential for OMC processes to address structural issues stemming from the gendered organisation of societies. Fuzsara's chapter draws attention to the dangers of focussing on specific measures such as female employment rates detached from their socio-economic context, since similar rates in different states do not necessarily indicate similar impacts or even similar 'problems' from a gender equality perspective. Thus while the EES may have helped to raise the visibility of gender concerns in the sphere of employment, provided a better evidence base on this issue, fostered the setting up of *ad hoc* institutions and promoted the participation of new actors it appears to have done little to tackle the structural problems of gender inequality. This analysis fits well with fears expressed elsewhere that the EU's approach to gender equality has been limited in scope: “the pursuit of gender equality within the EU has failed to be a transformative process. Anti-discrimination law has remained confined within the limits of liberal individualism, doing little to tackle the broader structural aspects of gender inequality” (Mullally 2003: 295). The failure to develop an over-arching ‘vision’ of gender equality which could support systematic, cohesive and structural analyses of the gender ‘problems’ in discreet areas and serve as the basis for the development of complementary and comprehensive strategies across different policy areas strips gender mainstreaming of its transformative potential and may render many initiatives ineffectual in practice.

A key concern is that there may be a significant disjuncture between EU gender equality policy and OMC processes: on the one hand it is questionable whether key gender strategy documents, such as the Framework Strategy and the Roadmap, offer a comprehensive over-arching vision, despite their gradually widening focus; on the other hand, it is not clear how much visibility or purchase such strategy documents have anyway in individual OMC processes. In the EES and the social exclusion OMCs the Lisbon Strategy seems to serve as the sole meta-narrative and gender equality does not appear as a ‘goal’ in its own right, but is referred to instrumentally in connection with the goals of the Lisbon Strategy.

However it is also necessary to look beyond the Roadmap, which is itself limited in its vision and scope, and to ensure that the ‘vision’ of equality developed is grounded on a firm understanding of current social trends. This is clearly evident in Guerrina’s chapter which analyzes activation policies within the context of demographic trends and clearly demonstrates the danger that increased participation may translate into further downward pressure on birth rates. The persistent failure of national and EU work-life balance measures to bring about real change in the distribution of unpaid work remains a major challenge for gender equality policy.

There are some signs that the European Commission is beginning to grasp the challenge. The Annual Report on Equality Between Women and Men, 2008 (European Commisssion 2008) recognizes the need to focus not only on job creation, but also on job quality. In addition it links employment activation to the quality of services available to help to address reconciliation issues, particularly childcare and social care services, and makes important points about the affordability and accessibility of these services.

It is important that the Lisbon Strategy addresses these issues. This strategy has been seen to be increasingly influential in determining the direction of OMC processes, and is also influential in setting the direction of policy for areas falling under the Community method, as Beveridge illustrates by reference to the Structural Funds. Thus the real challenge is to ensure that the Lisbon Strategy itself embodies a gender perspective which is transformative. The successor to the Roadmap could play a key role in articulating such a perspective, but political will is also required to ensure that it does inform the Lisbon Strategy.

Strengths and Limitations of 'Soft' Approaches

The 'soft' character of the OMC arises in all the contributions to this volume which raise many issues regarding the usefulness of soft law in sensitive policy areas such as gender equality. Various chapters demonstrate that while the OMC holds many theoretical promises in fostering policy learning and transfer, promoting partnership and promoting deliberative modes of democracy the results have been all together rather disappointing, particularly beyond the OMC's role as a propeller or catalyst for innovation. In particular, while the EES has served to give political prominence to gender equality, a critical examination of its first decade shows that there are a number of shortcomings some of which, in the words of Rubery (2005: 403), "may not be susceptible to resolution, either because of a lack of political will or because of the presence of contradictory objectives".

Aybars, O'Connor and Serrano Pascual all conclude that OMC has contributed to the establishment of a 'euro-discourse' around areas previously dealt with solely by Member States, a process of 'cognitive europeanisation' (Radaelli 2000, as quoted by O'Connor). Aybars argues that the significance of this should not be dismissed. On the other hand, a significant weakness of the OMC lies in the fact that this process may be contained almost wholly in exchanges between the political elites of the EU on one side and the Member States on the other, and may filter down only rarely into political processes within the Member States. Thus, as Serrano Pascual notes, any convergence attributed to OMC processes is likely to be a convergence of ideational elements – vision and concepts – rather than of political resources such as institutions and rules. This will be particularly true if participation is limited to a narrow elite – while wider participation, and particularly the involvement of actors at the national and sub-national levels could induce greater socialization of these parties and wider diffusion of ideas, this opportunity is lost if the process is more narrowly confined, with national reports being produced solely for EU consumption, or as a 'window-dressing' exercise.

O'Connor argues further that for the EES to successfully promote gender equality reforms are required: at the ideational level the tensions between the 'gender equality' dimensions of activation policies (as currently conceived) and a broader gender mainstreaming strategy embracing issues such as women's representation need to be resolved; while in implementation greater attention to monitoring and the involvement of stakeholders is advocated. Without strategic direction and robust monitoring, there is a risk that national policies amount to little more than administrative reform or 'rejigging' of measurement procedures (cf. Chalmers and Lodge 2003).

Many academic commentators on OMC have focussed on the absence of enforcement mechanisms, which is often seen as an inherent limitation. Voluntary or motivated compliance is regarded as insufficient on its own to ensure the adoption of measures to pursue the agreed goals, particularly in times of economic recession or political instability. However both Beveridge and Aybars argue that it is necessary to take a wider view of compliance and the factors which may induce greater compliance if OMC is to be assessed accurately. Moreover, the apt comparison may not be between traditional 'hard' law measures and OMC processes but between traditional 'soft' measures, new governance developments in non-OMC areas and OMC processes.

One potential benefit of OMC processes is the production of better statistics, knowledge and understanding of the problems under scrutiny. Fuszara points to the importance of this in states which might otherwise be inclined to argue that no problem exists. While some improvement is evident in this regard it is clear that more needs to be done.

It is difficult to assess whether tools for peer pressure and benchmarking may be *per se* sufficient to motivate any targeted policy change on the part of Member States. In some instances OMC guidelines and norms may be used at national level to consolidate already existing domestic policy objectives. In others, the vague nature of benchmarks may simply give scope for creative compliance and window dressing rather than motivate substantive change. This, combined with the difficulties of accessing reliable statistical data besides that generated through this process, and the need to relate the reported performance to its broader social and economic context, makes the comparison of Member States' performances, and assessment on the impact of OMC processes very difficult. Szcszyzak (2001) highlights the dangers of relying on OMC products such as benchmarks in this respect. In this book Aybars argues that while procedural changes can be detected, substantive change is harder to attribute at Member State level, while Koldinská concludes that the wide differences in the structure and quality of Member State reports makes effective comparison impossible.

Both Fuszara and Koldinská point to the relatively weak political support for gender equality and relatively weak capacities in policy-making in general as factors which limit the impact of 'soft' processes in new Member States. Both raise issues about the quality of the interactions which take place between Member States and within the new Member States, suggesting that this deprives OMC processes of much of their potential. But Fuszara also refers to the need for politicians to be convinced that the 'model' or 'good practice' promoted by the OMC processes is indeed 'good practice', since their agreement and support is essential for soft processes to succeed.

Overall the picture is mixed. It is clear that OMC has been 'successful' in maintaining the momentum for a process of policy-making at the EU level in areas where previously there had been limited intervention of the EU: in both the EES and the social inclusion OMCs there is clear evidence of repeated cycles of policy-renewal, monitoring, assessment and learning. While the Lisbon Strategy has undoubtedly given political priority and urgency to these particular OMC areas it may also be the case that the nature of the OMC process itself – its cyclical nature, its inter-governmentalism, its relatively 'simple' policy-making processes and its ability to accommodate diversity between different states – contributes to this success. However, as a soft mode of governance the OMC also has certain weaknesses, which are evident in relation to gender equality. Political commitment is variable, and vulnerable to economic recession and political stagnation. Where the promotion of gender equality coincides with broader economic goals such as higher employment, action at a national level may be fairly easy to ensure. However, many gender equality issues call into question existing social and family policy and these are often highly sensitive policy areas where, in the absence of any strong orientations and any element of compulsion, consensus is unlikely to be forthcoming and political action can prove very difficult. In these situations OMC processes appear to be particularly weak.

Actors

The two main institutional players of the OMC are the European Council and the Commission, respectively. The former has a pre-eminent and coordinating role to ensure overall coherence and effective monitoring of progress. Although the Commission plays an important pro-active and methodological role in shaping and defining the structure of the coordination process by moulding the behaviour of the various actors involved, channelling conflicts and fostering consensus building, the European Council and the Member State entrusted with the Presidency of the Union will, ultimately, determine the future scope, development and thus implementation of the strategy. Indeed, on a number of occasions the proposals put forward by the Commission have been rejected by the Council adopting the guidelines,[1] indicating the highly political nature of this process. This means, first, that the political players will have greater influence on Member States' actions in the field of gender equality by comparison to the Commission than is the case under the Community method and, secondly, that a great deal of political lobbying takes place behind the scenes at EU level in relation to the future direction of OMC processes.

Beyond this there has been a certain degree of institutional reform with the creation, for example, of the Employment Committee and the Social Protection Committee at EU level and *ad hoc* bodies created at national level. However, the central role given to the European Council and the Commission suggests that, to an extent, the "'open method' relies on already established societal actors, with the risk that it merely reinforces existing power structures and cleavages rather than encouraging wider 'openness'" (Chalmers and Lodge 2003). The minimal involvement of the European Parliament and the ECJ have contributed to an impression that the EU institutions are less transparent and less accountable in relation to OMC processes, than in respect of traditional 'community' methods of law and policy-making.

Besides this, OMC appears to promise wider involvement of different stakeholders including civil society and the social partners in a multi-level policy-making process. As with other aspects of soft coordination processes the main problem is defining our understanding of and delimiting the degree of 'openness' of this more participatory form of democracy (Serrano Pascual in this book). Two key questions arise: first, whether this increased participation is evident in practice; and second, whether the involvement of more actors has contributed to greater openness, in the sense of giving more actors influence within the policy-making process. There is clearly a risk that, if managed badly, wider involvement of stakeholders could actually make OMC processes more opaque and vague.

1 The first guidelines were adopted by the European Council. Subsequently, they have been adopted by the Council of the European Union.

Given the key functions of participants, it is pivotal to determine who should perform these roles and yet little attention is paid to how and why certain stakeholders are chosen (Fredman 2005). A definition of civil society can be found in the Commission's White Paper on European Governance (Commission 2001), but different OMC processes invite a different mixture of inputs. The lack of clear procedures may favour stronger or better-organized groups of civil society. However this may raise questions about how representative certain groups are, as illustrated by the UEAPME case in the context of the European Social Dialogue.[2] Linked to this are issues of accountability and the wider question of how far OMC processes can or should seek to enhance the participation of women in decision-making; a constituent part of EU gender equality policy.

A particularly strong role is given in the EES to the social partners and Velluti's chapter emphasizes the importance of their involvement for the effectiveness of labour market modernization policies. In practice though, the social partners' levels of engagement and concern with gender equality is extremely variable. Velluti demonstrates, on the trade union side, a very wide disparity between Danish and Italian trade union organisations in this respect. On the employers' side there is less evidence available: while some have championed 'flexicurity' and may pride themselves on their 'family-friendly policies and 'equality and diversity' measures, there are undoubtedly large divergences within and between Member States, in terms both of the attitudes of firms and their engagement with/by the State in policy development and implementation e.g. under the EES.

However there is little evidence, either within the EU strategy or the national reports of any awareness of possible gender bias arising from the lower representation of women in trade unions and collective bargaining, or from the patchy commitment of employers organizations to gender equality (Rubery 2002: 515; Velluti, Koldinská and Fuszara in this book). A significant contrast can be made with the Structural Funds governance where the issue of the participation of women and men is subject to regulation.[3]

Moreover, there is little evidence suggesting that the contribution of the social partners, civil society and other stakeholders is significant. In some cases they have not been given the opportunity to be involved in the EES due to their weak position in domestic politics and policy-making processes. In other cases these stakeholders, particularly the social partners, do not appear to be interested in developing gender equality policies of a transformative nature (Koldinská and Fuszara in this book). This is the case in Southern Mediterranean countries and Central Eastern European

2 Case T–135/96 UEAPME v. Council [1998] ECR II–2335. The case concerned a challenge to the legality of the Directive on parental leave by UEAPME, which claimed to represent the largest number of small and medium-sized employers (SMEs) at pan-European level. UEAPME's main contention was that since it had been involved in the first consultation procedure it should necessarily have been involved in the second consultation process, given the fact that the interests of SMEs were different from those of UNICE.

3 For example, the European Social Fund Regulation provides as follows (Art. 6): "Member States shall promote a balanced participation of women and men in the management and implementation of operational programmes at local, regional and national level, as appropriate."

states either because of the universalistic principle of equality sanctioned in their Constitutions or because other policy concerns are considered to have greater prominence than equal opportunities issues. Here there appears to be significant diversity at national level. With regard to representatives of civil society little or no effort has been made to secure the participation of stakeholders, particularly in Central Eastern European countries. This casts doubt on the real potential for deliberative democracy within the OMC. Borrás and Greve (2004: 345) argue that:

> rather than constituting a democratic watershed in EU politics, the OMC runs the risk of ending up in a sort of 'democratic legitimacy limbo', at the crossroads between the insufficient accomplishment of the deliberative and participatory democratic ideals, the virtual non-existence of democratic representation channels (by the European/national parliament(s)), and the absence of output legitimacy owing to its indistinguishable results.

These are particularly important issues for the effective implementation of policies at national level. If, as is argued here, both the OMC processes and the concept of gender mainstreaming are in need of clearer definition in respect of their nature, purposes and goals (including a removal of existing and inherent tensions and contradictions) then equally there is a need to carefully define the roles and contributions of different actors (Koldinská, Fuszara and Serrano Pascual in this book). This in turn would serve to give a clearer understanding of the form of deliberative democracy envisaged and being promoted under different OMC processes. An obvious counter-argument can be made here: defining these processes more closely may end up undermining their intrinsic nature as experimental forms of governance and introduce stagnation. It seems that a balance must be struck between these competing objectives. Clearer definition of processes to ensure that the required capacity building, knowledge resources and transparency are realized may improve the effectiveness of the OMC processes: overall, decision-making processes in the OMC must remain sufficiently untrammelled and responsive to reduce any significant risk of ossification.

Methods of Implementation – the Contribution of the OMC to Gender Equality

The OMC has come to assume great significance in EU gender policy. A number of distinct functions are performed within the iterative framework of the OMC:

- the articulation of policy goals and guidelines
- the development of national reports
- the negotiation of policy recommendations
- the development of indicators
- exchange of best practices, regular benchmarking and peer review
- the monitoring of Member States' performance

In relation to gender equality, the use of these governance tools has been combined with and strengthened through the inclusion of gender mainstreaming. This has confirmed the role of the EU in placing equal opportunities and gender mainstreaming firmly on the policy agenda. By doing this, the EU has maintained its traditional role of championing gender equality, tailoring its approach to fit that of the new policy areas in which OMC has created a role for the EU institutions in guiding and coordinating Member State activities.

As a result gender equality has had prominence within the EES and, to a lesser extent, the Social Policy Agenda. In the first years of implementation of the EES, equal opportunities were included as one of four key policy areas on which to develop the employment coordination process named "pillars". The "Equal Opportunities" pillar included policies aimed at fostering gender equality, reducing gender gaps and promoting gender mainstreaming (Aybars in this book, Figure 4.2). Moreover, a gender mainstreaming approach was extended to all four pillars to ensure a gender dimension to all measures adopted and implemented in the context of the EES. This was particularly significant given the broad scope of action of the EES which establishes a nexus between different EU policy areas going beyond the fields generally covered by social policy, and it was evidence of a commitment to the promotion of gender equality at Community level. This in turn was reflected in a commitment at national level as demonstrated by the first national reports.

However, in subsequent redesigns of the EES, equal opportunities ceased to be a pillar in its own right, becoming gradually compromised and weakened as a consequence of the various reforms at EU level. By introducing three new 'overarching key objectives' at the beginning of 2003 the importance of gender equality was crucially weakened: from being a principle and a fundamental right it was reduced to a policy objective under 'quality at work' or as part of the goal of "attracting more people to the labour market and making work a real option for all". Moreover, after the integration of the EES into the new Lisbon Strategy, there is only very little explicit reference to gender equality. The new integrated guidelines do not include a specific guideline on gender equality. Gender mainstreaming, gender gaps and the need to balance work and private life are still mentioned but have been moved to the introductory paragraph or are dealt with less explicitly, under headings such as 'life-cycle approach' (Rubery, 2005; Aybars in this book, Figure 4.2).

Evidence from the Member States shows that Member State attention to gender equality declined to match the reduction in focus in the Integrated Guidelines (Fagan *et al.*, 2006; O'Connor, Velluti, in this volume).

These developments indicate the importance of continuing political will and suggest that, at EU level, the scope of the OMC is only marginally determined by the objective needs and requirements of a given policy field to which the OMC is applied and is determined rather by broader EU policy goals or by reasons of good governance.

The expansion of the use of OMC from the employment field to other policies areas (Laffan and Shaw, 2005; Szcszyzak, 2006) has been accompanied by a transfer of practices developed in one area to others through the development of structural indicators, exchange of best practices, benchmarking, peer review and the use of Scoreboards which serve to rate the performances of different Member States in implementing policy[4] (Beveridge in this volume). The coordination of annual cycles of monitoring and review has opened up the possibility for measures in one area to be influenced by developments in another in a more direct way (and in a more immediate way) than was previously the case. It might also help to address the issue of coherence, and lead to clearer reporting of initiatives by Member States.

However, for gender politics the integrated approach may be somewhat double-edged. If the contribution of measures to promote gender equality can make to overall economic performance, or to the social agenda, can be kept firmly to the fore of the discussions of the Commission and the Council, then such measures may receive priority attention. Given the centrality of issues such as the gender pay-gap, women's employment rates, childcare and the organization of work to meet the needs of women with caring responsibilities, it is clear that the urgency with which some of these issues are being addressed and the use of targets are potentially of great benefit. On the other side, it is easy to foresee that, in addressing the many issues which have to included under the Lisbon Strategy, the key institutions might lose sight of the centrality of gender to many of the issues with which they grapple.

Similarly, at Member State level, the OMC brings both benefits and pitfalls. Since the Member States retain a high degree of autonomy in deciding how to address the recommendations of the Council, there is a more consistent, medium-term approach to many of the issues concerned which may be of benefit in both political and practical ways. From a political standpoint, where there is a risk that gender might 'slip down' the Council's agenda in any particular round of review and recommendation, Member States will generally respond to 'annual' recommendations by making some alterations to policy but not by wholesale abandonment of existing policy programmes – there will be revision, rather than renewal. The greater continuity and consistency which therefore exists at Member State level may act as insulation against more swinging policy shifts at the higher level. Moreover, when policies are picked up and 'adopted' by other non-state actors within the Member States, these activities might acquire their own momentum, as seen in the case of Danish Trade Unions (Velluti in this book).

At the same time national autonomy operates within a framework in which economic, social and employment issues are dealt with together and in which there is significant peer pressure for conformity with EU objectives, at least at some level. This may in turn act as insulation in the future from some of the more radical policy swings at national level which might otherwise have occurred with successive changes of government – the 'European' economic model may become too firmly established in the practices and bureaucracies of the Member States for any individual government to be able to resist wholesale its basic tenets.

At the same time this pressure to conform is mitigated by the tendency of Member States to adapt OMC goals and policies to 'fit' existing national policy styles and socio-political culture. Thus on a practical level, the degree of autonomy which exists within the OMC, together with the medium-term timeframe which

4 e.g. The Internal Market Scoreboard has been keeping track of Member States' progress in transposing Internal Market Directives, <http://ec.europa.eu/internal_market/score/docs/score16bis/score16bis_en.pdf>.

operates, may encourage both diversity of national practice and innovation in policy-making at national level. This was demonstrated clearly in Aybars' chapter. Fuszara and Koldinská, by contrast, show not strong adaptations to fit national policy styles but weak adaptations which reflect a lack of political will to bring gender equality dimensions of OMC processes to life. The resultant diversity can be seen as both the strength and the weakness of the OMC. It is a strength if, by fostering the development of 'bespoke' solutions, a good 'fit' between new and existing measures results, thus improving the likely success of the new measures. Moreover the ability for the Member State to retain influence over the shape and content of new measures may improve high-level political commitment to values such as gender equality, even where there is little appetite for equality politics on the ground. On the other hand it is a weakness if it simply reflects an ability of Member States to ignore significant elements of OMC policies or to switch their support on and off as domestic policy circumstances change. Finally, as Fuszara'a chapter illustrates, the concepts of autonomy and diversity might simply serve to mask what is essentially an unequal relationship between so-called 'peers'.

Further issues are raised by the OMC's inherently weak capacity for enforcement. Looking at the record on gender equality, it is clear that the performance of some states has been distinctly laggard, with some issues presenting greater challenge than others (O'Connor). While this weakness may have been a necessary requirement for the establishment of any EU mechanisms at all in some of the policy fields in question, there is an ever-present question of how much deviation can be tolerated before confidence in the ability of the EU to provide the necessary leadership in these areas is lost. A second weakness stems from the fact that under the OMC generally, and particularly where benchmarks and targets are deployed, there is a tendency to focus only on the weakest performers in any particular policy-field. This has the unfortunate result that some better-performing states may take the view that they have achieved enough, even where their performance falls short of an ideal. In relation to gender equality this is aggravated by the failure of the institutions to articulate any ideal or 'vision'.

Gender Equality, Gender Mainstreaming and the OMC: Some Prospects for the Future

This book looked at the interface between gender equality and the OMC, principally in the fields of the EES and the social exclusion strategy, and examined how effectively the OMC has served as a means for the promotion of gender equality in the EU. The contributors have shown that, while gender equality is still gathering momentum and there is space for a positive outlook on gender equality in the EU, political commitment to the promotion of gender equality within these areas has been variable over time, and the quality of the gender focus has also varied. On the one hand this seems to stem from the ever-evolving nature of the OMC processes which undergo regular re-orientation to reflect changing political demands, changing externalities and developing understandings of the 'problems' and the 'solutions'. Notably this appears to have caused a decrease in the visibility of equal opportunities following the redesign and reform of the EES on successive occasions (Aybars in this book, Table 4.2) and to have produced conflicting rationales and discourses around the Employment Strategy (O'Connor in this book). On the other hand, variations in commitment and focus may be explained in part by vagueness in the way in which the EU articulates the value of gender equality (Beveridge, Guerrina in this book) and the rather open-ended way in which gender mainstreaming is defined as a strategic tool (O'Connor in this book).

A number of specific needs have been identified to address these shortcomings. These included greater clarity in the objectives of the OMC processes and the role of gender within these, and similarly clearer reporting requirements. In addition, the success of the OMC will depend on the continued development of a good evidence base on gender issues, including appropriate indicators, targets and assessment tools.

Despite these shortcomings, the mainstreaming of gender equality into OMC areas has resulted in a much clearer understanding at both EU and Member State levels of the significance of these areas from a gender equality perspective and this in turn has strengthened the case for EU action in these areas. It is not fanciful to argue that, even without other Lisbon-related issues, the OMC has performed a useful service by focussing on the gender dimensions of employment activation policies, social exclusion measures, health and pensions. Gender mainstreaming within the EU has been strengthened by the creation of OMCs in these areas, as this has enabled the Commission to extend its gender equality agenda to encompass areas beyond the scope of EC competences but of immense importance from a gender equality perspective. Besides providing a wider platform for gender mainstreaming, the OMCs have already resulted in new tools, many of which have also been adapted and utilised by the Commission in gender mainstreaming initiatives in non-OMC areas.

However, the use of OMC processes in these key areas produces limitations. Mainstreaming opens up the possibility of reconceptualizing proactive strategies, such as those required to tackle gender equality, as positive duties rather than as mere political choices. Rather than seeing gender equality as dependent on individual (negative) rights such as that not to be discriminated against in access to employment or in remuneration, the traditional EC approach, and positive duties place an onus on the state to address systemic and institutionalized disadvantage. This approach "casts the responsibility on the state to remedy those deficiencies, not because of proof of breach of an individual right, but because the state has the appropriate power to do so" (Fredman 2005: 49). As yet, though, mainstreaming duties in EC law are fairly weak (Beveridge 2007) and have little or no purchase in OMC areas. Gender mainstreaming in these areas is "highly dependent on political commitment and vulnerable to the vagaries of political change" (Fredman 2005: 42). Lombardo and Meier (2007) conclude:

> the broadening of the policy areas beyond the labor market in which the EU could intervene, through gender mainstreaming, and the deepening of focus in order to tackle the structural conditions of gender inequality and to challenge the gender dimension of

political power, through positive actions, have been inversely proportional to the binding nature of the measures adopted.

The OMC has other inherent limitations, many of which also stem from its 'soft' nature. The chapters in this book demonstrate that there is considerable variation in the level and form of attention given to gender by different Member States in their OMC instruments. While the possibility of accommodating or even promoting diversity between states may be one of the suggested strengths of OMC processes, the chapters here suggest that these differences arise not because of different policy choices made by states, or because of differences in their social and economic position, but due to their historic attachment to particular welfare state models and their variable capacities to address problems of gender equality and bring about societal change through policy processes. Thus states with a strong attachment to gender equality are likely to display that in OMC processes and may harness OMC processes to further embed that commitment, while those in which gender equality has had weak support historically are unlikely to pay it much attention in OMC processes This suggests that OMC is not a strong promoter of gender equality and raises questions about the appropriateness of relying on OMC processes to advance a supposedly core value of the EU.

However another limitation to the role of OMC in promoting gender stems from the long-standing failure of the EU to develop a clear concept of gender equality and a clear understanding of what gender mainstreaming requires at EU and Member State levels respectively (Beveridge, in this book). The failure of the EU to articulate a clear and over-arching concept of gender equality not only makes it difficult to specify what the goals are in this area but also makes it difficult to state what place these goals should occupy in OMC processes. In any case, while a convincing argument can be made that OMC processes should comply with 'core' EU values such as transparency and accountability, it is clear that they do not always: the experimental nature of these processes may mean in effect that they are often 'beyond governance'. If this is the case then even a strong consensus that gender equality, clearly conceived, is a core and over-arching priority for all areas of law and policy-making, would not guarantee its respect within OMC processes.

Until this is clarified the OMCs will simply provide yet more sites within the EU polity where competing concepts and understandings of gender equality and gender mainstreaming can be fashioned. As noted above, in the OMC processes examined in this book it is the Lisbon Strategy which is most likely to fill the vacuum and influence the way in which this is done and the embedding of a stronger vision of gender equality in the Lisbon Strategy is needed to realise the potential of OMC to advance gender equality.

The existence of a multitude of sites for political activity on gender equality within the EU, and the absence of an overarching vision of gender equality, stems in part from the continued fragmentation of legal competences between different parts of the Treaty and between the OMC and non-OMC activities. Many writers acknowledge the usefulness of OMC in overcoming the absence of competence in the fields which are important to the EU. From a gender equality perspective, however, it is clear that the resulting distribution of competences, and its implications for the tools, policy-making methods and array of actors involved in a particular field is neither logical nor helpful. The lack of a clear and direct competence in key areas may result in a move away from a gender perspective in some areas (Lombardo and Meier, 2007), and resort to sub-optimum approaches.

As things stand there are strong disconnects between OMC processes and the EU *acquis communautaire* and developing constitutional discourse, which increasingly confirm gender equality as a fundamental right and gender mainstreaming as a constitutional guarantee. There is little evidence of awareness of this in OMC documentation, which tends to articulate a more instrumental approach to gender issues. In particular, OMC is premised on principles of better regulation and good governance, rather than on a rights-based discourse, and hence can be characterized as standing outside the regular governance frameworks of the EU. Some writers have identified this as a general weakness of OMC and have proposed that governance of the OMC should be 'regularized'. This would offer some way to address the disconnects which currently exist, and go some way to addressing the current unevenness in the distribution of competences. A positive duty to have regard to issues such as gender equality could ensure that activities such as the OMCs are underpinned by clear and non-derogable fundamental rights, prescribing the normative guidelines within which policy must operate (cf. Fredman 2005). De Búrca (2003) argues that courts could have a proactive role in ensuring that policy-makers take into account rights and that derogations to these rights must be fully and openly justified. Such measures might help to ensure that gender mainstreaming measures are based on the recognition that gender equality is *in primis* a fundamental right. However, such initiatives would amount to a radical departure from the inter-governmentalism and experimental 'exceptionalism' which characterize the OMC and are unlikely to find favour with Member State governments in the near future.

References

Borrás, S. and Greve, B. (2004), 'Concluding Remarks: New Method or Just Cheap Talk?' *Journal of European Public Policy* 11(2): 329-336.

Chalmers, D. and Lodge, M. (2003), 'The Open Method of Coordination and the European Welfare State', Paper No. 11, ESRC Centre for Analysis of Risk and Regulation, London School of Economics and Political Science.

Commission (2006), Commission Staff Working Paper, Roadmap for Equality Between Women and Men 2006-2010, Impact Assessment, Brussels, SEC(2006) 275.

Council Decision (2005), of 12 July 2005 on Guidelines for the employment policies of the Member States (2005/600/EC).

De Búrca, G. (2003), 'The Constitutional Challenge of New Governance in the European Union', *European Law Review* 28: 814-839.

European Commission (2001), *A White Paper on European Governance* (COM (2001) 428 final).

European Commission (2008), *Report on Equality Between Women and Men 2008*, Brussels, 2008.

Fagan C., Grimshaw D. and Rubery J. (2006), 'The Subordination of the Gender Equality Objective: The National Reform Programmes and 'Making Work Pay' Policies', *Industrial Relations Journal* 37: 571-592.

Fredman, S. (2005), 'Changing the Norm: Positive Duties in Equal Treatment Legislation', *Maastricht Journal of European and Comparative Law* 12(4): 369-397.

Laffan, B. and Shaw, C. (2005), *Classifying and Mapping the Open Method of Coordination In Different Policy Areas*, July 2005, Project No. 02/D9, NEWGOV, New Modes of Governance Project, Project No. CIT1-CT-2004-506392, <http://eucenter.wisc.edu/OMC/Papers/laffanShaw.pdf>.

Lombardo, E. and Meier, P. (2005), 'Implementing Gender Mainstreaming in the EU: a Battle of Policy Frames?' Contribution to ECPR Joint Sessions of Granada, 14-19 April 2005; Workshop on 'The Future of Gender Equality in the European Union'.

McGlynn, C. (2006), 'Work, Family and Parenthood: The European Union Agenda' in Conaghan, J. and Rittich, K. (eds) *Labour Law, Work and Family* (Oxford: Oxford University Press).

Mullally, S. (2003), 'Beyond the Limits of Non-Discrimination: Promoting Gender Equality' in Costello, C. and Barry, E. (eds), *Equality in Diversity, The New Equality Directives* (Irish Centre for European Law, Ashfield Publications).

Rubery, J. (2002), 'Gender Equality and Gender Mainstreaming in the EU: The Impact of the EU Employment Strategy', *Industrial Relations Journal* 33: 500-522.

Rubery, J. (2005), 'Gender Mainstreaming and the OMC. Is the Open Method Too Open for Gender Equality Policy?' in Zeitlin, J. and Pochet, P. (eds) with Magnusson, L. *The Open Method of Coordination in Action. The European Employment and Social Inclusion Strategies* (Brussels: PIE-Peter Lang).

Szyszczak, E. (2001) 'The New Paradigm for Social Policy: A Virtuous Circle?' 38 *Common Market Law Review* 1125-1170.

Szyszczak, E. (2006) 'Experimental Governance: The Open Method of Coordination' 12 *European Law Journal* 486-502.

Index